M000082882

Endorsements for
Jump First Think Fast

"In the five decades I have been working, I can't think of any business executive, who has been such a meaningful mentor as Frank O'Connell. He taught all of us how to define goals, understand creativity, have positive attitudes, and love our work. There are so many successful executives who owe their fruitful and rewarding careers to Frank. We were all so very lucky."

—Lois Whitman-Hess, HWH PR

"Frank O'Connell was successful because of his commitment to goal achievement, flexibility, and ability to employ proven marketing techniques. Frank thought outside the box and has worked assiduously to maintain a mentoring relationship with me and other fellow team members."

—Robert P. Kirby, former CEO of Oroweat/
Arnold Brands, Inc.; Dairy Division, Borden Inc.;
Murray Bakery Products; Castleberry/Snows Brands Inc.

"Like Mentor in Homer's *Odyssey*, Frank tutored us in the realm of possibilities, preparing his cohorts for grand adventure and its rewards and perils. As the result, our ventures over four decades yielded both extraordinary shareholder returns and professional development."

—Sam K. Reed, CEO of Keebler Foods Company,
founder of TreeHouse Foods Company

"'When the internal speed of an organization is slower than the external speed of the market, the company will eventually fail.' This is one of my favorite quotes from Frank. Creativity, energy, optimism, and fun continuously infuse Frank's life. I've been blessed to work with and learn from Frank, a motivating leader who energizes organizations, turning them into winners."

—**Kosmo Kallerekos, managing director**
at Baring Private Equity Asia,
former founding member and senior partner
of The Parthenon Group

"*Jump First, Think Fast* describes how Frank approaches his life. It is his instincts, risk-taking, and ability to do things differently that impressed me. I learned a lot about how to just jump into things. His stories are both practical and personal. I urge readers to enjoy the stories and learn. I certainly did."

—**Chris Walsh, founder of CW Resources, Inc.**
former VP of operations for Reebok,
former Sr. VP of operations for LA Gear,
former managing director for Nike/
Taiwan and managing director of Nike/China

JUMP
FIRST
FAST
THINK

AN UNCONVENTIONAL APPROACH
TO HIGH PERFORMANCE

FRANK J. O'CONNELL

WITH RICH MARIN

Worth
BOOKS

Jump First, Think Fast: An Unconventional Approach to High Performance

Copyright © 2022 by Frank J. O'Connell

All rights reserved. No part of this publication may be reproduced, stored in a retrieval system, or transmitted in any form by any means, electronic, mechanical, photocopy, recording, or otherwise, without the prior permission of the publisher, except as provided by USA copyright law.

No patent liability is assumed with respect to the use of the information contained herein. Although every precaution has been taken in the preparation of this book, the publisher and author assume no responsibility for errors or omissions. Neither is any liability assumed for damages resulting from the use of the information contained herein.

Library of Congress Control Number: 2022910732

Print ISBN: 978-1-63763-107-2
E-book ISBN: 978-1-63763-108-9

Cover Design by Bruce Gore, Gore Studio, Inc.
Interior Design by Bill Kersey, KerseyGraphics

This book is dedicated first to my mother, Virginia, who endured the worst of me, saw the best of me, loved me anyway, and correctly identified my life as a carnival. Next, to my wife, Barbara, who endured the worst of me, saw the best of me, loved me anyway, joined my carnival, and never looked back.

And this book is dedicated to my children, Beth, God rest her soul, Kim, always giving to and saving humans and animals, Sean, whose humor and brilliance is astounding, and Mack, the wild card in the bunch. The grandchildren will be mentioned in the next book because they weren't around when these things happened. I love you all and thank you for your support.

CONTENTS

FOREWORD

Note from a Friend

My good friend Frank asked me to read the beginning of his career life story, written for him by professionals as an "airport business advice" book. It didn't feel right to him. It didn't read right to me. Frank and I have known each other for almost thirty years; we both have dual degrees from Cornell, and both of our families hail from the Finger Lakes of New York. I felt I could do Frank's voice justice.

He's not a preachy sort of guy who takes himself so seriously that he thinks people need to take notes when he talks. Frank is a successful titan of business who did what he did and got where he was going because he loved what he was doing. He was and still is passionate and driven about every minute he spends on this earth. I admire that and decided to help him tell his story exactly because he does not preach from some business gospel. What he does is use every ounce of his experience, throws it at the problem at hand, and tries like the devil to solve the problem (and one look at Frank's smile, and you just know there is some devil in there). Innovation, that thing made of perspiration and inspiration, is his stock and trade. Frank is the Chieftain of Innovation. Sometimes he succeeds and sometimes he fails, but it is never for want of passion and genuine effort.

This book is a memoir of Frank's business life. It's about the amazing stories of his interactions with the movers and shakers of our times, of the trends that have set the course of our existence these past fifty years, and of the subtle nudges he gave to those movers and movements that actually "moved the needle."

I don't mean to overstate Frank's importance to human civilization. In fact, the greatness of the man is that he would smile, scoff, and self-denigrate any attempt to suggest that he has moved the needle of mankind. But for a simple farm boy of humble origins, his "light touch" affiliation with meaningful trends, brands, and ideas makes his career a veritable hallmark of his generation of business leaders. And the best part about it all is that Frank never sacrificed a moment of fun for himself or anyone near him. He is a testament to the power of innovative thinking.

Rich Marin

■ **CHAPTER 1**

(1990)
PUMP IT UP

On a lonely bridge in eastern Washington state, two athletically clad men stand on the railing over the rushing waters hundreds of feet below. They both have long bungee cords wrapped around their ankles, and they are both very nervous. One man bends over and pumps up his Reebok Pump athletic shoes with the basketball-shaped pump on the tongue of the shoe. Then, they dive off the bridge like Acapulco cliff divers, heading for the steel-gray waters below. The bungee goes taut and snaps back. The man with the Reeboks hangs from the bridge upside down in silence. The other bungee goes slack and comes back up with nothing but a pair of empty Nikes. The announcer says, "The Reebok Pump. It fits a little better than your ordinary athletic shoe." Every mother's son just fell to his death off the Spokane River Bridge.

Our New York ad agency group, along with the San Francisco office of Chiat Day, came up with the bungee jumping commercial.

In 1990 I was the president of Reebok Brands North America and felt the advertising needed to be as bold and dramatic as the Pump shoes. To the credit of Paul Fireman, Reebok's founder and CEO, he supported producing and running the commercials. When we had applied for clearance to run the commercials on the three major networks, one refused. We knew in advance that it was all pretty controversial, as it implied people dying from a bungee jump. My marketing team was very concerned. On the other hand, I thought the response was fantastic news. Controversy is always a friend to advertising. The controversy would surely send viewers to the other two networks to see the commercial. Calls came into those two networks, calls came into the company; everyone thought the commercial was outrageous. Outrageous was good. We needed outrageous. I wanted outrageous. That is exactly what I got, and what happened next made marketing history as the Reebok Pump took off like a rocket ship.

The commercial only ran six times and cost $500,000, but it caused Reebok to sell out of every pair of $180 Reebok Pump shoes we had in inventory around the country. This created a fresh playing field in the consumer's mind and was uber-cool—now there was an alternative to Nike. The day after the ad ran, Arsenio Hall, a TV trendsetter, spent twelve minutes on his show talking about the ad and the shoes. The public reaction was so remarkable that the networks pulled the commercial as too controversial. That is the definition of outrageous. For me, it was a near-perfect outcome for branding the new urban chic shoe.

We held a press conference in Atlanta for the product launch. It was in a building with a three-story atrium. The press was having drinks and food when we asked them to look up, at which point two guys jumped off a ledge. One jumper was wearing Nikes and the other Reeboks. They dove off the atrium supports three stories up and came within a foot of the floor. No one came out of their shoes, but there was that moment of doubt among the crowd, all of whom had seen the commercial. It was dramatic and it drove home our point. Jump first, think fast. Outrageous.

. . .

Playing from the second spot, like Reebok did with Nike, is always a challenge in any market, but let's stop and think about this in the context of risk and reward. People in the investment world always think and structure their business in this very productive and universal context because everyone can usually agree that one comes with the other. And yet the ratio of one to the other is rarely the same in different circumstances. You can take lots of risk and have little chance for reward, but that is usually just called being stupid. You can get lots of reward and have minimal risk attached, but that is almost always called lucky, or maybe privileged. Most of business is about the balancing act and trying to get as much reward as possible with as little risk as possible, and this takes continuous market awareness and strategic thought.

The context of brand positioning is just the sort of context that demands lots of strategic thinking. By definition there is only one market leader, so everyone else is playing catch-up. Not being the market leader is the position that most businesses find themselves in, and it's perhaps the most troubling because of the tantalizing proximity to success. No one exemplified this notion better than Avis with its "When you're only No. 2, you try harder...Or else." Avis's ad agency, Doyle Dane Bernbach, chose in 1962 to embrace Avis's second-place status as a compelling means of emphasizing *their* customer service. It was very memorable, which is good in advertising-speak.

Everyone wants to work for the market leader or become the market leader. I didn't get out of business school and decide to go find underdogs and play from the second spot. I needed a job and took it. But brand marketing finds you in that place eventually, and my turn in the breach came after fifteen years of honing my marketing and business skills, when the opportunity at Reebok came calling. Every career has many turning points, but the Reebok chapter has always seemed to me to be my Rubicon. And this ad was the moment of truth that would lead to the creation of the new Roman Empire ... and also my ignominious defeat. Those are the moments that seal your fate, and my fate as a marketer took direction from that.

• • •

The '80s had been about burgeoning technology, led by the silicon chip industry, global capitalism with Reagan and the actual and symbolic breakdown of The Berlin Wall, and a shift in personal values to an emphasis on health and exercise. In many ways, my career path, which had begun in the mid-1960s, was perfectly consistent with these trends. I was engaged in all of them—tech, globalization, and running as fast as I could every day. In some ways I was surfing on the leading wave of most of these trends. On reflection, I'm unclear whether that was a case of me following the trends closely or me being one of the trendsetters that led the way over the decade. It was probably a combination of both, but when I was more aware of it (and it did not escape my attention), then my next step was in exactly that direction.

It was Gerry Roche the famous Heidrick & Struggles executive recruiter, who formally reached out to me. Gerry was heading the search for a president for Reebok Brands. I had maintained contact with him throughout my career since my days at Carnation. It was important to be known by and to be in the databases of the top recruiting firms, and no one was bigger in the field than Gerry. After securing a job through a firm like Heidrick & Struggles, you are on the radar screen for future positions. The top firms and the executives they consistently hire and source as candidates are like an elite club.

This was a club of which I wanted to be a member. And they seemed to want me as a member.

My friend Joe LaBonte, who I knew from when he was President of 20th Century Fox, which had backed my video game company, and was then president of Reebok International, touted the position to me by saying during our initial phone call, "You will be known as Mr. Reebok." Joe was banking his comment on his three-year tenure at Reebok, working for Paul Fireman, chairman and CEO. It had been a turbulent ride, to say the least. To the world, Paul Fireman was Mr. Reebok. The unwritten plan was for me to replace Joe LaBonte as president of Reebok International, and Mark Goldston, who had been hired as the head of Marketing, would replace me as President of Reebok Brands. Reebok was on that first wave of the personal exercise trend, and the industry growth was eye-popping. Paul was the creator of Reebok as we knew it.

Every picture you see of Paul Fireman makes him look like the smallest guy in the room, and one with a slightly pudgy waistline to boot. Not exactly the icon of a sports-shoe empire. But Paul often looks that way because he is standing with athletic giants. In many ways, this is the story of the man. He is a complex guy with issues (who of us cannot be thus characterized?), but he also had that entrepreneur's drive and zeal accompanied by that "syndrome" of not wanting to let go. He is the guy who likes standing with giants, and while he often suffers physically by comparison, it doesn't preclude him from standing proudly, smiling from ear to ear, beside them. The story of Reebok is inextricably linked with that of Paul Fireman.

• • •

Reebok, as I came to see it, had no truly differentiated image. Nike was threatening to dominate the market. That market, while driven by technology, was surrounded by entertainers and high-profile athletes, neither of which Reebok had in its stables. Reebok was losing market share and was being heavily discounted at retail. I was afraid the serious athletic shoe buyer was no longer considering Reebok versus Nike in its purchasing decision. Brand awareness was falling, and the most recent advertising was the corporate campaign (as opposed to a product campaign) of "Reeboks Let U.B.U.," which was considered by many a colossal failure. With no truly differentiated shoe in a few years and in an industry ruled by product innovation, this was a bad omen for Reebok. The company needed to get back its mojo, and that would require a dramatic roundhouse punch.

Paul Fireman was a street-fighting product guy. It all started when, at a trade show, he met with an Italian designer who had come up with a shoe design. Paul asked me if I would meet the designer and review his concept. I remember this rough prototype for the pump, with tubes and fluid flowing through it. I quickly concluded that we could never manufacture a shoe taking this approach, but it did trigger a concept in my mind.

I talked with our designers about using some type of bladder that could be inflated with air and surround the foot. I was a skier, and there were similar concepts used in high-end ski boots where ankle support was of the essence. Ankle support was key in many sports; indeed, high-tops were born of that very concept. The advantages of an adjustable system were obvious in terms of ankle support, but naturally it needed to be lighter in weight than a ski boot. Also, since no two feet are the same size and shape (including differences between the right and left foot), adjustability was crucial. Incidentally, while everyone was familiar with ski-boot bladder technology, this was decidedly *not* the physical model that drove the concept.

Many stories surround the origin of the Pump. As with most great inventions, there is an endless list of people who claim to be responsible for the invention. I don't begrudge them their due and trust that they will grant me the same respect.

Nike already had Air Jordan, which was a huge success but a totally different technology. They also had a shoe with a bladder that was inflated with a separate pump, much like those used to pump up water floats. It was a clumsy design that wasn't popular. The trick would be to find a technology that worked better than those already in existence.

I came away from the show and wrote a general concept brief describing the idea and the end benefits. Then I started to look for the best outside non-footwear technology firm known for innovative solutions through the application of materials. Business Week had done an article on the top innovative technologies companies. Luckily one of them, Design Continuum, was located in Boston and appeared to have a perfect profile for the challenge. I contacted them and told them about the project. They immediately said, "But we don't know anything about making shoes." I said that was a good thing. We knew how to make shoes, and what we needed was someone who understood technology and material science. We hired them, gave them my concept sheet, and asked if they would get back in a few weeks with their preliminary thinking. Their website does a nice concise job of describing their four-step approach to the challenge through a design-thinking lens. They came back with a rough prototype that was spot-on—a polyurethane bladder with a built-in, off-the-shelf pump in the shape of a basketball. At that point, it was time to put them together with the internal design team (the Shoe Dogs) who knew how to turn it into a manufacturable, cost-effective, and safe athletic shoe.

I decided not to have the Pump development run through the traditional product development bureaucracy. I had learned from my other product development experience that it was best to have a small, carefully picked SWAT team representing each functional area (design and development, operations/costing/manufacturing, marketing, and sales), reporting directly to me. I established what was a high-speed SWAT team. I was the process director and needed to be the barrier buster. I needed to push for revolutionary solutions and then let the process slip back as needed but never bog down. Reebok was not used to rigid deadlines.

Athletic footwear companies typically have difficulty dealing with the integration of technology in the design and manufacturing process. Thus, it is critical to get outside technologists to work with the internal "Shoe Dogs" (guys who spend their life thinking only about shoes), who design the shoes around the technology such that it can be mass manufactured, resulting in a high-quality shoe at the right cost. We concluded that the most difficult shoe to apply the Pump technology to, due to its already large size and sturdiness standards, was a basketball shoe—ironically, the shoe that would most benefit from added ankle support. Basketball shoes take a lot of punishment, and a two-hundred-pound guy jumping and landing required a design that would both last and protect against breaking an ankle. I decided that we needed to send the Design Continuum people and our Shoe Dogs to Korea to work together with the production team in developing prototypes that we could launch quickly.

The team started sending me samples on an expedited basis. There was a group of Reebok employees who regularly played basketball, and they volunteered to be the guinea pigs for the prototypes. The early prototypes came back to me the next day all torn up after only one game.

The design requires sonically welding two halves of the bladder together. The weld had to be strong enough to hold, since giving way under pressure would likely result in a broken ankle. We were fortunate to find a small manufacturing and engineering firm with a very smart engineer by the name of Eric Stahl at the helm. We met with him at his company in Springfield, Massachusetts, on a rainy

Saturday. He was using sonic welding in a white room, producing medical devices where a weld failure would be life-threatening. We saw that he had the technical and manufacturing capability, but we told him we needed millions of bladders. Furthermore, we were uncomfortable relying on a single source for such a critical component. In the end, we needed to take a risk. We did, and Eric delivered. Had we not taken that leap, it would have taken us months to find and qualify a second source with the capability we needed. As a side note, Eric became a friend, and coincidentally, owned a home in Woodstock, Vermont.

The Pump was born. A whole book could be written about it. It was the vehicle that brought the Reebok brand back to its original luster. The Pump was all about design and product development—both crucial components of the athletic footwear business—and we nailed them both.

The built-in pump looked like a basketball in the tongue of the shoe. There was a release valve in the shoe's heel. The design engineers assumed we wanted to hide the pump. Quite the opposite. We wanted to expose the technology, making it a design feature. The early prototypes had a valve in the heel that made a hissing sound when the air was released. The engineers wanted to make the release of the air silent. I said no, based on a series of experiences, including in the toy business. I believed the hissing sound made the technology more believable. Also, I observed that when you gave people the shoe, they put their hand in the shoe and pumped it up so they could feel the bladder inflating and then pushed the release valve and loved the hissing sound it made, almost like it was an interactive toy.

The last, and some would say the most critical, step was to make the advertising and communication as bold as the product itself.

With technology and design in hand, I turned next to the marketing and advertising campaign, which as I've said, had to be as bold and provocative as the shoe. We needed to create a new playing field where we could beat Nike (the nemesis that never faded).

What drives fashion in the athletic footwear business is not the fashion runways but the courts in the hood. Reebok learned this lesson early on. They would test and introduce shoes, first in the city stores, before launching nationally. We researched inner-city athletic heroes, who never played in the big leagues but became neighborhood legends. Guys who just played their hearts out. Reebok had a smart program of refurbishing inner-city neighborhood playgrounds. They often had interesting names, like Lamar Fontaine Field. There was always speculation that the athletes found in these inner-city playgrounds might have been better athletes than their major-league counterparts. There was strength and honor in the hood. So Reebok hired inner-city kids as design consultants. They wore dreadlocks, and they knew hip when they saw it.

Chiat Day had been Reebok's agency for many years. They were an outstanding creative agency under the direction of Jay Chiat. However, they had just taken a hit with the U.B.U. campaign, since, as explained, it was very controversial and panned by the retailers (mostly due to a lack of product orientation). Even though I felt it was brilliant in holding Reebok's awareness until we got some new shoes, we were on the edge of searching for a new agency. But we nevertheless agreed to give Chiat Day a shot at developing a Reebok Pump campaign.

The typical approach to creating an ad campaign is to agree on a direction for the agency. Then the agency goes off on their own and develops various alternative approaches. Finally, they make presentations to the management team, who tries to shoot holes in the campaigns. I decided to take a different approach and create an internal competition between Chiat's offices and my own management group, assigning one member of my team to partner with each of their offices. It was a unique approach, to say the least.

The direction I gave the San Francisco team was that we needed a product demonstration that exceeded the uniqueness of the Pump product itself. I asked them to give me an advertising campaign that their other clients would *never* run. I felt we would never beat Nike on the court (in the NBA or in the hood), so they needed to come up with a new playing field (our own) where we could win and be the U.B.U. nonconformists, all at the same time. The San Francisco office came up with a whole series of crazy things like running with the bulls in Pamplona, where the Reebok runner outruns the Nike runner. When they came up with the bungee side-by-side, Nike versus Reebok, with guys jumping off a bridge and only the Reebok jumper snapping back up, we knew we had something. The result was the bungee jumping commercial.

The Pump commercial's dramatic presentation of a new shoe and new technology compared favorably to the cerebral and not-street level nature of U.B.U. Most states had outlawed bungee jumping, making it all the more intriguing. We made the management presentation, and most of the people who saw the ad were horrified. The Reebok public relations department commented that every mother in America would be calling me to complain, and all I could say was, "Great!"

We introduced the top-of-the-line Pump at $180. We were consciously using what was called a pinnacle pricing strategy with a plan to later introduce less expensive versions. The initial distribution went to inner-city stores, where we purposely limited the inventory and distribution to create scarcity and buzz about the product. Kids would be lined up outside the stores before they opened to try to buy a pair from the most recent shipment. We tightly controlled the allocation of product, putting up with the wrath from the big retailers who were fighting for an unfair share. There were constant fictitious rumors about shipments to retailers who were spying on one another. Buzz, buzz, buzz...

The ad had worked like a charm. We finally had Nike on the run.

Even though we had tried to avoid going up against Air Jordan on the court, the court had come to us. In the highly televised NBA slam dunk contest, Boston Celtics rookie, Dee Brown, went over to the bench and pumped up his Reeboks in full view of the audience. It was the tipping point for the Pump.

This ad and all that went into it not only changed the course of Reebok, creating billions of dollars in shareholder value, but it also changed the course of my career.

• • •

If there is a major theme that runs throughout my background, it is the ability to take concepts and solutions I have learned in other businesses or industries and translate them into my current business. By any other name, this is the essence of innovation. Some people say that there is nothing new under the sun. I say that there is always something new to be learned from cross-fertilization of ideas between industries. For me, the common thread has always been an understanding of consumer behavior and retailers. There are other areas that provide equally rich knowledge transfer, such as operations. Certainly, the knowledge of how to build and motivate a management team transcends industries.

I am often asked about the notoriety of having run these well-known companies, how I felt about being the president and CEO, and so forth. I'm taken aback by these questions, as my title has never been what brought me satisfaction. I think I have always had the ability to separate who I am from what I do for a living. That's the only way I can stay grounded.

I find my brain is like a radar screen that is constantly scanning, pulling some remote thought or experience and applying it to the current situation. Sometimes the experiences and ideas are stuck in my head as vignettes or little stories. This often provides unique solutions, especially when I'm dragging the ideas from one industry to another, such as from greeting cards to toys. I often think about executives who spend their entire career in one industry, wondering how they gain fresh perspectives and ideas from the huge and changing business and social universe. I have had numerous interchanges with these executives and find it takes only a few minutes and questions to see the narrowness of their views and exposure. I come away screaming (if only to myself), "Why don't you hire some young people from other industries and proactively do things that expand your horizon?"

My favorite approach is to ask these managers if they have been to India and China. And have they taken their families? I am constantly honing my questions for these insular managers. If you work at increasing the number of positive responses, you will begin to melt the ice of isolation around you.

I am wired differently. This sounds like an introspective analysis, but it's really just a personal observation. I started to recognize when I was at Cornell that I thought differently and had a different perspective and picture of the world from most people. It's hard to define, but I saw life through a broader lens, open and fueled by new and different thoughts and experiences. I had an innate ability to understand the consumer and was completely intrigued by consumer behavior and psychology. I can easily place myself in the consumer's shoes, or perhaps I have never left those shoes. No matter what executive level I have achieved or what company I have run, I have always stayed grounded with the mass consumer. It has become a bit of a mantra in every business I look at, I ask, "What do you know about your consumer? Do you have any research?" I am constantly blown away by how little both the big corporations and start-ups really know about their customer and ultimate consumer. Also, the type of consumer is changing fast, and the demographic shift from the Baby Boomers to the Millennials is a speeding bullet train of change that many companies can't see.

At times my view of the world is a bit of a kaleidoscope. Ideas seem to flow like a stream. I can get stimulus from every person and thing around me. I think in half-baked ideas, analogies, stories, and vignettes, and I build quickly from others' ideas. That is random thinking at its finest.

A big part of my style and unique view revolves around humor. I treat everything with humor and think in humorous terms. I find humor adds to the fluidity of my thinking. I don't take myself too seriously (important for us all). When I am in an intense meeting where there are strong people with differing points of view, I try to melt the ice with humor, loosening the grips to improve the chance for a collaborative solution. I am known for treating major business catastrophes with perspective and humor. I remind you of my line, which is—*business is not life-threatening*.

CHAPTER 2

(1943–61)
MEANWHILE BACK
ON THE FARM

I have carried so many lessons from the farm and my hometown of Ovid, New York, that they are almost hard to enumerate. Where and how I grew up has had more to do with my success and who I am than anything that has happened to me. I vaguely remember wandering around our barnyard as a toddler, learning how to walk where creepy crawlers and chickens ruled, falling down and briskly relocating off the deck when something came after me. I started life with two solid stakes in the ground: my mother's love and guidance, and everything that growing up on a farm offers. These have proven to be valuable life traits over the years. Farming is nothing if not innovative.

Confidence and being secure in knowing how to make a living came to me shortly after learning how to walk. That may sound like an exaggeration, but it's not. The cause-and-effect cycle is so much more evident on a farm, where you put in the effort to grow or raise something and then you eat it or sell it. This wasn't running a paper route or starting a social media company while sitting at a computer . . . it was the ultimate in entrepreneurship. Doing chores made things grow. Not doing chores caused things to die. The lessons were simple but never forgotten.

Our farm was in Ovid, New York. Ovid is a medium-sized town of less than forty square miles and 2,300 residents (it peaked at 3,400 residents in my youth), located in Seneca County between the two largest Finger Lakes—Seneca and Cayuga. In other words, it was in the middle of nowhere. Growing up on a farm in Ovid provided one lesson after another. It was my mother and older brother, Dan, and I doing all the learning as we went. One day we learned how to castrate sheep.

There's a reason for everything you do on a farm, and nothing is done casually; it's always done with purpose. We were raising the sheep for wool and slaughter, and excess testosterone was simply not helpful. This was a case of changing the things we could change. This may seem trivial to hardened farmers, but to a young, impressionable boy, it was all shocking (the castration especially) and had the effect of opening and healing the wounds of youth with daily regularity. Innovation was always at the top of my mind.

The day after we castrated the sheep, we watched from the kitchen window as a hailstorm destroyed our entire bean crop, which was about to be harvested. There was nothing to be done and we learned the inverse about accepting the things we cannot change. But tragedy not only breeds resilience. It also breeds ingenuity.

We raised laying hens and when we hit the worst market in forty years, instead of wholesaling our eggs, we sold them door-to-door on an egg route we built. Every Friday my mother drove us around the route to make deliveries. Going straight to retail was not a gimmick we did to be cute. This was no lemonade stand on the corner; this was economic life or death, and life came from getting those few extra pennies per egg that retailing afforded. Marketing innovation helped us survive when other farms didn't. Don't get me wrong, we always managed to have fun while we did it (we were always riding pigs, washing cows, building huts in the haymows, and driving tractors from a very young age), but farming was serious business, and we always knew where the fun began and ended when the serious business came into play.

A farm is a 24-7 sort of place. One wet summer we couldn't get the tractor and bean machine on the fields to harvest because the fields were simply too sodden. Time for an alternative solution. We rented a bunch of Gravely Garden tractors with sickle bars, hired kids from school, and harvested fifteen acres literally by hand. The crop was saved. We solved the problem with our brains and our brawn.

Hard work is the essence of farming. There is no substitute for it, no chemical additive or magic potion to lessen the load. When you mechanize, you do so to plant more acreage, not to make your day shorter. And the beauty of it all is that you see the progress you are making as well as the impact of your mistakes in real time. You can't misinterpret or ignore causality on a farm. I quickly came to love the satisfaction of seeing and making progress and, yes, money.

Almost every meaningful endeavor in life requires great effort. There are so few instances of things coming easily or with pure luck that "winning the lottery" is, indeed, the appropriate expression for those rare lightning-struck examples. Farming makes this all very clear. You wake up at dawn or before, you break your back for twelve hours, and then you pray that your luck will not be bad and undo all that you have worked for. This is not praying for the roulette wheel to make your fortune; this is praying for the gods to not whimsically prove that man is but a mere pawn in nature's game. I have always said that nature is my boss and I am happy with the odds she offers.

We were always trying to cheat Mother Nature out of a win without abusing her as our most important partner. I remember at lambing time bringing sick lambs into the kitchen and putting them by the radiator in hopes that keeping them warm would keep them alive. It worked. Severe winters and bad snowstorms were more the norm in upstate New York in those days, and Ovid seemed to get at least its fair share. This forced us to find ingenious ways to get our far-ranging cattle fed. One time we had to take advantage of a government-supplied airdrop of hay down to the cattle or let the winter take them. Losing the cattle would have meant losing the farm. And then there were the run-of-the-mill hardships like frozen pipes, something we learned to avoid at all costs. Once again, hay was the most common solution, but mixing in a bit of naturally bio-reactive manure didn't hurt either. ABI— Always Be Innovating.

Farming is also a team sport. While Mother worked at Cornell to earn a living, running the farm back in Ovid was mostly left to Dan and me. We had very different approaches to doing business. Dan was older and naturally more frugal and conservative. He always wanted to buy old machinery at auction and spend our otherwise peaceful winters (when we could catch up on our educations) busting knuckles repairing the old, worn machines. His form of innovation was a bit more hardscrabble than mine. He wanted us to do everything ourselves in his vision of parsimonious good business. He was the original "Make versus Buy" kind of guy.

While Dan was tight with money, Mother knew money was dear and that we simply had to do what needed to be done. At one point, she determined that we needed some extra money for necessary repairs on critical farm equipment, so she unilaterally decided that we needed to turn our house into a tourist home by renting rooms whenever there was demand. We had a sign on the road that offered rooms for rent and below it another offering "Farm Fresh Eggs."

This had several very real impacts on me. To begin with, there was the lesson of flexibility, since room sales were the determining factor on where I would sleep at night. This also made me somewhat less attached to my possessions as I watched my favorite bathroom cup get used to soak one lodger's false teeth overnight. You see, we had only one bathroom, so this was not just about camping out for a night or two; it was about learning to share what today would be thought as unsharable personal space. Hello, Airbnb. What this did for my business sense was to give me a hard lesson early on about the importance of cash flow in every enterprise.

Diversity is also learned quickly on a farm. As small boys, Dan and I worked with the hired hands, when we could afford them. These were rugged and earthy men. Their vocabulary and demeanor were not the same as Mother wanted us to use in polite company. We learned a lot of practical things about farming and machinery from these men, but also learned a more "manly" vernacular and manners than Mother wished we had. She was unabashed in commenting to us when she noticed our vocabulary changing for the worse. She once asked how we could be outside working all day and not come in to go to the bathroom. While she was not a prude, she did have her standards of civility and reminded us that we were fortunate to have acquired indoor plumbing and that we had damn well better plan on using it. I think we found the limits of her manly trait indulgence when Dan and I each came in with a plug of chewing tobacco in our cheeks and a touch of tobacco spittle on our chins.

I guess I was sort of a farming overachiever in that I didn't just join the FFA (Future Farmers of America) and 4-H (Head, Heart, Hands, and Health), but became the local Ovid chapter president. Mother always encouraged us to enter projects and win smaller—and eventually larger—prizes. Building on success was a big theme in our household. I went all the way to the New York State Fair with my pet roosters, who were literally covered with ribbons. I went so far in the poultry world as to being made a judge in the Laying Hens Division (all that egg route work had paid off). I even won a trip to New York City as Poultry Man of the Year. It may sound like a lot of chicken shit today, but at the time it was quite a big deal. I strutted my stuff through the Fulton Fish Market (I guess there was no poultry market at the time) and was even elevated to international competition at the Toronto Winter Royal Fair. Those Canadian boys sure do know their chickens, so that was all she wrote. But back on the farm in little old Ovid, we turned a small, smelly chicken coop into an operation raising three thousand broilers per quarter and six hundred laying hens and pheasants.

Growing up on the farm in Ovid and learning about life from my mother and my best friend, Walt, and my brother, Dan, I gained the confidence that I could solve any problem or pass the best and the brightest by outworking them.

Virginia Rapp Davidson Smith O'Connell Govern (aka Mother) lived ninety-seven glorious years, spending most of those years in her beloved upstate New York. She was married three times: to an attorney; to a farmer, my father, Daniel M. O'Connell Sr.; and to an engineer, George Govern, whom she put through college at the age of 40 and set him on a course to becoming named City Engineer of Auburn, New York. Her careers spanned the breadth of college administrator at Cornell, dairy farmer, and mother to two strapping farm boys. Mostly what she did was encourage and motivate all the men around her.

Mother had learned about life the hard way. Originally from Buffalo, New York, she was married first to an attorney from DC. It became clear early on, when their bank account dwindled, that he was having a love affair with the blackjack table, so she packed up the house and left for good. Her second husband, my father, Daniel, endured a long sanitarium bout with TB before he met my mother and then died of cancer at the young at age of forty-three after only five years of marriage. That wrenching and unexpected harsh reality left her on a farm with two boys to raise. It was pretty gut-wrenching for my brother and me, too.

When a friend of my father, Roy Weston, showed up, she was sympathetic and trusting enough to mortgage the farm to invest in Roy's business. But Roy proceeded to hightail it to Brazil with the money, and while he was eventually apprehended with a small portion of the money, it was a very hard but lasting lesson about trust for all of us.

Her third husband, George, who achieved one of the highest scores on the Civil Engineering exam while studying at Manhattan College, had been with the Army Corps of Engineers and worked hard to help us run the farm while trying to make something of himself with her support. But he ultimately fell to alcoholism and all that that entailed for her and the family. All of these experiences served to make my mom an understanding mother who knew the difference between peccadillos and major problems and character lapses.

My mother was the best mentor, motivator, and matriarch of the family anyone could ever have had. She taught me about working hard, the value of ambition and education, the importance of innovative thinking and, mostly, the imperative of unconditional love. She was not highly educated (though she promoted and supported it with all her men), but she was always wise and a good business woman in the end. She had a tolerance for young boys that made growing up a learning experience rather than a series of crimes and punishment.

She understood how an altar boy, presiding over a Christmas midnight mass, could walk behind Monsignor Sullivan in the procession, lean forward, and end up catching his cassock on fire in the process. I wanted to get home and open my presents! She accepted that tipping over the outhouse on Halloween and being chased by the cops was something that just had to be done. And when I was coming of age, using a fake ID at Katie and Harry's Bar at the age of fifteen for some mild refreshments after a basketball game, and the state police raided the joint, she came to "bail out" (we were only *almost* arrested) both me and the local justice of the peace's son. She went above and beyond pleading my case to not be thrown off the team, even though the valiant effort failed. She was mother, father, and pal to us when we needed any of those.

Except for gum-chewing, which I use for concentrated thought, my farm-boy traits are mostly good and valuable. The experience being president of the FFA and 4-H taught me Robert's Rules of Order and how to run a meeting and form committees. Those lessons have stuck in my head, and I still use them in board meetings. When I experience the typical boardroom drama from a bunch of suits trying to intimidate me, I smile and think of the beautiful reality of the farm. I admit to occasionally wishing I had a cattle prod to help the process along.

A high energy level is a gift, but it still needs to be directed. I do my most creative thinking and take my riskiest, boldest moves early in the morning, just as I did in the Ovid farmlands. I can chart my biorhythms, which tell me when to do various tasks: After exercising early in the morning, I face my most difficult situations and do my creative thinking and problem solving but want to be alone (lots of space in Ovid). By 10 a.m. I am ready to meet and talk to people. I seldom ever go to lunch (it takes too much time and nobody on the farm eats lunch) but have pushed myself at times to do so and to be more social. I meet with groups early in the afternoon and save routine tasks or the urgent but unimportant for late in the day as the sun sets over Seneca Lake. I don't procrastinate but suffer from the reverse plague of wanting to get it done now. I can drive people nuts by wanting everyone to stop what they are doing to focus on completing my task. After all, I managed to command all the attention there was in good old Ovid.

In other words, the farm and Ovid, strangely enough, prepared me for a life in the fast lane of innovation, and the first entrance ramp was a mere twenty-five miles south in Ithaca on the Cornell University campus.

CHAPTER 3

(1961-66) GOING TO CORNELL

The town of Ovid and Cornell University have more in common than meets the eye. The transition was The Cascadilla School. The school was also considered by the local community to be something in between a prep school and a reform school, all at once. Getting "sent to Cascadilla" in Ithaca was as much an indicator of juvenile delinquency as it was upward mobility.

Any objections I had about making a long daily trip and leaving my comfort zone in Ovid were overcome by an unpleasant incident. I managed to get into a car accident doing one of my usual stunts, this time in the Lodi Cemetery. My girlfriend at the time was in the car and was injured. Taking one too many stupid risks had the result of thrusting me into an even bigger risk of leaving Ovid High School for the strictures and seriousness of Cascadilla. I was fortunate to get the "air cover" of Walt, Dan, and five other Ovid boys "deciding" to go at the same time. This made it seem less personally impactful and socially outcasting. At age sixteen, I went off to Cascadilla with a 1956 Oldsmobile Convertible, with glass-packed exhaust pipes and teardrop fender skirts. It made the miles figuratively fly by down Route 96.

Maxwell Kendall was then the headmaster of the school. While he was a great academic and great headmaster, as a dairy farmer himself, he came to school smelling of cow shit many mornings. It never bothered us farm boys since we sometimes came to school smelling even worse. Mr. Kendall was in the habit of doing write-ups predicting what each student would likely do in their lives. His assessment of me in those days was that my openness and sense of adventure would lead me down paths others would not go because of their skepticism. He went on to suggest that these traits would propel me a great distance in life. Never underestimate the value of having someone in authority characterize your potential in a positive light.

When it was time to apply to Cornell, Mr. Kendall's assessment carried a great deal of weight with the admissions staff. You see, many of our teachers at Cascadilla were faculty spouses, so it really was like a Cornell "farm team," to make an appropriate sports pun. The most likely Cornell College to which my crowd applied was, naturally, the School of Agriculture. Not only was the farm life our guiding light, but there was the added issue that as a state or land-grant college, it was more affordable for New York State residents compared with the tuition cost of the endowed colleges. At the time, the college was tuition-free for New York State residents living on farms.

Once admitted to Cornell, the real differential advantage for me came in the form of Professor Wendell Earle. In addition to being an important academic and life advisor to me over the years, he eventually helped me double register my senior year into the Graduate Business

School (where MBAs were being minted). That would prove to be pivotal to my later career goals. For years the only undergraduate business program at Cornell was the Agricultural Economics area in the Agricultural School.

A major stabilizing factor for me during those early college years was my very early marriage (we were each seventeen years old) to Gail Young. It's an age-old story. Boy meets girl and they fall in love. Girl gets pregnant. Girl and Boy decide to keep baby. Girl and Boy decide, contrary to the "plan," to get married sooner and start life together. But naturally, there's much more to the story.

The Young family was quite different from other local families. They had an aura of wealth. They were from the Shaker Heights section of Cleveland, Ohio, where the family patriarch, Ray, was a successful machine tool business executive. The family lived on a beautiful property, Nundawaga Farm, on Seneca Lake about ten miles away from Ovid. This stood in stark contrast to our 250-year-old farmhouse, where we put hay bales around the foundation in the winter to insulate against the cold. But in the summertime, when Gail and I were dating, and later after we were married, we lived with the Youngs at the lake, water skiing and generally having a good time. It's no wonder that Ray Young quickly became a father figure to me. I had never known anyone so successful or with such a big house, new cars, and water skiing boats. Gail's brothers and sisters were all smart, interesting, fun, and artistic.

My decision to marry Gail was mine and mine alone. It was difficult for my mother because it was certainly not in her life plan for me, and, more importantly, it demarcated that my life had moved independently into my own hands.

One fact that is undeniable is that very few students my age entered Cornell in marital bliss. It was so unique that I became an unofficial counselor to other young married couples.

Such was Gail's commitment to this new life with me that she gave up her full scholarship to art school at Syracuse University to work at the Cornell Research Library (not a bad job at all, and probably above my pay grade at the time). I sold my Oldsmobile convertible in favor of a Ford Falcon station wagon. When our first daughter, Beth, was born during a January winter storm, it was only our first semester on the Hill. I rushed Gail up to the West Hill Hospital in that wagon, pushing its limits. In fact, the blessed event came most inconveniently during my first semester final exams. Imagine my surprise when I ran into one of my professors in the father's waiting room. This seren-dipitous bonding experience certainly didn't hurt my grades that first grading cycle. Our daughter, Lauren Beth, soon became part of the whole educational experience.

We were all living upstairs in my Aunt Margaret's house. This was one of the Greek revival homes in downtown Ithaca on West Buffalo Street. We had the second floor to ourselves, and I could build a study in the attic. I took the conversion of the attic space into my study very seriously. I knew I would need quiet space to work and think. After sneaking some spare plywood and chain from a local construction site, I made a desk by chaining a piece of finished plywood to the ceiling. I was very proud of this suspended desk, which seemed very cool, but was about as stable as my country-boy psyche in the big leagues of Cornell higher education. Luckily, my farm training made it sturdy enough to last five years and get me through not one, but two Ivy League degrees.

I spent many evenings up in the attic at my makeshift desk, studying late into the night. A neighbor next to us, also a Cornell student, had a small motorcycle, which he would take out at night to escape from the rigors of studying. I would hear him roar up West Buffalo Street and wished I had the money for a motorcycle, which seemed so liberating and fun. I heard him return with the exhaust pipes loud against the night and vowed that someday I would own a bike just like it.

My life's third foundational stake in the ground was going to Cornell. It exposed me to a bigger world and changed my life. The combination of an Ivy League education, a supportive and mostly stable home environment (I was responsible enough to keep my head down and be at home when not in class), and an unusual group of professor mentors took me to another planet. My professors somehow thought me a more serious student since I was a married man who carried a diaper in my back pocket rather than a handkerchief. I gained great confidence in those years and came to feel that I could learn and do just about anything if I just worked harder than everyone else. I also learned that despite my free-spirited ways, I had the capacity for the hard thinking work I needed to do, and I knew when I needed to apply it.

As I got into my courses at Cornell, I found that I loved the work and was overwhelmed by business curiosity. Cornell is a big research university that has global reach, but the agriculture school felt like a small, friendly college on a day-to-day basis. This made it a perfect environment for me by being comfortable yet mind expanding. I worked as hard or harder than everyone I knew, and it showed up in the form of good grades. My areas of greatest interest were marketing and consumer and creative product development. I seemed to have a great affinity for those arenas. Even then I sensed that I saw things differently than my peers. I could somehow climb above the fray and see a bigger marketing picture than others easily saw. Maybe it was the farm, maybe it was the attic study, or maybe it was just that my head was forever in the clouds.

This all culminated in some clear mileposts of success beyond just grades. The first was that I was granted the Heinz "Pickle" Scholarship. This should tell you a lot about the Cornell Agriculture School, where food science was one of many serious activities that were sponsored by the world of massive food companies. As they say in their marketing materials, they pride themselves in "applying the principles of science and engineering to ensure the nutritional value, safety and quality of foods in the United States and around the globe." But that doesn't stop it from sounding funny when you get a pickle scholarship.

Professor Earle secured a summer job for me with Jewel Tea Company in Chicago. These were the days when internships did not exist, and the normal summer work was the sort of construction labor I had been doing. But Professor Earle thought it was important to my future that I learn how to sell directly to the consumer, and the summer job with Jewel Tea was selling at its most basic, which was door-to-door.

I was twenty-one years old when I was assigned a sales territory with Jewel in Harvey, Illinois—as Jim Croce would say, "On the south side of Chicago, in the baddest part of town." Whatever you know about Chicago and its problems today, I bet they were worse in 1965 during the Civil Rights Movement. By this time, our second daughter, Kim, had joined the family. I found a dinky little run-down, one-bedroom apartment, and we settled ourselves in for the hot summer ahead. Selling an array of two hundred staple grocery items to 250 customers door-to-door during race riots was certainly an education in itself. The job involved "owning" your own route, ordering products and maintaining an inventory in your garage and managing receivables and payables. It became a small family business very quickly.

Few people in marketing or business (for that matter) ever get the rich opportunity to sell directly to consumers. Most never have the chance and will spend their entire career designing products and programs to sell to consumers without ever having been at the coalface. The same is true about retail. You should always live where the consumer touches your product. I was once interviewed for a senior job with a consumer products company in a grocery store.

Knowing grassroots products, brands, merchandising, and pricing is important in any industry.

Running the Jewel Tea Home Shopping route taught me more than just selling door-to-door and learning how to jam my foot in the door. In every new leadership job I've had since that summer, I would first ask to spend time as close to the customer or consumer as possible. I start by spending time in the field visiting stores and riding routes and talking to customers with no data screen or company person telling me about the customer. You learn quickly that this is the one chance you get for an honest and unvarnished market appraisal.

The Jewel Tea method of selling was one of the only ways the customers I had that summer could buy food on credit, so extending credit and making collections was a meaningful business conundrum. You wanted to make the sale with your differential advantage (this is what made operations like Rent-A-Center great), but people would move overnight and try to stiff you. This was real life and real business. I learned all the tricks of tracing people and collecting, including showing up on Saturday or Sunday when the husband was at home. I must say this sometimes worked to my advantage and sometimes ended with a size-twelve boot in my ass.

Through all this I also learned about building franchise value. I significantly increased the value of my route over the summer by building revenue per customer, getting new customers and decreasing receivables backlog. Fundamentally, this is how every business builds value. When I look at the current and many prior attempts (some successful and some not so much) at home shopping services (direct, on television, and now online), I think back to this experience. I wonder how many college students today would ever consider a summer job selling door-to-door for the value of the experience. Most prefer to spend their summer at an internship, sitting at a computer studying purchasing patterns, thinking they are learning the market. Ha!

In my senior year in the Agricultural School, I was in the top 10 percent of the class and on the Dean's List. Professor Earle and another influential advisor to me, Professor Lawrence Darrah, encouraged me to double register in my last year of undergraduate with the graduate Business School, and thereby get both my bachelor's and MBA in five years. Each year, they took a limited number of students into this relatively unique program within the Agricultural School. It was a tough call.

On the one hand, my family of four was living on fumes in our little upstairs apartment on West Buffalo Street. On the other hand, my work at Jewel Tea had convinced me that it was important to get as far up the corporate food chain as I could, and I knew enough to know that an MBA was all the rage in that world. Being able to get the MBA in one year instead of coming back in a few years for two years seemed like a no-brainer to me. Gail was ready to get away from Cornell and student life but agreed that we could suck it up for another year while we were already settled into a rhythm on West Buffalo Street (with a decent support network just up the Lake), so I applied for dual registration and got in.

When you are in the academic groove, you are in the groove for undergraduate work or graduate work, no big difference. What was different was shifting from a state agriculture school to a broader-based endowed college like the Business School. The older students (many had come back from the working world to get their MBAs) were strangely familiar to me, based on my experience at Cascadilla School. But this was a more consistent, business-focused group of people who were far more like-minded. I thoroughly enjoyed Business School and the relevancy of the courses. It was nice to have some case studies that weren't about farms and food science. This all gave me great confidence in my ability to learn about a situation quickly and adapt to an environment. The experience took me squarely out of the "farm world" and showed me how enjoyable it was to interact with people from every walk of life. The farm was deeply rooted in me, but it was good to learn what was beyond the farm.

CHAPTER 4

(1966-80)
PACIFIC HORIZONS

I took my first job out of school with Carnation in Los Angeles. Gail and I didn't know much about Los Angeles, so deciding where to live in this sprawling urban metroplex was a challenge. I was barely twenty-three years old, with a newly minted MBA from Cornell, a wife, and two little girls. The headquarters for Carnation were located at 5045 Wilshire Boulevard in downtown LA, in a stark white building with huge palm trees growing up the side. There was a popular ice cream bar on the first floor known for its homemade Carnation ice cream.

The office was on the edge of the area called Hancock Park, known as the poor man's Beverly Hills, with beautiful brick mansions on every street. Hancock Park was simply too expensive for almost anyone who worked at Carnation to live in. Most of the young executives commuted over an hour to and from their homes in the San Fernando Valley, which was more affordable. Some of the Carnation executives lived in the buttoned-up community of Pasadena, which was the quintessential upscale American suburb with sidewalks and white picket fences. But that wasn't a good fit for Gail and me. It was too expensive and too staid. Instead, we found a nice little rental house in North Hollywood on Magnolia Boulevard from which to launch a search.

Chatsworth is in the northern part of the San Fernando Valley, set against the backdrop of the San Gabriel Mountains of the Sierra Nevada Range. It is a rural place, more exurban than suburban. There were lots of farmers and horse ranchers in the area. The one made me feel at home and the other made me feel like the cowboy I wanted to be. This made it seem perfect, but mostly, Gail was happier in that sort of setting than the craziness of LA proper. So off we went.

The Valley was a happy place for us for a couple of years. I used this moment of being in the great Western landscape to launch my motorcycling hobby; I bought a used Honda Scrambler, a bike I artistically painted green. It would be my first of many and was both the realization of those Ithaca attic dreams and the start of a lifelong love affair with the freedom of being on two wheels. I rode my motorcycle every day down to the Ventura Freeway to carpool an hour and a half farther to Carnation. This was in keeping with the commutation patterns of the expanding footprint of Los Angeles County, and thus seemed as natural then as it seems absurd today.

Gail and I also enjoyed riding the Honda Scrambler around the rustic hills and canyons of Santa Susana Pass and between Topanga Canyon and the Pacific Ocean. Once I got comfortable with my riding abilities, I traded the Scrambler for a classic Triumph Bonneville and realized how much I truly loved riding—the thrill of being in the open air and the freedom I felt on the bike.

Gail decided not to work outside the home to be with the girls more, which allowed her to pursue her interest in art. We were in the heart of hippie land, so there was a constant supply of artistic and interesting people wandering here and there (kind of like a year-round, unstructured Burning Man Festival). Gail never owned a bra—ever—but had plenty of Birkenstock sandals. She was truly a hippie's hippie, who went so far as to mow the lawn topless without a care in the world. She taught art and exposed the girls to art. She was less interested in the girls' formal education (peace out, baby!) and was decidedly more laissez-faire in attitude than I could ever possibly be.

Then, with a $1,500 loan from Gail's grandmother, Almeda Young, we took the plunge and bought a house (not much more than a shack, really) in the rugged and rocky hills of Box Canyon. It was up a winding dirt road off Santa Susana Pass at the Religious Sect (an old stone house). There were only two other houses on the lane at that time, and they were spread out among huge boulders and lots of tumbleweed. Sometimes at night, the sky was bright red. This was because our corporate neighbor, Rocketdyne, often tested their latest rocket engines, causing the ground to shake and the rocky terrain to echo like thunder.

The Box Canyon shack was funky but fun and had killer views of the San Fernando Valley below and the Santa Monica mountains to the west. It had been built by a movie-set builder mainly with 2x4s. It made me feel like we were living on a Western movie set (for all I knew, that had been its original purpose). The isolation and views were not the only benefits. By having some land, the girls (Kim in particular), could keep a horse named Rosie and a pony named Daisy, as well as the two Great Danes, Hannibal and Flower. Kim trained both horses to jump and do other incredible tricks. She became an excellent bareback rider and eventually got deep into barrel racing. A burgeoning cowgirl, she had the freedom to ride on the horse trails in the canyon. She discovered many old, abandoned movie sets in those wilds. Beth and Kim thrived and had lots of friends who often came over for playdates. This life seemed to suit them.

While we had a wide variety of local friends, there were few professionals like me. I found myself drawing closer to my progressively good friends at Carnation. Those young, like-minded guys and their girlfriends or spouses were originally shocked by Gail's predilection for directness. Gail was not prejudiced against anything, but she was very opinionated and didn't care what people thought of her or her comments. She tended to grumble and complain about everything except her hippie-like existence. While California was moving towards healthy habits and enlightenment, Gail was decidedly going in the other direction. If anyone commented that they were concerned for her health, she would say, "I know I smoke and drink too much, but who the hell cares?" The older she got, the more belligerent and set in her ways she became.

That was about the time I realized that my marriage to Gail had begun to seriously deteriorate. Gail was patently not interested in the junior executive lifestyle I was aggressively pursuing and, quite frankly, loved. She could level a cocktail party in under two minutes with some off-color comment. And here's the thing: she liked that about herself. She had zero interest in considering a move from Box Canyon.

Do you remember who else lived in Box Canyon in the Santa Susana Mountains? Yes, next to us was the Spahn Movie Ranch, with Charles Manson and his Helter Skelter Family, who was spending their time planning the Tate–La Bianca and Sharon Tate massacres. Right there in Box Canyon. This was the same place my daughters were going horseback riding every day. Hell, I even did business with them by buying a shack from them to use for our animals. They seemed a bit strange, but who wasn't out here in La La Land? Between Gail and the Manson family, I was the one who was getting boxed out in Box Canyon.

• • •

I occasionally stop myself and ask how I got wherever I was. In this case it was more logical than not. With graduation looming and five years at Cornell starting to feel like enough, I launched into the task of job hunting. To start with, in 1966, life was quite a bit different than today. Everyone wanted to hire MBAs. It was a hot ticket to the business world; there were less than fifteen thousand MBA grads in 1966, while today over two hundred thousand are churned out annually. The big concentrations in those days were accounting, finance, manufacturing, and brand management. Most of my classmates went into banking and finance in New York City or brand management at places like P&G and IBM (a category unto itself). Very few graduates went into operating roles in those days ...at least not directly out of school.

Unlike many of my friends who were more uber focused in their efforts, I spent most of my last semester at Cornell interviewing as many companies as possible for the experience and the exposure. I flew around the country at the invitation of companies, collecting offers from P&G, IBM, HJ Heinz, and Carnation, to name a few. It was a heady experience and may have been the time in my life when I was feeling more in demand than any other time.

In the marketing arena, Procter & Gamble was considered the Holy Grail. It had the best consumer product training in the world and was a sure fire path to leadership in brand management. I knew Gail was a big consumer of their products, most notably disposable diapers in those early years. But P&G was headquartered in Cincinnati and my visits there left me cold. I wasn't crazy about the culture, which seemed somewhat too regimented to me (not surprising given the size of the P&G operation).

IBM was a slick operation. Its shift from workaday business machines to computers that were supporting NASA in its push to reach the moon within the decade made it a very tempting place to start. The added advantage was that with my Jewel Tea sales training, I thought the famous IBM sales culture would serve me well. But the deal-killer was the Tom Watson white shirt, dark suit and tie culture that screamed conformity to this wild and crazy farm boy.

HJ Heinz held a soft spot in my heart thanks to my annual Pickle Scholarship stipend checks, which kept us in pickle juice and other important family condiments during the baby years. But those were the days when Pittsburgh was at its nadir, and the town seemed grim to me during my visits. All those years in upstate New York made me hanker for a more interesting, sunnier, and livelier place to start my "real" life.

And then there was Carnation. My farm and agricultural school training (not to mention my Jewel Tea route) made me inherently like the food business. I'm reminded of the old Barneys commercial where the little boys ask one another what they want to do when they grow up. Babe says he wants to be a ballplayer. Fiorello says he wants to be mayor of New York. But Barney just says, "I don't know, but you're all gonna need clothes!" Well, I don't know either, but you're all gonna need food!

Carnation had an accelerated MBA training program, which would get me to responsibility faster than other places. And wow! They were offering me $10,000 a year to start. In 1966 that was serious money for a twenty-three-year-old with a family of four and lots of lint in his pockets. But most important, Carnation was in California. I will admit to having my share of palm-tree-itis. When I was landing at LAX and squinting out into the sunshine past the palm trees to the beaches of the Pacific, I said to myself that this could work. Like every kid, I felt that life was long and starting somewhere for a while was just that and no more. California would be a good place to start and then I could work my way back across the country over time.

While I've implied that all I had to do to get a job offer was show up, the truth is that you always need to impress people in person and go meaningfully beyond the you that's on paper. It's simple: demonstrate passion for the job and company and leave the interviewer feeling better about themselves. While I feel I could write an entire book on job hunting and interviewing, given my years on both sides of that desk, I'm guessing that what I've just explained in one sentence gets you 90 percent of the way to success. The other 10 percent, though, might be the difference between getting a good versus a great job.

I recommend you start with a self-analysis using a close friend who'll be honest with you. I was lucky. I had Gail, Walt, Dr. Earle, and my mother. They were all willing to be brutally honest with me about what I was good at, what I was not so good at, and what they liked and disliked about my style. I also encourage people to sit down, as I did, with their significant other and identify their five major priorities in life and how the proposed jobs fit in with those. The bonus is that you might also discover important things about your relationship.

This approach beats the hell out of simply identifying companies and trying to immediately figure out how to get in bed with them. Most young people today grew up in the age of computers and searching for everything online. That's great for learning about the company and building your passion base. But the real power lies in the face-to-face interaction. I honestly feel it was more important for me to have those personal interactions than it was for the companies. It would be hard for me to advise anyone to apply for a job online, sending off a resume. Even if I could have gotten the job of my dreams that easily, I'm not sure it would have allowed me to properly judge if it truly was or wasn't really my dream job.

At this point, all I cared about was that Carnation wanted me, I wanted Carnation, and I was going to California.

The Carnation Company, run by H. Everett Olson (at the time, in the prime of his career) was a highly successful and profitable food conglomerate that had grown from a family dairy farm in Washington state to a public company based in Los Angeles. They sold milk products (condensed milk from "contented" cows), Contadina tomato paste, and Friskies pet foods. I immediately felt at home with this company. Its roots were on the farm and its head was up in the clouds of Wall Street. Its core was consumer products, and I immediately sensed my point of differential advantage. My time on the farm, my time at Cornell's Agricultural School, and my Jewel Tea hard-earned skill in understanding the consumer all set me apart.

But there was something else as well. My wild and crazy ways allowed me to think creatively, to think big and get ahead of the competitive crowd. As an MBA, I had been trained to think strategically and conceptually. I felt primed to not just change a product here or there at the margin, but to revolutionize the company and the industry. As presumptuous as this sounds, that was my mindset.

I found that to advance quickly you needed to do two things. First, you needed to develop an area of expertise. Second, you needed to stick your head above the crowd and the day-to-day by making strategic observations regarding the big picture. This caused people to see you and your contribution differently from the herd. Work hard at your daily tasks and don't be afraid to make intuitive observations that are not completely supported. This feels a bit risky at first, but it is the beginning of building your personal brand. My frankness was evolving.

• • •

The best part of Carnation for me was the accelerated training program which they had started for new MBAs like me. My sponsor was the head of sales, Tim Crull, and he allowed me to work in all areas of the business: sales, merchandising, market research, marketing, advertising, and product management. This was a huge opportunity and a boost to my education and career development. I got to do meaningful consumer research on products that succeeded and failed. Studying product failures is perhaps one of the most valuable research exercises for a wannabe brand manager. It exploded my curiosity and gave me an appreciation for consumer research methodology.

One such product failure was Calico Cow, a flavored evaporated milk (chocolate, vanilla, and strawberry). Carnation had a huge evaporated milk and condensed milk business that was in decline due to changing consumer patterns—most notably, more refrigeration—and they were trying to use underutilized capacity. Frankly, the killer for any food product is simply the taste. A sweet, flavored condensed milk tasted artificial, and this taste killed the product.

I started to learn that my role in business would be to guess how consumers would react to a stimulus, like a change of flavor in condensed milk. In other words, how to *avoid* guessing. That should lead to opportunities for learning branding, positioning, and eventually a rigorous and disciplined process for new product development. To this day I can't wait to read research reports on anything with which I'm involved. I love and hunger for consumer and market research and learned quickly how to design all sorts of studies to get information. I also learned how often we all misjudge the consumer. Today, the first thing I tell an entrepreneur if he wants me to invest is, "Show me your consumer research."

Very soon I became the product manager for the newly formed Instant Products Division and Carnation Instant Breakfast, developing the brand into a wide range of flavors, which was a breakthrough in the cereal business. I was able to force our way in between Post and Kellogg's in the cereal section of grocery stores. Coffee Mate was another brand in the division, which remains the most popular nondairy creamer in the world. This division became a very profitable growth engine for Carnation and was the beginning of a huge trend for Carnation and the market worldwide. I like to think that in some small way, my seminal research got out ahead of a trend that ultimately led to Nestlé—a world leader in candy that was seriously eyeing the nutrition market—eventually paying a handsome price for Carnation years later.

I loved my experiences at Carnation. It was the perfect launchpad for my career and my unconventional life. They were highly supportive, encouraged mentoring, and advocated a sophisticated, research-oriented learning environment. But with all this, they were still quite a conservative company.

As president, Tim Crull, kept a record of every MBA and their career path. I saw him stand up in front of an audience of trainees, including myself, and address each by name and give a brief recap on their career aspirations. I was blown away that he could remember us all and had that much interest in us. He eventually left and became CEO of Norton Simon, Inc., but returned to become CEO of Carnation when Everett Olson retired.

In my first presentation to Everett in his office, I had included a wrong number. Everett let his half-glasses slide down his nose and threw my proposal at me, saying, "Come back when the numbers are right." He then punctuated the matter-of-fact statement by angrily putting out his cigarette in front of me. I learned a valuable lesson that day. Everett regularly told his VP of Sales that his situation analyses were "bullshit." No holds barred. I was in an agency presentation when he eviscerated the head creative director so badly, he couldn't speak and had to sit down. God help you if you didn't know the Nielsen numbers for your product and category cold. Good lessons all.

I learned that I love and am comfortable with ambiguity and blue-sky futuristic thinking. I found out early on that my point of differentiation was to be able to conceptualize strategic views and articulate them in fashion that got a "*Wow!*" reaction. But I always made sure my numbers were right.

CHAPTER 5

MAKING BREAD WITH LITTLE RED HENS

I spent three years honing my brand management skills at Carnation, but I started to feel antsy. Gail and I made the decision to end our marriage. I packed up my clothes, jumped on my Triumph Bonneville, and moved into a place at Playa del Rey Beach with three great guys with whom I worked at Carnation. I found myself launched into the world of a single man with kids. Our split was amicable, and I drove out to Box Canyon on weekends to pick up the girls, who quickly adapted to my new lifestyle. I bought a beautiful classic white 1965 Porsche 356C and began a different phase of my life.

At the same time, I pursued a brand management opportunity at Hunt-Wesson Foods out in Fullerton, CA, so I moved to Laguna Beach and shared a house with another junior executive I met there,

John von Leesen, who readily accepted me and my two daughters, who visited on weekends. The company immediately placed me in the Frozen Refrigerated Division, running the Wakefield Alaskan King Crab business. I was exposed to managing large fishing boats in the Bering Sea and spent many days in Alaska on king crab boats and in fish processing plants way before the Alaskan pipeline had taken off. I figured out how to charter flights into New York on a Boeing 747 to short-supply fresh king crab and seize a market opportunity. A fun experience was hiring a well-known television personality and chef, Graham Kerr, "The Galloping Gourmet," to develop a series of frozen crab-based meals.

About a year later I shifted over to Snowdrift Solid Shortening, another Hunt-Wesson brand. Within the company I became known as "Mr. Grease," selling 30 million pounds a year. I could tell from booming sales in the Southeast where my market was, so I arranged a visit to a place in Nashville called The Hut, which was a famous old recording studio that produced radio commercials with June Carter Cash. After a couple of run-throughs, she politely recorded our "Madison Avenue" version of the commercial, then told me how she would have done it. It turns out that she was an incredible baker who had used Snowdrift her entire life, as had her mother. She clearly knew the Southern consumer. She started her version of the commercial by playing her guitar and saying in rhythm, "You tired of humped-up, puny biscuits? Shriveled-up chicken? If you want to please your man, use Snowdrift."

That day I also spent time with Johnny Cash and met their daughter Rosanne, who had just turned sweet sixteen. She had just gotten her license, so we let her drive us to lunch at Morrison's Cafeteria. I flew back to Fullerton and convinced my boss, Ed Krakauer, and the president and CEO, Ed Gelsthorpe, to run June's version of the radio commercials. They were a big hit and sold lots of "grease."

From grease, I went in the opposite direction towards health foods. I had been spending some of my evenings trying to raise money to start a health and natural foods company. While meeting with potential investors, I encountered Robert Fell, who was a senior executive at a company called Archon, a newly formed health and natural foods conglomerate. It had been started by David May of May Company, Clair Boothe Luce, and August Busch of Anheuser-Busch among others, all of whom wanted to provide healthy food to the masses. They convinced me to not start my own competing company but to go to work for them, handling the combined marketing of six companies they had aggregated. It wasn't the start-up I was looking for, but it did give me my first exposure to the wonders of stock options. Nothing like a taste of equity to get your juices flowing. I was twenty-nine years old when I was hired as director of marketing for Archon's Family Natural Products Grocery Division, with a cool office in Beverly Hills, a block away from Rodeo Drive. That sure beat crabs or grease at the time.

I found an ad in the *Los Angeles Times*, where four "professionals" were looking for a fifth to share a house in the Hollywood Hills. I met the guys one evening at this amazing Spanish-style home, which had at one time been the home of the Belgian Consulate, on Mulholland Drive that overlooked the San Fernando Valley. One of the roommates (the Master Lessor) was a pool cleaner, one was an IBM sales guy, one was a bit part actor, and the other was a painter who drove a huge Brougham Cadillac and cleaned parking lots at night. I took my space in the children's wing and settled in. With a pool and fun places to play hide and seek, Beth and Kim loved coming there on weekends, and the roommates, who had their own assortment of kids, readily accepted all of us. It was quite an experience, which included having my beautiful 1965 Porsche 356C stolen out of the front driveway. It was recovered a few days later, but the new engine had been stripped out of it.

I settled in as the head of marketing all of Archon's brands and reported to Robert Fell. My job included marketing natural bread mixes, Hunza Teas, El Molino Mills Flour, Radiance Natural Vitamins, and Marly-Savon Clair Cosmetics. My job was to bring them to the mass market under the umbrella of Family Natural Foods. I loved the health foods business and enjoyed being in an entrepreneurial environment, working with people who had a bit of gray hair at the temples and had made their marks as founders of these companies, but took the risk of joining a venture such as this. It opened my eyes to owning equity, and I figured out that this was really how you made any money.

One day on the toilet paper holder in a stall in the men's room, I discovered on a yellow legal paper an outline for liquidating the company, apparently left by the CFO. I saw the "handwriting on the stall" and started making my own plans for departure. I had learned a lot. The best part of my time at Archon was meeting my wife, Barbara, who worked for the VP of sales. She managed to see through all my crazy transition issues. She appreciated my 1965 Porsche 356C (my babe mobile), loved riding behind me on my Honda 500 motorcycle, and saw through the synchronized lighting, music, and fireplace in my Hollywood Hills bachelor pad. Luckily for me, she lasted a lot longer in my life than Archon.

I worked with several executive recruiters who sent me all over the country, interviewing with consumer products companies, and I eventually landed in the office of Bob Kirby at Oroweat in South San Francisco. I was there to interview for the brand-new position as the company's first-ever director of marketing. I was thirty-one years old. Bob was a Harvard MBA trained as a commodities trader at Continental Grain. He knew markets, just not consumer product markets. I was offered the position, and in negotiating my employment agreement, the deal I struck with Bob was that I would teach Oroweat what I knew about food marketing and new consumer product development, both of which were not highly respected in the baking business. At that time, advertising was considered dirty and somewhat unnecessary.

In exchange for these secrets of the universe, I wanted to eventually gain general manager experience. This was the beginning of a turning point in my career. It became the most important mentoring relationship of my career, and Barbara and I formed a lifelong personal relationship with Bob and his family. It's safe to say that the Kirbys have been our guiding lights in many ways for many years, starting with what would be my seven years at Oroweat.

Oroweat was owned by the Continental Grain Corporation (CGC), one of the big, highly secretive grain trading companies. The book *Amber Waves of Grain* was about CGC and the infamous Russian wheat deal. Michel Fribourg and his family owned the company. They decided that since they knew everything about grain and therefore the cost of goods for grain-related products such as flour, they should vertically integrate and buy bakeries. A logical, but not easy, path.

Continental Grain bought Oroweat from two founders: Ed Nagel and Herman Dreyer. Herman had two college-educated, highly competitive sons, Walt and his younger brother Pete, who grew up in the business. This led to some interesting founder and family dynamics which provided great humor and a cultural challenge. Having a brother, I understood the dynamics, including people calling each other "rubberheads". However, I also learned a great deal from Bob (aka RPK) in how he managed the situation and the family, who were experts at producing high-quality, natural, wholegrain bread and rolls, as well as French bread, bagels, and muffins. Bob always valued the heritage and legacy of the family companies he bought and fiercely protected the quality of the products.

I also had a real immersion in learning the direct store delivery (DSD) system. The bakery was headquartered in South San

Francisco and made hundreds of different fresh products daily, all of which needed to move first on large transports from the bakery to individual route trucks, where the drivers delivered the product to the stores and merchandised the shelves. Again, I found the best way to learn the DSD business was to go to the depot at 4:30 in the morning and ride the route trucks with the salespeople delivering to stores. RPK knew a lot about finance, M&A, and commodities. I knew a lot about the consumer and new product development.

As I prepared to begin this new opportunity at Oroweat, I first rented a cozy apartment on Russian Hill, at the corner of Hyde and Union, in San Francisco. Barbara flew up with the girls on some weekends, but the commute and uncertainty of making a commitment took its toll on the relationship. I became fully immersed in the company and found myself fully committed to the marketing role I had been hired to do. Living in the city was fun and exciting, and I met a lot of fun and exciting people. But eventually I had my fill of city life and agreed to move with our CFO, Paul Carter, and his friend from when he worked at Memorex, Jack McCaskill, into a hexagonal glass house they had built in Saratoga, California. Jack McCaskill was quite opposite from Paul in personality. Paul grunted and Jack chatted merrily. While building the house, Paul wanted to do everything himself and take shortcuts (another "tell"), and Jack wanted to do it right. There were many classic moments, like Paul hanging the kitchen cabinets upside down and never changing them. Maybe Paul was dyslexic, since he also managed to wire the house electrical box backwards, resulting in him blowing out all the lights in the community and then calling the electric company from a pay phone to complain.

It was at this point that I finally had my epiphany about Barbara, whom I had left back in LA when I relocated to San Francisco. During one of my mother's visits, I took her and my stepfather, George, to dinner at the home of a cute gal I casually dated who lived in Oakland. This triggered my mother into action. She gave me her speech about playing the field: "You could catch a foul ball." She was warning me about bringing home floozies. Unbeknownst to me, my mother had kept in touch with Barbara even during our separation. Mother was very direct with me on the ride home from dinner, saying that no one compared to Barbara and that I should call her. And so I did. We reconnected and were married six weeks later.

I had many interesting experiences taking Oroweat into a twentieth-century marketing, branding, and positioning mode. I hired Honig-Cooper & Harrington, an edgy advertising agency with big accounts like Levi's. This led to a high-profile advertising campaign in the Bay area using billboards with a loaf of Oroweat Honey Wheat Berry Bread suspended over the San Francisco skyline. It was a test using our Southern California market as the control subject. For some reason, the route salesmen distrusted advertising, so the route drivers in the control market set their sights on boosting their sales to beat the test area. It played on the natural competitiveness of Northern and Southern California. I quickly learned that this was a great sales tactic, regardless of which way the test went. All we had to do was threaten a region by saying that if they didn't get their sales up, we would have to start advertising. As Art Linkletter always said, people are funny.

There were a lot of people to educate and convince that all this marketing, consumer research, and advertising "nonsense" made sense. Ed Nagel, one of the founders, had a reaction to the advertising campaign and told Bob Kirby, "Frank is a nice boy, but he is going to ruin the company." When interviewing agencies, Bob would ask what happened to the stock price of their most recent clients. He educated a few Mad Men who hadn't bothered to think about shareholder value.

Eventually we made significant progress in understanding the consumer. This included conducting a sophisticated segmentation study, which revealed a whole new way to define the baked goods section from the consumers' eyes, recognizing the growing popularity of whole-grain and natural ingredients. It became a power tool for us with major supermarket-chain executives and made Oroweat the knowledge leader for the category. This led to more shelf space for the Oroweat brand, which meant we were kicking the butt of the big bakery boys.

This was when Bob came through with his commitment to me. At age thirty-two, I was promoted to general manager for the Pacific Northwest for Oroweat in Seattle, Washington, which was composed of a bakery in Seattle and warehouse in Portland and the Stone Burr Milling Company, which did the milling process of cereals and grains. This process preserved the nutritional value of the product. Bob Kirby took a big risk promoting me to the GM position. It was the first time a GM reported directly to Bob instead of to the founders, Walt or Pete. New guy, new town, new chain of command, unhappy founders. The general manager in Seattle was departing, and I was parachuting in at the same time. Bob had one very important last commandment for me: "Don't get creative." He wanted me to let the organization teach me how to be a GM. Lucky for him, I didn't listen.

Barbara and I had been married only three days when we packed up and moved to Seattle and rented a nice apartment in Redmond, across Lake Washington from the office. I traded in my Honda 500 for a new Honda Gold Wing, which Barbara and I could use to explore the beauty of the Pacific Northwest.

While baking might not seem like the most glamorous industry, I soon discovered that running a regional business as a GM was complicated. Producing hundreds of wholesome, fresh bakery products daily and distributing them through a complex DSD to thousands of stores was both challenging and intriguing. We controlled our own plant, making perishable product, and we had a fleet of transport trucks taking the product to depots where hundreds of company-route delivery trucks and personnel merchandised the product on the store shelves and pulled stale product for resale through a network of thrift stores.

The company CFO, Jim Cairns, described the GM job by saying that it required one hundred decisions a day and that I should try to get 50 percent of them right. It was people-intensive with many departments reporting to the GM. Typically, the route drivers and plant workers were unionized, testing a GM's negotiating skills at contract time. The financial reporting and cost accounting systems were complex. The baking process, which included understanding how to maintain quality, was complex. Jim also told me that I would begin to understand the P&L dynamics the first month I missed budget. It's always good to have something to look forward to, right?

When I arrived, I was told there was a grumpy old head baker I would probably want to fire. As it turned out, I found that the old baker understood fermentation, the heart of the baking process, better than anyone. So naturally I ignored common wisdom and Bob's warning about creativity, and I started to work on new products with this old baker. Together we forged a relationship that was surprisingly productive and enjoyable to boot. I would come up with the ideas: beer bread, pear bread "com-pear," and such, and he would develop the formulations to make them work. He also had a few good ideas of his own that no one had listened to for years. He never told me my ideas were crazy.

He's the one who convinced me to go to baking school. I wanted to better understand breadmaking, so I went to the American Institute of Baking in Manhattan, Kansas, at Kansas State for two weeks of classes. This gave me a basic understanding of the functions involved in each step of the baking process along with production techniques. I would call Barbara and then need to run, as I had hundreds of loaves of bread in the oven. I was especially interested in fermentation since, as with wine, it is such a critical element to baking good bread. It all came in handy quickly.

Not many weeks after becoming the GM, I was in my office on a Saturday when I got a call from the GM who headed the Southern California division. They were negotiating with the Bakery, Confectionary, Tobacco Workers, and Grain Millers' International Union, and things weren't going well. As a result, the union was getting their sister locals in other regions to stop working in support of their efforts. This was called a sympathy strike. The GM warned me that my union workers would be stopping work in a couple of hours.

Nothing I had learned in business school was coming to mind. My next bizarre thought was, *Could I staff the bakery with my administrative non-union staff at least to process today's production?* I set up a series of chain calls with my direct reports. They, in turn, called all their people to get volunteers.

The workers would all be leaving the plant in an hour. While it was a strike, it was not against our plant, so they probably wouldn't be antagonistic. I called our normal catering truck company and asked if they could get some trucks to our plant and when the workers came out, to tell them that the food and drinks were on Mr. O'Connell.

Then I went into the plant and talked to the workers. Their union officials were informing them of the strike, but I wanted to be highly visible and talk to them personally. When the workers left the plant with the dough rising, they went outside and hung around for the free food at the catering truck. I went into the bakery and started to work the machines and ovens with my skeleton administrative crew. We had been on the production floor hundreds of times, and we weren't sure we could do it the right way, but we had to give it our best shot.

Thousands of pounds of dough had been set and would continue to rise. We had to keep the dough moving, pulling it from the fermentation room, into the dividers, in and out of the proof box, and then into the slicers and the baggers. If this all didn't happen at the right time, it would be a disaster. The yeast didn't know we were on strike.

I went out to the catering truck and started asking the bakers what to do. They were so intrigued and amused by our attempt to run the bakery that they gave us instructions. I kept running out the back door of the bakery to get instructions from them and communicating it to our team.

Despite all that help, we progressively made every mistake you can make in a bakery. We pulled the dough too late from the proof box. The dough balls were too large coming out of the divider, making loaves that were too big to get through the slicers and then the baggers. It was like Lucy and Ethel at the candy factory. We had to keep pushing the oversized loaves off the conveyor belt to prevent the line from plugging while pulling new trays of dough from the proofer sooner to get smaller dough balls. Very quickly we were literally knee-deep in loaves of bread. Eventually we got a batch right and the loaves went through the slicers into the bagger.

We worked all night and kept the bakery operating, albeit at a low production volume. I hadn't thought through how to staff a second shift with the small number of admin people we had. We solved that the first night by working a double shift, but far worse was that the strike went on for several weeks. We pretty much burned out our little team. I slept on the small sofa in my office for three nights.

During those few weeks, I worked every station in the bakery. I had burned my arms from improperly flipping hot bread pans out of the oven, releasing the bread onto the conveyors. Not only was the experience invaluable, but it built mutual respect with the bakers. We appreciated and understood the breadmaking process and their challenges far better than any study or analytical measures could have taught us. From that point forward, mutual trust provided for greatly enhanced team communication.

• • •

I loved my time as a GM. You make something every day that people enjoy. You can walk into the bakery and see the product being made and then go outside and watch the trucks leaving for the stores. Baking is an art as much as a science, since fermentation is a variable that requires a magic touch of sorts. The DSD system is less random but so expensive that you feel the need to treat it like a piece of fine art. It requires intense daily handling of product from the bakery to the store shelf. And the best part of the job is that you get to take hot bread home, so your kids know what the hell you do all day.

The motto of the Food and Agriculture Organization of the United Nations is *Fiat Panis*, "let there be bread". If you work in the bakery business, your life revolves around bread. I even named my first-ever company car the "Bun Mobile" (a silver and maroon 1975 Ford LTD with velour seats and crank windows). You would be surprised how much creativity and innovation can be put into bread.

We decided to expand into the pita bread business. I came up with the idea of hiring women, especially flight attendants, to run the routes. I thought flight attendants were good communicators and could sell store managers shelf space and displays. (Contrary to popular company opinion, I had no plans to dress them like belly dancers). The good communicator part turned out to be true, but there was a challenge regarding driving the route trucks. They all had floor stick shifts and clutches, and fewer flight attendants had truck-driving skills than I had hoped. I used to sit in my office at the end of the day with the head of our garage, looking out the window and listening to the grinding gears and tortured transmissions as our new route drivers downshifted to pull into the parking lot. *Fiat Panis* perhaps, but not Fiat trucks.

This was the era of the high-fiber diet with emphasis on the prevention of cancer of the colon. Bran'nola Bread was the first bread that was high in fiber but also tasted good. That old head baker developed the first high-fiber bread that people actually liked. I came up with the name—a combination of granola, known for good taste, and bran, known for fiber. When researching the name, we found a guy who had just taken est training had registered the name for a cereal product he was developing. We paid him $100,000 to get the name. *Fiat Panis ... Ooooohm.*

I contacted David Reuben, the then-famous author who wrote *Everything You Always Wanted to Know About Sex But Were Afraid to Ask.* He had just written *The Save Your Life Diet* about the importance of fiber in your diet. His father had recently died of cancer of the colon. I had copies of his book sent to the homes of the grocery buyers; their wives read the book and talked to their husbands about the importance of fiber. After that, our calls on those buyers were much more productive. Eventually the brand went national and grew to be a $500 million product. *Fiat fucking Bran'nola Panis.*

We also expanded the short distance into Canada with frozen bread. That effort had its moments since we would fly in and out of Canada from Lake Union with a young kid and his pontoon plane. We had a number of experiences, including losing the radio midflight, requiring me to visually scan for other aircraft we might bump into. There was even one time when we were not able to get airborne because the pontoons somehow had gotten filled with water. It was all worthwhile, though, since it allowed us to win the contract for supplying the Trans-Alaskan Pipeline with bread.

We opened the Denver market, shipping frozen bread in refrigerated trucks from Seattle. I went into the bakery late one night, which I occasionally did to see the night shift workers. I opened the back door of one of our transports and saw it loaded with pallets of Coors Beer, which the driver was backhauling from Denver. This was when Coors was still regionally distributed. There's a great joke about the Vatican changing the Lord's Prayer from "Give us this day our daily bread" to

"Give us this day our daily Bud." I was torn as to whether to applaud the entrepreneurial ingenuity or punish the corporate larceny.

Managing the tractor-trailer drivers was always a challenge, especially since we self-insured our trucks. They were independent cowboys who loved talking on their radios. One night in the middle of nowhere, two of them were playing around and literally ran into each other. They were unharmed, but they did a fortune in damage.

The Seattle general management experience led to my being promoted to head a new Central Region with five bakeries. This required a move from Seattle to Denver. Barbara and I had built a custom rustic/contemporary home on Mercer Island, where Beth and Kim came to visit us often. But I flew to Denver and Barbara put the house up for sale by owner and sold it in one day. We were off again.

Bob Kirby had acquired this array of bakeries, including Arnold Bakeries in Greenwich, Connecticut, and had moved the corporate offices there. The Central Region consisted of bakeries in Florida, Colorado, North Carolina, and the Stone Burr Milling Company in Seattle. The gem of the group in Denver was the Star Bakery, which was bought from two brothers, Rudy and Sam Boscoe. They were quite a pair with offices separated by a shared bathroom, probably just like how they grew up. And just like at home, they screamed at each other through the doorway every day. One way I got them to make a decision was to get them in my car and then go for a long drive. They never forgot anything the other had ever done wrong. Having a brother, I truly understood this interaction. Although they had sold Star Bakery to us, they remained actively involved, thus the challenge of managing a family-owned business with the family still involved.

My time spent in Denver was another traditional steppingstone up the corporate ladder. Regional management has similar and different challenges from the GM role I had so enjoyed in Seattle. As most good managers will tell you, "It's all about the people, stupid."

That's not to be confused with, "It's all about the stupid people." I had to form a new Central Regional Office, which meant I had to build a team. Sometimes that's easy and sometimes not so much. I got off to a rocky start with my new CFO, a critically important position when you work for a numbers wonk like Bob Kirby. Denver's altitude sits at more than five thousand feet, and the poor fellow died of a heart attack on the first night he arrived. They say altitude can kill you, and that's apparently true, especially so if you have a weak heart to begin with.

Shortly after moving to Denver, our oldest daughter, Beth, who was then sixteen, came to live with us. Gail had remarried and Beth wanted a change, so we became a family of three, with a teenager under the roof. No need to describe the dynamics, but you can only imagine.

At Arnold Bakery, the corporate brass frequently jumped on the corporate plane to fly around and visit the various bakeries they had bought for budget reviews, so it was standard procedure for them to schedule a visit to us in Denver. There was a famous story about one such budget meeting scheduled with Bob Kirby, who was president of Arnold-Oroweat, and the top-level management in the company. A few days before their arrival on the jet, I took my management team out to lunch, and then after a few glasses of wine, took them to Shepler's Western store in Denver where we picked out a beautiful, expensive Stetson Western hat for each of the members of the corporate team that was scheduled to be at this meeting. We arranged to have all the hats sent to them at the Greenwich, Connecticut, headquarters along with a poem that read, "Let it never be said, that these hats were given, instead of getting out of the red." We also sent a bandolier with pencils to Bob Kirby, who had a habit of throwing pencils, especially in budget meetings. The hats were specifically chosen for each individual's personality: Sherriff Bob, Diamond Jim, Fearless Fred, Buffalo Bill, and Gentleman Jack. For several days we got nothing but radio silence from corporate, so we were naturally concerned that they were less amused than we were. But a week before the budget meeting, Jim Cairns the CFO wrote his own poem and had it sent to us by special delivery. I won't post it here as it is somewhat long and mimics the tone of "Twas the Night Before Christmas." It begins with "Twas the night before budgets..." It ended with, "There's one burning question, Let's get to the facts, Where in the budget, Did they bury the hats?" It referred to me as Robin Hood and my team as the merry men. The next day, the corporate jet landed in Denver for the budget meeting. My whole team was dressed in Robin Hood garb, complete with green tights. The corporate group was all wearing their hats. I had hired a local high school band to play *Hail to the Chief* as Bob got off the plane. The group had had a bit too much to drink on the plane, so when one corporate executive stood up in the door of the plane to wave his hat, he fell backwards into the plane. That was an encouraging start. I also used another trick, which was to find an interesting place to hold our budget meeting, such as up in the mountains, as well as a cool place to eat, like a wild game restaurant.... anything to divert them from focusing too closely on the numbers.

• • •

Bob was busy back in Greenwich. He had bought Arnold Bakery, the largest roll and bread plant in the world, located in Greenwich, Connecticut, in the less tony part of town by the Portchester, New York, town line and adjacent to the toll booth on Route 95. There it competed with the Lifesavers plant as to which could dominate the nostrils of the rich and famous residents of Greenwich. The plant was a monument to the founder, Dean Arnold, right down to the beautiful tile floors.

After a couple of years running the Central Region in Denver, I was invited to take leave of my regional manager role to head up the newly consolidated marketing function at headquarters in Greenwich. I was thirty-six years old and had been taught by the best all of the skills needed for general management, especially in a complex region like the one in Denver. At the corporate office, the marketing focus was to ratio-nalize the brands (position the brands against target consumer groups), which were now plentiful, following a stream of acquisitions. We needed to consolidate advertising and spur new product development. As an example, Arnold ran a famous poster campaign in the subways—"You don't have to be Jewish to love Levy's" (rye bread). The poster showed a robed choirboy eating a slice of Levy's rye. It worked in New York, but it was doubtful it would fly in Denver.

I was reluctant to leave general line management responsibility, but Bob convinced me it was the best use of my talents. The needs of Arnold needed to be met. It would have been difficult to bring someone in from the outside (unless they had their own Robin Hood suit). Again, Barbara put our home on Monaco Parkway up for sale by owner, sold it in a week, and after watching the moving truck leave the yard, we packed up the Honda Gold Wing and headed for Greenwich.

Beth preferred to stay in Denver and, with Gail's consent, we agreed to let her do so. We found a charming and updated farmhouse complete with paddock and horse stalls in Westport, Connecticut, (home of Paul Newman and Neil Sedaka) and settled in. It was at this point that our youngest daughter, Kim, who was fifteen, asked if she could live with us, so we moved her back to Westport from Box Canyon, along with her horse, Rosie, and pony, Daisy. They were quite the talk of the Fairfield County Hunt Club, where we boarded them until we closed on our house. Once Kim was enrolled at Staples High School, she worked at the Hunt Club after school mucking stalls and making friends in the horse community. One friend at the time was Clea Newman, Paul's daughter.

At Arnold Bakery we were able to make significantly higher margins than the industry standard with our consolidated marketing, scale, and wholesome products. We also managed to do so while maintaining superior taste, texture, and quality.

We had acquired a number of whole grain, French bread, roll, bagel, and English muffin bakeries and had a panoply of brands across the country. It's always a great spot to be a market leader. Jack Welch, who was just up the road at GE, used to say he only wanted to play from the number one or two spot in any industry. I would go further and say unequivocally that the number one spot was decidedly more fun. We had lots of business fun at Oroweat in those days.

• • •

Bob Kirby's departure from Arnold/Oroweat ranks as one of the great mysteries and tragedies of the twentieth century . . . at least to me. It was a difficult time for me and others in the company. I was close to Bob and owed him a lot for all the risks he took in putting me in growth positions. Suffice to say I never had a better mentor in my career and may rightfully have to claim that almost everything good I know about business, I learned from Bob.

Ray Rudy became our new president of Arnold-Oroweat. Ray was with P&G and General Foods and later was a founding partner in 1995 of JW Childs. Ray's CPG strength was in contrast to Bob, who had a strong business, financial, analytical, and transaction background, and he was learning marketing.

I had no problem working for Ray. He was careful not to crowd me in marketing. We were able to build a good marketing department hiring people from Pepsi, General Foods, Richardson Vicks, and other good consumer product people who were commuting to NYC from Connecticut. You might say being local was a differential advantage for us. We did a search for a new advertising agency and ended up with Jerry Della Femina, who wrote a popular book, *From Those Wonderful Folks Who Gave You Pearl Harbor*. He was considered to be the last of the Madison Avenue Mad Men. It was a trip dealing with Jerry, but I don't remember any spectacular advertising campaigns in particular. No "Plop, plop, fizz, fizz" that I can recall.

Innovation comes at you in different ways. Sometimes a bungee jumping commercial makes all the difference. Other times, the Mad Men fall short and it's the old baker who figures out how to make the artisanal bread rise.

• • •

For the first years of my life, I had equated work with the production of food. Indeed, from eggs, broilers, and proverbial fatted calves, I had, with the help of Cornell's agriculture and food science programs, graduated to consumer-packaged goods of all sorts. Frozen foods, snack foods, convenience foods, baked goods, and health foods had been my focus, but the expertise I had been accumulating was really about marketing and selling these foodstuffs to consumers. Understanding the consumer and their wants and motivations has always been a fascinating subject to me. My job was understanding how to capture consumer sentiment, translate it into products with inherent demand, and then effectively and efficiently deliver them to consumers at a mutually beneficial price point. Along the way I had also gathered a fair bit of knowledge and experience in general management, knowing that it was a key to advancement, and an ability to fully implement my most creative product ideas.

However, I was starting to feel it was time for me to move on from food and the baking industry to a new and faster-moving consumer product category. Our modern world had progressed well beyond a survival economy, but food, while still an interesting product category with lots of room for creativity, was a tad stodgy. I had recognized by that time that food operations were always likely to be dominated by more flinty-eyed businessmen like Bob Kirby. Cost and quality control ruled the day. Marketing and product development were important and nice to have, but simply not the driver of overall leadership. My brain moved at a pace that needed more elbow room. And then there was that "fun" thing about me. It was always a bit of a double-edged sword in the food business. I needed to let my fun side out to run a bit more freely. Bob Kirby had already left Arnold Bakery for his next food industry position at Borden's. With Ray Rudy from General Foods now running the Arnold Bakery show, it was decidedly less fun for me and seemed like the right time to move on. So, I decided to leave the baking business and, whether consciously or opportunistically, I was introduced to the toys and games business.

The opportunity came at the hands of Ed Krakauer. I had worked for Ed at Hunt-Wesson Foods in Fullerton, California, when he was a senior vice president. He later left and went to Mattel, Inc., where he was head of the new electronics division. When I contacted him about my desire to look outside the food industry, Ed encouraged me to take a serious look at the electronic game industry, both because it would be a good career experience and because he felt my personality fit the industry well. Mattel was looking for someone to head up sales and marketing for their electronics division. I was aware of the opening thanks to Ed, and he really teed me up with the company as a "great fit." The division had been formed to house the growing hand-held video games business, which included Mattel's new and much heralded Intellivision video game console.

At this point in my career, I was thirty-eight years old and had moved from New York to Los Angeles to San Francisco, remarried, moved to Seattle with Barbara, moved to Denver, and then moved to Greenwich, Connecticut. The opportunity at Mattel would take us back to Los Angeles, which wasn't such a bad thing, as I remembered the palm trees I had spotted on my first flight out there. We ended up buying a house in Hancock Park, just a few blocks away from my first job at Carnation Company on Wilshire Boulevard. Kim moved with us back to California and enrolled in the local high school. She found an after-school job at the Silver Lake Stables close by, and she was a happy camper. She had donated her horses Rosie and Daisy to a nonprofit organization, as it was obvious that taking them with us would have been a challenge because of their advanced ages.

I had an interesting interview with the president of Mattel, Ray Wagner, who spent the time testing my creativity aptitude and my feel for new product development. It wasn't walking the grocery aisle, but it was a penetrating process. I must have done something wild and crazy enough, because he offered me the job. I better understood the unusual interview sequencing (since I would not be working for Ray directly) when it was explained that I would be working for the newly appointed president of the electronics division, Josh Denham. Josh's background was operations and, apparently, Ray insisted that he be teamed with an experienced marketer. Business seems always to organize itself around the people rather than the strategy. Who's to say which is better?

When I joined Mattel in 1980, I knew very little about the toy and game business. Too little to recognize the challenges Mattel faced. That awareness gap is never obvious from the outside looking in and may not have deterred me in taking the spot, but it's always good to remind yourself of what you may not know when you jump into the deep end of a new pool.

Intellivision was Mattel's new video game console designed to compete with Atari, the gold standard in video gaming in its day. It had its own game software and was different from the handheld game category, which was less expensive with small display screens usually dedicated to one game (e.g. football). Each format had its own challenges.

Intellivision had recently been introduced with a tiny advertising budget compared to Atari. It was not selling at a pace that would interest the distribution network; thus it risked being delisted by retailers before Christmas. Mattel's handheld games had missed their annual drop-dead delivery dates for the development cycle. This meant that the most popular handheld games like football and hockey would not have new products to sell during Christmas in a very competitive, new product-driven category. There was little to be done to avoid a terrible Christmas season. We had nothing but obsolete product to offer.

This certainly was not the food business. I had to learn a lot very fast. First, when over 75 percent of your product is new every year and a big percentage is sold during the Christmas holiday season, you must be an innovation machine and a slave to the product development and business cycle (and meet all deadlines without fail!). You need to be bold enough and risk-tolerant enough to produce millions of units of something you probably have never produced before and may never produce again. The only sin worse than missing deadlines was having a hit product with insufficient supply to meet the demand.

An even more precarious facet is that the product development cycle generally takes three years. The first year is about sourcing and concept testing new ideas. The second year is heavily focused on design, engineering, prototype development, and game-play testing, with the added wrinkle of component sourcing and costing. The third year is all designing and building the production lines and deciding where the product will be produced most optimally. And that all presumes the market hasn't moved or that the competition hasn't gotten to your finish line first.

Product manufacturing outsourced to China adds a communication and timing complexity overlay. This naturally makes this entire process even more challenging. There are many variations to this timeline depending on a spectrum of possible sources for the underlying idea. If the concept is based on intellectual property such as a popular movie, TV program, character, or sports league/legend, this further complicates things, as the shelf life can be that much more fleeting or suffer an unexpected mishap or reversal. There is little difference if these ideas or models have been invented by Mattel or are a turnkey product purchased from third-party developers (both are equally possible, but neither mitigates the risks).

So it is fair to say that the product development cycle managed by project managers drives the company. This was both new and inviting to a marketing person like me and yet gave me more than a modicum of sheer terror. I recall the days of installing PERT (Program Evaluation Review Technique), a project management process. The system links the interdependency of each step, shows the impact on the overall schedule of any slippage, and directly assigns account-ability to a person or department. There is generally very little slack time and thus if a drop-dead date is missed, the introduction date will often slide to the next season.

The Intellivision story was a high-stakes game, involving both hardware and software, that Mattel was not used to playing. To begin with, the name is a combination of the words *intelligent* and *television*, purposefully positioned so that parents would be supportive based on the theory that it would increase their children's brainpower.

I went to work for Mattel in October of 1980. I had just come aboard as senior VP of sales and marketing for the electronics divi-sion, and there was trouble in paradise. Intellivision was shipping and Mattel had the distribution channels, but the sell-through was not going well. Also, the defect rate was running high (close to a whopping 20 percent), and the heavy returns were not boding well for profits or future sales. As you can guess, the theory was the classic razors and razorblades; get a large installed base of consoles/machines ASAP and sell millions of units of software. That was hard to do if the razors kept failing.

Intellivision was positioned as an electronic computer system, prom-ising an eventual keyboard that would change your life. Remember, in 1980 we were still pre-PC, so this strategy was more earthshaking than it sounds today. I remember feeling that the product positioning was confusing and problematic. The initial games were sports: NFL Football, Major League Baseball, and Golf with a chaser of Blackjack, Backgammon, and Poker. While there were some basic software modules that came with the console, the real challenge was filling in an array of games and programs that would be available for sale.

I had a quick market research study done comparing our archrival Atari to Intellivision. The results said that the consumer viewed Intellivision as a game-playing machine with superior graphics and sound to Atari. It was not viewed, as we thought, as a computer that was going to intermingle with and change their lives. Somehow, Mattel thought that consumers should buy it and wait for the keyboard...even though the company had no experience with home computers and what they could or couldn't do for people, or their kids, with or without the darn keyboard.

Mattel's promise to deliver the ever-delayed keyboard became somewhat of a joke. Obviously it wasn't a physical constraint to manufacture a keyboard; it was the interface and what the console could do with a keyboard attached. Surprise, surprise—personal computers and the attendant operating systems and application software are a complex business unto themselves, well beyond the electronic game unit of the folks who brought you Barbie dolls.

In keeping with that issue, in 1981 Mattel Electronics became a separate company. We had a lavish party at the Marriott, featuring a rising and relatively unknown comedian named Jay Leno. Like all good pay-for-play comedians, he tailored his set to our business. As he started to riff, he delivered the killer line by asking the question—"Do you know what the biggest lies are? 'The check is in the mail.' 'I'll still respect you in the morning.' And 'The Intellivision keyboard will be out in the spring.'" Funny stuff...but not really funny to a fledgling stand-alone business.

At least we had the hardcore gamers with us, right? Not so much. It was clear that the awareness of Intellivision among those hardcore gamers was low, and many gamers were intent on buying the Atari system and weren't even considering Intellivision. Not good. I knew I needed to make some bold moves. First, Intellivision had superior graphics to Atari, so we needed to do a serious head-to-head comparison of Intellivision versus Atari. And second (it was then November, just before Christmas, so time was incredibly tight for this first all-important holiday season), we needed to immediately jack up the advertising budget by millions of dollars to promote awareness.

The head-to-head advertising concept was considered radical, requiring Mattel's board (still the mother ship) to weigh in to modify the advertising agency protocol. Obviously, blindly spending millions in advertising in November, not knowing if it was going to work, was a big risk. What seemed desperately necessary to me (given the shortening development cycle of the infant tech sector) seemed recklessly risky to others. Amazingly, I was able to convince management and the board that this was our one shot. If we didn't sell a reasonable number of consoles and get an installed base during that Christmas season, the Intellivision platform and future game cartridges sales were doomed.

The immediate challenge was coming up with a provocative TV commercial that was relevant to electronic game players and could be conceived and produced on the run. Remember that in the early days of Atari, the game players (and many of the games) came from the stand-up arcade games. Then, once hooked, the gamers would buy a home console. So we came up with the idea of having popular writer George Plimpton make a head-to-head comparison to Atari on screen. Intellivision had strikingly superior graphics, which provided for a bold demonstration. The head-to-head technique also allowed us to piggyback on Atari's millions of dollars of advertising and extreme popularity. Plimpton had become very recognizable and well-known for his book *Paper Lion* (which was later made into a film starring Alan Alda of M*A*S*H* fame) and his attempts to try various high-risk stunts. I wanted to approach him directly and found out he was at the La Costa Resort in Carlsbad, south of LA. I could circumvent his agent and talk directly to him, as rude and forward as that sounds now. As it turned out, he was an avid game-player himself. He invited me to his hotel. I loaded my car with both the Atari and Intellivision systems and a load of games. We spent a fun evening playing games. He turned out to be a real gamer. Much to my surprise, without checking with his agent, Plimpton agreed to do a series of commercials for us.

The next challenge was confronting the board with the reality and immediacy of the jump in advertising spend to do the TV commercials I had already sold Plimpton on doing. The chairman of the board approached each new idea as a skeptic and was good at generating long lists as to why an idea wouldn't work. I figured out quickly that the best way to deal with him was to start my presentation with all the reasons my idea wouldn't work. It got his head going up and down in agreement and took away his arguments when I launched into my presentation on why we had to do it.

The marketing strategy worked. Demand for Intellivision consoles far exceeded our production capacity. Sales started to take off before Christmas. It became apparent that we couldn't meet the holiday demand. We didn't want to lose sales to Atari, so we came up with the idea of selling empty Intellivision boxes to put under the tree and later, when production caught up, we would deliver the actual Intellivision console. It sounds crazy, but it worked. We had a successful Christmas season and were solidly on the gaming map. I then turned my concentration on developing razor blades—I mean, game cartridges.

CHAPTER 6

ADDICTIVE, HABITUAL, ARRESTED DEVELOPMENT

Designing video games was certainly a new new-product development process for me. We had an internal development team that grew to perhaps one hundred people. The status of game development software at that point was rather crude. There were probably less than one hundred people who could program for the Atari system. The open-source concept was not yet on the scene, and independent third-party software was just emerging. Most system architectures were closed, meaning that if you were a third-party developer, you had to legitimately reverse engineer the system to be able to develop software or games.

Most games were initially developed by a single programmer who developed the game play and wrote the code. This meant they had to be good at conceptualizing the game and developing the game-play protocol, the graphics, the sound, and the writing of the code. A programmer was normally good at one aspect but not usually all five. Also, the process was that they would work for months writing code before you saw enough of the game to even begin to know if it was any good. In the early stages, developers worked on whatever game appealed to them personally, regardless of the marketability of the theme. My market research training got the heebie-jeebies over this approach. Often, after months of work, we would find ourselves declaring a game unmarketable, based either on judgment or consumer testing.

Designing a new approach to video game development became a long-term passion I really enjoyed. Throughout my career, innovation and inventing new approaches to product development have captured my curiosity more than most things. I have had the luxury of testing many of these approaches in a variety of consumer product fields, so I am confident in my feel for the area.

I started by working with our marketing team to develop a consumer-driven strategy versus whatever whims happened to strike our game developers. Until that point it was the typical hit-driven approach, with everyone copying the latest high-selling game. This was the beginning of segmenting the market into types of players and levels of play. We then matched the type of players to categories of games, such as hit-and-detect versus strategy games. The critical element, of course, was always the quality and compulsiveness of the game play. There was an interesting quixotic aspect that was either present in the game (and sensed by the gamers) or not.

We developed a mixed strategy based on the competitive sales rates of various types of games and those that best took advantage of Intellivision's unique features. We hired IBM to help us design a better, more efficient development process and a set of development tools. The idea of product development driven by trade shows came out of this experience. I learned about how trade show deadlines drive the completion of demo prototypes. Engineers can't stop engineering, best defeats better, and that means the product is never done. But when you must deliver a working version for a trade show, it drives breakthroughs and an endpoint to the engineering. I would hypothesize that the reason the Japanese are such world leaders in innovation is that they work feverishly to achieve breakthroughs just in time for trade shows.

My experience at Mattel taught me about innovation on demand. The Consumer Electronics Show takes place in Las Vegas every year in January. It is the biggest show of the year and in many ways a make-or-break battle for retailers open to buy for the next season. The pressure is immense. It is a showmanship game of who can best capture the buyer's imagination.

I also learned early in my career how to use trade shows to find new innovations and products. I would organize my marketing and new-product people to walk the show. Yes, to do blatant competitive espionage, but also to look for new ideas. Often the best ideas were found in the inexpensive section of the trade shows, deep in the bowels of the convention center. Here, independent inventors often could only afford to rent card tables. It took some imagination at times to see how the technology could be turned into a real product. Inventors who did not even have the money for card table booths would shop their products or inventions to the various competitors on the showroom floor. There was always a buzz about somebody in the underground of the show with the next great thing.

What is game play and how does it relate to habitual behavior? I may not have been peddling drugs at Mattel, but it was the next best thing. My view of the toy and game business, and the consumer product business in general, is that of inducing habitual behavior. It sounds bad and is clearly detrimental when applied to a subject such as overeating. But this was just having healthy fun. Over the years there have been scary studies regarding the hours people spend in front of video screens and especially playing video games. Now it's Facebook and other social media sites, not to mention texting continuously, that have done a great job of forging the new breed of habitual behavior.

In fact, forming habitual behavior may be at the heart of marketing. When people would ask me what I did, I used to say, "I predict consumer behavior to a stimulus (product or service)." If I can predict consumer behavior, then I can develop products and distribute them in such a way that they get into the path of the consumer and *voilà!* a purchase ensues.

It is a bit of a distorted view of the marketing world, but at times I see all these marketers and product developers competing to convert the largest possible share of your mind, time, and pocketbook to their habitual behavior. We have lots of pretty names for it: brand essence, brand loyalty, repeat purchase, religion, dwell time, stickiness, fans. We worry about it when we see it as addictive behavior: drugs, alcohol, sex, smoking, eating, kids with TV, then kids with video games, cell phones, texting, and social media. We don't put other repetitive, thoughtless behavior into the same category, like buying Nikes, etc. Maybe we should think about that.

Atari was founded in 1972 by Nolan Bushnell, an engineer who became famous by developing the first video game, *Pong,* for stand-up video game machines. He sold it to Warner Communications in 1976 and went on to found Chuck E. Cheese. In 1977 Atari introduced their color graphic cartridge-loaded game machine, which sold for $200. They were Mattel's stalking horse in the gaming world.

In 1982 Atari began a search to replace their president, Mike Moone. I was on the gaming "screen" by then, so I was asked to interview, along with a large number of other candidates. I was not offered the job and, of course, always wondered if they were just trying to get competitive intelligence (why else would they not hire a great guy like me?).

At that point I concluded that, strategically, Mattel was in the software business and not the hardware business. Given Intellivision's continuing 20 percent defect rate, the challenges of developing a keyboard, and home computers coming on strong, this was a safe conclusion. That, combined with the growing competition from independent computer gaming companies, made me question Mattel's capability to compete as a hardware developer and manufacturer.

I started to push Mattel to strategically switch to becoming a software developer for the industry, producing games for the largest installed base of other brands' consoles. This direction was accepted by the brass, and we decided to produce video games under the M Network banner, starting with games for the Atari platform.

Atari was suing everyone in sight who was trying to develop games for their console. The company had a famous lawyer, Skip Paul, known as "Sic 'em Skip" who purposefully kept a high profile, aggressively suing developers. Atari had a closed architecture system which they wanted to keep a secret. Thus, to legally develop third-party software or games, you had to reverse engineer their system. I recall that there were only roughly one hundred people (inside and outside of Atari) who knew how to program for the Atari system.

The challenge was to find engineers who had legitimately and independently reverse engineered and documented the architecture. I put out the word in the gaming underground that I was looking for the architecture. One day I got a call from a guy who said that he and a small, geographically dispersed team had done it. We arranged to meet him someplace in the hills outside of LA (very clandestine).

The test was to both play a standard Atari game in their system and to take a game they had developed and plug it into an Atari console. The key was the ability to use all of Atari's features. The test proved successful under both circumstances. The next step was to have our engineers validate their proof that they had not stolen the architecture but had developed it from scratch, which included showing all the proper documentation. This checked out and I began negotiations. I quickly made the team millionaires, and we got our Atari kryptonite.

I also headed the marketing for tabletop games at Mattel, which included the infamous Dungeons & Dragons, the very controversial fantasy role-playing game. I got to know the developer, Gary Gygax, who became quite famous. One day I found the press, loaded with TV cameras, outside my door after several people had died, supposedly by losing their identity in a D&D game. The press was trying to suggest that D&D was to blame. I made the statement that fantasy was healthy for children. Yikes!

The Mattel Electronics Company grew rapidly. My recollection was that in the time I was there, the company grew to $500 million in revenue. We also continued to develop and produce hand-held electronic games in addition to consoles.

Why did the cross-fertilization of ideas become such a distinctive element of my thinking and career contribution? There were so many ideas that were potentially transferable from one industry to another. When trying to find a solution to a problem, all sorts of analogies would pop into my head. They were never the same. But whether similar or applied in an entirely different way, I felt they could be used to create a unique solution.

Generally, the flow of ideas comes to me in involuntary ways, but I have learned triggers to opening the flow and consequently being more receptive to capturing the ideas. Some people who know me would say I have Attention Deficit Disorder or ADD, or maybe not. My mind is constantly jumping and pumping at a high rate of speed. I love to be asked to come up with solutions (even harebrained ones, occasionally). It's part of the process of being thrown into situations

I don't know anything about. I seldom mention half of the ideas that come to me. I have found the ones where there is a high risk of looking stupid are often the best. Why? Because these are the ones that are not occurring to others and therefore sound stupid to them. Remember, most of those people were often there for the problem generation phase, so they tend to be defensive. I am constantly pushing myself to take the risk of mentioning those ideas. My best and most fun days are those where I am involved in a heavy dosage of idea generating.

I guess this all says that I am *not* a serial thinker, but more of a random thinker. There are times I feel that life would be easier if I could be less random, but I would never change that at the expense of my ideation capabilities. As for Mattel, my random walk into gaming was coming to an end. Mattel was swell, but I was hearing the siren sounds of the entrepreneurial spirit.

CHAPTER 7

DELVING DEEP INTO VIDEO

There are very few aspects of Americana that are more American than the movies. Other countries make and watch movies, but no modern culture defines itself around the movies more than we do in the United States. And what aspect of late twentieth-century pop culture is more American than the video game and video gamer, with their droopy pants, layered T-shirts, piercings and body ink, and the ubiquitous askew flat-brimmed cap. This was my kind of space.

I had a definite strategy and business plan for the video game business. People are forever asking me about my new and different ventures: How did I know how to do that? How did I know the strategy? How did I know how to write the business plan? How did I uncover that key element of success for the video game business?

The bottom line is that I didn't know. Here's a shocker for you: no one ever knows. The stint at Mattel gave me a short but helpful education in the business. After that, it's about instinct for the market, being unafraid to jump into the unknown and then making sure to learn everything there is to know about the market as you go. I would work 24-7 until I felt I fully understood the business, always searching for the "perfect" answer. I'm not sure I would spend exactly ten thousand hours at it, but I would certainly make Anders Ericsson (and maybe even Malcolm Gladwell) feel good about his theory of deliberate practice making perfect.

As explained, initially I wanted to develop video games based on popular TV, movie, and other entertainment properties for the most popular dedicated video game maker, Atari, and the rapidly emerging personal computer market. This concept was not as novel as I had hoped, as entertainment companies were getting the same idea. They were beginning to develop their own video games or license their properties to video game developers, so I would not be without direct competitors.

Where do ideas come from? There's that whole perspiration to inspiration ratio people like to talk about. For me it's a blend. Obviously, the perspiration and inspiration are both there in significant measure. The other key ingredients I find necessary are cross-pollination (adapting ideas from one business to another) and good people management. The people element cannot be understated. Releasing your ego and believing that ideas often come from lots of sources is important. I always believed that gathering a creative and diverse team was a key element of successful ideation.

What was at least a bit more unique in the gaming space was my idea of developing games that looked like movies, and to do so with teams that had experts with a variety of critical skills instead of having the game built by a lone wolf designer/developer. The teams were to be composed of a director, a game concept / game play developer, a graphics expert, a sound expert, and a coder. Also, the process would not be shooting from the hip; it would involve consumer testing at all stages, a science I had come to trust. I just hoped I was bringing the best of both worlds together, though some might wonder if I was doing the exact opposite. The confederacy of experts could be a confederacy of dunces if I was not careful. The creative spark of unleashed video game fabrication could get doused with the cold water of process. My kind of challenge.

My goal was to develop the passive movie version and the interactive version, the game, at the same time. There were a variety of sound business reasons for doing this, as there were some development efficiencies and marketing-related benefits. From a creative standpoint, the best practices for good game development were just emerging. I hypothesized that good passive and interactive entertainment could have common elements that reinforced each other. Furthermore, I felt that minor modifications to the passive game form could create the platform for much more powerful games. If you introduced the movie/TV passive version at the same time as the interactive game, you could leverage the marketing dollars and reach a much larger audience. The awareness and consumer demand could benefit from the launch of both mediums. You had two shots at success. A bad movie didn't mean a bad video game and vice versa. The different mediums and the creative development spark could make all the difference. The concept was not without successful examples, as evidenced by some video games becoming movies (like *Tron*).

After I resigned from Mattel Electronics, we set out to focus on a new video game business. Barbara and I, feeling like we were the first entrepreneurs ever to set forth on the fantastic voyage, left behind our fully furnished Hancock Park micro-mansion, which we leased to actor Sean Cassidy and his family. In its place, we rented a simple two-bedroom apartment in San Jose in a modest apartment complex. Keep it cheap. We even rented all the furniture, pots and pans, dishes, and silverware.

This parsimony proved less of a bargain than we had thought. All too soon the pots and pans had sprung leaks. I'm not sure I even knew that could happen. But it seemed somehow emblematic of the transient California lifestyle. It was like buying expensive Italian loafers, only to find that walking in them would wear through the soles in a week. What this experience did do was remind me how focused we had been on starting our businesses versus enhancing our immediate lifestyle. We worked long hours and the apartment was incidental. Almost everyone has those moments in their evolution.

By this time Kim had graduated from high school and left for Colorado to attend Lamar Community College. We had seen a segment on *CBS 60 Minutes* about this small community school and their very successful program in Horse Training and Management. A natural for Kim, where she spent the next two years riding horses, training them, breeding them, and making lifelong friends.

Back in Northern California, one of my first business partners was Paul Carter. I had lived with Paul at his hexagonal glass house in Saratoga before Barbara and I were married, back when he and I worked for Oroweat. He was the bright young former CFO at Oroweat, who had an MBA from UC Berkeley and an undergraduate degree in electrical engineering. He had the financial background I did not have. Paul was not married at the time, and we would fly up to San Jose on weekends or Paul would fly to LAX to spend hours working on a business plan for a video game business.

The second partner was John von Leesen (JvL), my former roommate while at Hunt-Wesson, who had overseen all media buying. He was smart and a good negotiator and financially astute, but in a different way from Paul. John was particularly anxious to join us to take a shot at being an entrepreneur. John joined us in our initial strategy meetings, as we contemplated putting together an entrepreneurial business in which the three of us would be partners.

Since both Paul and John were mostly financially oriented and I was the only one with marketing and video game experience, there was some overlap and even redundancy between them. I should have recognized that in a start-up, there is no room for redundancy. As Don Valentine put it, "Three's a crowd." This was the first of many lessons (aka mistakes) learned about starting up a start-up. There are always trade-offs between picking relationships and loyalty over skill sets, and sometimes vice versa. Also, start-ups must remain lean, and the human dynamics of three partners leads inevitably to that odd-person-out place we have all witnessed and all dread. Note to self: pay attention to human dynamics.

Barbara and I initially funded my share of the partnership business with some of my bonus from Mattel, but we quickly began looking for outside funding once we realized how quickly money can evaporate in a new venture. Because the two presumed partners, Paul and John, were both former roommates and business colleagues of mine, this should have boded well for really knowing my partners. Little did I realize that my choice of partners would later produce such heartburn. Note to self: look more carefully before you leap.

Nevertheless, we set about the challenge of reverse engineering the Atari system. We hired a couple of engineers in our Los Gatos office and began the reverse engineering process. I always think of Captain Kirk telling Scotty to put the warp engines in reverse and Scotty saying with his Scottish brogue, "She can only take so much, Cap'n." But mimicking the Atari system and documenting it properly was the tech fundamental that would allow us to legitimately develop software and legally defend ourselves against Atari's undoubted and looming legal wrath.

Our company was called Decision Making Systems, which, in hindsight, seems somewhat less artful and kitschy than I usually like. I took my business plan under my arm and began the search for capital. I was also hoping I could get more than just money. I wanted some strategic relationship that would accelerate us on the path to success. That said, I can't kid you, just money would still be an okay thing at that moment.

I was trying to keep a low profile and work in the underground for competitive reasons and to keep Atari at bay for as long as possible. I needed to hire game designers and programmers from competitors and wanted to strike fast and avoid being sued. I spent time lurking in the halls of Atari to try and recruit their best designers. Wait, are you getting this picture? This is like Jack choosing to go into the Giant's lair and run between the legs of the Giant, trying to sneak his lunch out from under him, reassuring himself that he is invisible. Ballsy, but maybe not so smart.

I learned many lessons about the "unusual" values and motivation of game designers. These insights became important when I was trying to convince a game designer to leave Atari and come to a fledgling start-up. For example, in one instance it was guaranteeing a designer that he would be sitting by a window. Another guy needed to know that there would be a couch by his workstation. This seemed weird at first, but when I realized that he worked late and would sleep on the couch, I wondered if I shouldn't go out and buy more couches for the other designers.

Don Valentine from Sequoia Capital, the famous venture capital firm that discovered and backed Apple, contacted me. That's like the head cheerleader calling you for a date. Don located me by hearing of my activities in the underground and offered to look at backing the company. To some this would seem like the Holy Grail. To others, venture capitalists are leeches to be avoided at all costs. The typical game was to fund your venture with family and friends and perhaps some form of debt if possible, to get the valuation up before going to the venture world. Also, to maintain that 51 percent control if possible. I was too new to this entrepreneurial arena to have a point of view, so I took the meeting, as they say.

One of Don's first observations was that, for a start-up, we had three relatively high-level people. I immediately realized what he was saying, that at most it should be me and one CFO and administration

Dan O'Connell senior and Virginia Davidson on their wedding day, 1936

Dan and Frank O'Connell with their mother, Virginia O'Connell, on
the farm shortly before Dan O'Connell senior passed away

The farm in Ovid, NY

Frank on the way to his first communion, Ovid, NY

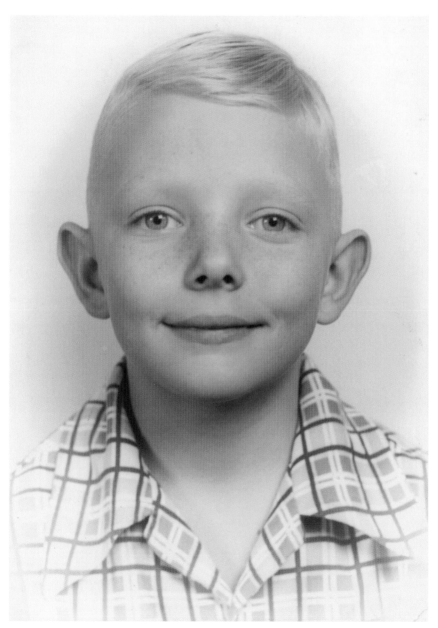

Frank O'Connell, age 9

Dan, Frank, their dog, Rex, and a friend in front of the barn at the farm in Ovid, NY

A teen-aged Frank O'Connell at the barn on the farm, Ovid, NY

The big barn at the farm in Ovid, NY

Frank on his way to Camp Drum NY for National Guard Training, 1957

Carnation Instant Breakfast

Frank and Gail at Frank's
Cornell graduation, 1966

Frank under the hood of Don Peck's Ford Mustang in the race track pit

Don Peck, brother of Gregory, and Frank O'Connell,
crew chief, on the race track with the Ford Mustang

Frank and Gail's house at Box Canyon in Chatsworth,
California, overlooking the San Fernando Valley, 1968

Frank on his 1970 4-cylinder Honda CB750, traveling through California, 1973

Frank on his 1970 4-cylinder Honda CB750 traveling through
the Death Valley National Park in California, 1973

Snowdrift Solid Shortening
by Hunt-Wesson Foods

Hunt's Manwich Sandwich Sauce

Early dating years: Kim and Beth join Frank and Barbara for a relaxing moment, 1973

Barbara and Frank at their wedding, December 1974

Frank O'Connell and his 1965 Porsche 356c in San Francisco

Oroweat Baking Company logo, 1973

Barbara and Frank O'Connell chat with renowned chef, James Beard,
and others at an Arnold-Oroweat Baking Company event, 1976

Bob Kirby, former President of Arnold-Oroweat and Frank's mentor

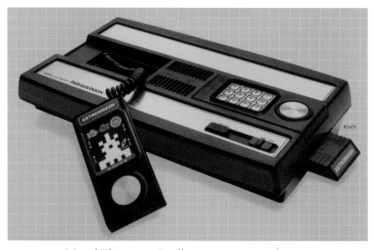

Mattel Electronics Intellivision game console, 1982

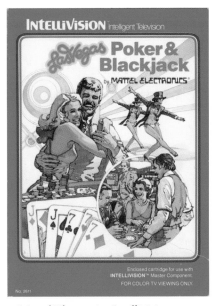

Arnold-Oroweat Bran'nola Bread

Mattel Electronics Intellivision game cartridges for *Poker & Blackjack*, 1981

Mattel Electronics handheld video games

Frank in the lobby of Fox Video Games with employees gathered for coffee, 1982

Famous George Plimpton ad comparing Intellivision's superior graphics to Atari

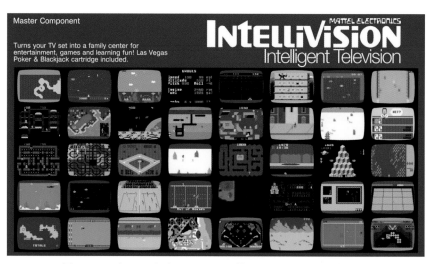

The original Mattel Electronics Intellivision game console, 1981

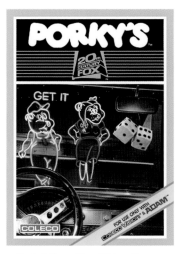

Porky's from Fox Video Games

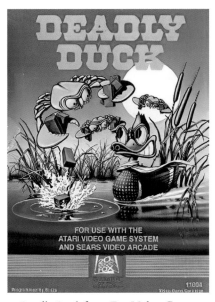

Deadly Duck from Fox Video Games

Fox Video Games booth at CES Las Vegas, 1983

M*A*S*H from Fox Video Games

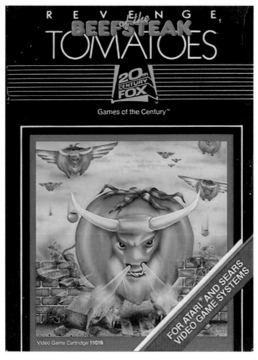

Revenge of the Beefsteak Tomatoes from Fox Video Games

person. John, meanwhile, continued to delay putting his investment into our company and seemed reluctant to make the commitment to join us and relocate from Los Angeles to Silicon Valley. This led me to making the decision to not have JvL join the venture. Paul, who had put in his financial share and lived in Saratoga, had more of the CFO experience we needed, and I would be CEO. It was a difficult decision, and an even more difficult conversation, for which John has never really forgiven me. I never saw or heard from him again.

Eventually, Don offered to put in $2 million, but he wanted 51 percent of the company for doing so. That implied Paul and I had $2 million of intrinsic value in the company, which felt good, but we would lose control. I weighed giving up control so early, in exchange for the advice, experience, and network that Don and Sequoia could bring. It was a hard thing to do, but I ultimately turned him down. I placed a high value on control, since it was one of the principal reasons I wanted to become an entrepreneur. Hindsight makes me wonder if I did the wrong thing, but we'll never know now, so onward and upward.

This is a whole other learning curve subject. Since that time, I have watched or been involved with well-known venture firms repeatedly. The venture capital firms, especially those in Silicon Valley, that provide involvement, direction, and especially relationships significantly increase a start-up's chance of success. I come down in favor of using a good VC, understanding that in an adverse situation they will always put their own interests first. But no entrepreneur worth his salt goes into a venture expecting an adverse situation, and in that event the clarity of a seasoned VC might do more good than harm, even for the entrepreneur. So, yes, my advice is to take a smaller piece and relinquish control, if necessary, for increasing your odds of success. A larger pie is better for everyone.

With all due respect to Don Valentine and my other mentors up to this point, none of them was the big money man I next met. My raising capital efforts led me to a meeting with Marvin Davis, the Denver oil man who owned Twentieth Century Fox Film Corporation. This meeting was arranged through Bob Fell, who had been my boss at Archon. Prior to my arrival at Archon, Bob had hired Barbara in the grocery products sales department, and they had become friends. After Archon, we kept in touch with Bob and later, after moving to San Jose, Barbara and I went to visit Bob at his home in Santa Barbara. Bob was well-connected in the entertainment community and hung out with people from the upper echelons of Beverly Hills. During our visit, I told him about my video game venture, and he mentioned his relationship with Marvin Davis and offered to arrange a meeting.

My skill in raising capital, something I consider a core competency throughout my career, has always been an important starting point for me. I think there is a misconception about the "magic" of raising capital. Yes, you need a compelling and rational proposal, but your passion for making the project successful is what overpowers the rational. I can always sense when I reach the point in a meeting when the room goes quiet and I am looking directly into the eyes of the investors. That's when I know I have hooked them.

The meeting with Marvin Davis took place on the lot of Twentieth Century Fox in Century City. It was quite exciting to go to Marvin Davis's office at the studio. I recall while I was waiting for him, a shoeshine man came by and asked if I wanted a shine. I found this quite amusing and gave him my shoes. He disappeared someplace to shine my shoes. A moment later a secretary appeared to escort me into Davis's office. The shoeshine man was not yet back, so I went into Marvin's office in just my socks.

Marvin was a very large man, to say the least. He immediately made me feel comfortable. A second later the gentleman arrived with my newly shined shoes, and I realized he had Marvin's shoes as well. Marvin had been shoeless behind his desk all along.

In that meeting, I described my idea that the world would gravitate towards interactive entertainment. Marvin knew I was a video game specialist, but he was not too shy to bluntly ask, "What exactly is interactive entertainment?" It may seem hard to believe that there was a time when that term was barely understood, but the truth was that it wasn't often mentioned in common discussion, even in the entertainment business. I explained to him that someday there would be interactive theaters and that the interactive form would be far more important than passive entertainment (movies). He was intrigued enough that I moved on to explain my strategy of taking his current TV and movie properties and making interactive versions of them. Since I hadn't lost him yet, I went on to describe creating both passive and interactive forms simultaneously.

I reviewed the business plan and ended with the punch line that I needed $2–3 million in capital. We had already done a fair amount of the reverse engineering of the Atari system, so the time it took to market could be reasonably quick. The key component we needed from Fox was the interactive entertainment rights to their TV and movie properties, which were historically extensive. Other than the properties Fox owned outright in totality, they didn't know for sure if they owned the interactive rights, a question they had probably never been asked. It's hard to contractually capture what you don't yet know exists. I suggested that from this point forward, all their agreements should cover Fox owning the interactive rights to any property they contract or license. This was obviously breaking new contractual ground, as no one knew that those rights were worth anything. After the presentation, Marvin and his team had a hard time hiding their interest and said they would like to think about it and get back to me.

The meeting was at the end of the week. I got a call the next Monday saying that Mr. Davis was willing to invest $5–6 million (twice what I had requested) but wanted two-thirds of the company and control. I'm sure this was the voice of experience that knew entrepreneurs always need twice as much as they suspect. He also agreed to pay us back for our investment to date (which was clearly an inexpensive act of goodwill that he would use as a bargaining chip in later conversations). He would put all of Fox's past and future inter-active entertainment rights into the company. This was an incredible offer. I was very cool on the phone, saying I needed time to think about the offer. The truth was that I was so excited that I might have even peed my pants. I couldn't believe someone would commit that amount of money and assets to my idea. I recall later having a celebra-tion dinner with Marvin at the famous Chasen's Restaurant in West Hollywood, which was his favorite restaurant. He ordered ribs and I was struck by how he ate and how *much* he ate. It was no accident that he was a big man. Also, he ate most of his dinner with his hands. He made a comment about being able to be overweight if you were rich. Despite being a diabetic, he lived to the ripe age of seventy-nine.

• • •

We completed the investment transaction and launched the new company, Fox Video Games with the byline "Games of the Century." I was forty years old when I became president and CEO of Fox Video Games, with Paul Carter as CFO. We were to liaise directly with Joe LaBonte, the president of Twentieth Century Fox. He was more a busi-nessman than an entertainment guy, having previously been executive vice president at ARA Food Corp in Philadelphia, and at one point running the real estate unit for Fox. Bob Fell remained initially involved but not on a day-to-day basis. I later learned he was paid $250,000 in cash and another $250,000 in stock for making the introduction. Good for Bob. I usually make introductions for the sheer pleasure of connecting friends, so I guess I'll get my reward in another life. These were big numbers to me then and not-so-shabby numbers to me even now. It was part of my introduction to the entertainment business.

Marvin Davis and Fox Film Corporation lived up to every aspect of the agreement we signed. They sent money with the appropriate support we needed, but they never stalled or played games with us. This has always impressed me and is not so ordinary as it should be. I used to hear about some of Marvin's oil deals that sounded a bit sketchy, but I never had any issues with him in our business. Even in tough times, when the video game market was glutting, Fox was an upstanding partner. Through Joe LaBonte, they tried to help us with their powerful relationships, including with retailers. It was also a fun and entertaining relationship. We got to spend time at the studio or, as they call it, "The Lot." We had many lunches at the commissary and saw many more stars. We also got invited to countless entertainment events and were often flown on the Fox corporate jet. It felt like a relationship where everyone should have been making millions, but that proved not to be so easy.

We had the best of both the venture world (still owning 33 percent of the company) and of the entertainment world, earning very good salaries and driving two new leased 1982 XJ6 Jaguar sedans as company cars. Paul was a good negotiator, so he handled most of the deals. I had watched Paul negotiate with the IRS, where he knew the code better than the agent. I was once audited personally by the IRS. I found the perfect combination, which was to have Paul put the numbers together and then send Barbara to deliver all the backup documentation and sweet-talk the auditors. The outcome was benign.

It was interesting that when we went back to Don Valentine and told him we had gotten funding and TV/movie IP video game rights from Marvin and Fox, he asked if we would consider taking on Sequoia as an added financial partner. Fox was not sanguine to the idea, so we declined. In hindsight, accepting the offer might have been a good idea, as Sequoia knew a lot about how to make start-ups successful and we could have used their guidance. It might have made the difference in adding value to the company, but then we probably wouldn't have gotten those Jags either...

Flush with our fresh funding and payback of our investment to date, we aggressively moved forward. Paul Carter and I bought a new building in Santa Clara and leased it back to the company. Paul got a deal on used workstations. Barbara separately bought the independent telephone system and leased it back to the company as well. Paul knew enough about software development and electrical engineering to wire the building and put in a keycard security system that allowed programmers twenty-four-hour access but also tracked who was coming and going. Many programmers work at night or for long stretches, sometimes sleeping on couches and eating terrible fast food. We made sure there were bathrooms with showers. It's pretty much as depicted in The *Social Network* when Zuckerberg goes into his zone. Drugs can also be a problem, particularly when bonuses are paid. It is not uncommon for programmers to disappear for a few days. We had to plan for it. Tracking the hours they worked was not important, but software code theft was a serious concern, especially when Atari was still hovering in our thoughts.

We gradually moved the small group of engineers and programmers from the Los Gatos Tudor office building to the new building. Coincidentally, the executive recruiter for whom Barbara worked in Santa Monica accelerated their plan to open an office in Silicon Valley by subletting our office in Los Gatos. Barbara set up shop, hired a staff, and stayed there until the lease ended and then moved into new office space close to the airport. By then we needed to recruit even more people. Back to the hallways of Atari.

There were many challenges. First, Atari programmers were paid through royalties based on games sold. Thus, they had good incomes and were reluctant to move to a small start-up where a good game probably would not sell as many units as an Atari game with their massive distribution. Second, Skip Paul, Atari's attorney, was going directly after developers. However, game developers are an unusual lot and motivated by many nontraditional factors. We did have the Fox name and a chance to develop games based on entertainment properties. When we interviewed programmer candidates, we listened carefully for what motivated them, which often was not just money. We were willing to be very flexible in our agreements regarding recognition and our willingness to have their name appear on the game or in advertising, thus making them a gaming hero. We also were willing to pay higher royalty rates and guarantees. Programmers tended to move in clusters, so if you could convince one designer, often others would follow. We were fortunate to get a designer from Atari who had developed the famous *Battleship* game. As I recall, he wanted written into his contact that he could have a window and a couch.

We could hire a good engineering and software supervisory staff from computer hardware and software companies outside the game industry, where there was a lot more technical talent. They were not game designers, but they knew hardware and software development. The game industry, per Nolan Bushnell and *Pong*, was still very much a garage industry with the best game designers learning on their own.

I truly wanted to come up with a new game development approach that would open the process to allow for the contribution of multiple talents and disciplines to push the quality and game play experience. One individual rarely had the talent to optimize and take full advantage of the platform we were creating. I recognized there were two different types of individuals: those who wanted to work alone on their game and those who were willing to experiment as part of a development team. We split the building in two, devoting half the space to solo developers and the arranging the other half to optimize communication for team development.

The team development group was organized much like a movie production crew, with a director who oversaw the entire process and maintained the schedule and the process discipline. We hired experienced game designers but also digital experts from outside the industry for sound, graphics, code writing, and hardware. We also instituted a front-end strategy where we decided on the number of games and general themes in the various categories that were matched to target audiences as well as Fox properties that lent themselves to games. Much like movies or commercial production, we storyboarded the game concept right up front.

Storyboarding and this new process allowed us to test game concepts early. Thus, we could either modify the game or perhaps decide it was a loser and cut our losses early in the development process before taking the next very time-consuming and expensive steps.

• • •

When I was headlong into video game development at Fox Video Games, mutual contacts kept saying I should meet this guy, Steve Jobs, who had started Apple Computer. At that point he was just in the market with the Apple II personal computer, but he had only Macintosh on the brain at that point. He was up-and-coming, but nothing like the Silicon Valley icon he would become. The growing VC community of Sand Hill Road in Menlo Park also played a role. Indeed, it was Sequoia Capital that arranged for me to meet Steve Jobs.

At my meeting with the soon-to-be-legendary Steve Jobs in his famous one-room hovel of an office in Cupertino, I noted that, while he was certainly arrogant, he didn't strike me as much different than many of the other young entrepreneurs in the Valley, and thus I wasn't put off by him. We discussed my background at Mattel and experience with interactive entertainment. We agreed about the importance of understanding game play mentality. I also expressed that I had a reasonable amount of research connected to Intellivision regarding home computers and hadn't found that people wanted them in their homes. At that time, consumers seemed to use computers only for mundane tasks such as balancing their checkbook or inventorying recipes. I suggested that until there were better applications or more interest in home office uses, games might get the family to buy and use a home computer. Also, I believed that game play could be used to teach more complex applications, such as navigating a relatively new application called the spreadsheet.

Still not knowing exactly what Jobs was developing, I expressed two areas where Fox Video Games might be helpful to him. First, we could develop a series of games or become a dedicated developer to get a critical mass of games to market at the time of launch. There was typically a significant time before game software was available after the launch of a new piece of computer hardware. This would give him an application-driven sales boost. Second, if, like most computer hardware companies, he was going to keep the architecture closed, Fox Video Games could develop a system and a set of tools to help third-party developers get product applications to market more quickly.

Steve listened carefully and then proceeded to go to the chalkboard and draw a line from the left lower side of the board to the top right, expressing how he was going to build a multibillion-dollar computer company. I guess that chalk line was his sales ramp, though he never actually said that. Luckily, Paul had trained me in interpreting idiot-savant communications. Steve asked me to sign a nondisclosure agreement (NDA), which I did on the spot. He then showed me the Macintosh Computer icon interface he was building. Suddenly he was more savant than idiot. I knew it was a huge breakthrough in simplifying the user interface, and considerably more intuitive and user-friendly than the IBM and Microsoft word-based interface that had little or no graphics.

Steve seemed to be intrigued regarding what an entertainment game developer could bring to his computer party, and he agreed to send over his key lieutenants to our offices in Santa Clara to see what our gaming programmers were up to. He reluctantly agreed to have his team visit us with the Jobsian admonition, "I don't want my engineers wasting time with some bozos."

The morning of the meeting, the Santa Clara office looked normally quiet in the early morning haze as I pulled up in my leased Jaguar sedan. The day before had been a crazy day, so I had decided that an early morning to prepare for an even crazier day would be in order. As I walked into our open-space office, I saw Rick walk by in a T-shirt that caught my eye. It had a picture of a clown's face with a big red "NO" circle and diagonal across it, like a European no-parking sign. The programmers were an eclectic lot, and colorful statement T-shirts were hardly a rarity. As I headed to my cubicle in the corner, I noticed more activity than normal in the office at this early (or any other) hour. Programmers worked on their own schedule, and gaming programmers like we were employing kept particularly peculiar hours all around the clock, but butt-crack-of-dawn hours like this were never busy. Then I saw Esther with her normally unkempt frizzy hair walk by looking fresh as a daisy with her hair in a tidy ponytail. It wasn't her coif that surprised me as much as her T-shirt, which was the same "NO" message as Rick wore. I looked around and saw all the programmers wearing the same T-shirt. It was then that I realized what was under the "NO" symbol. It was a picture of Bozo the Clown. Sometimes you have to just sound it out. Bozo the Clown Stop? Stop Bozo the Clown? No Clowns? No Bozo! That was it! No Bozos.

When Jobs's team of engineers arrived at our offices, we had a balanced combination of well-educated computer engineers and game developers who had learned game design in their garage or had come from Atari or another computer game company. Steve called me following their "No Bozos" visit and said he was impressed with both the team and their T-shirts. He didn't expect to find that kind of engineering talent in an entertainment company. We continued to have dialogue, and then he invited me to his office for another visit. At that meeting, he showed me more features of what was to become the first Macintosh Computer. He said he had decided to open the architecture so that every third-party developer in the world would produce software for the Macintosh. It was a great idea, but it severely undercut the value of what I had offered as our competitive advantages for him. Ultimately, Steve made the decision not to proceed further with Fox Video Games. It was a big disappointment, but that's Silicon Valley.

• • •

The video game industry began to get crowded. Anyone who had a popular piece of content thought it should become a video game. They either licensed it to a video game company or set up their own new company. This included the other TV/movie studios Paramount, Warner Brothers, Disney, MCA, and, of course, all the major league sports teams. There were also two fast-growing independent developers, Activision and Electronic Arts.

Our team could develop games rather quickly. This was somewhat unusual in and of itself, but we also seemed able to get them produced without a major glitch. Maybe we were doing something right. Some of our first games, which were under development before the Fox deal, were *Fast Eddy, Worm War I, Porky's, Beanie Bopper,* and *Deadly Duck* (we used to say it took more than luck to play *Deadly Duck*). You know *Donkey Kong, Mario Brothers, Fast Eddy, Porky's,* and *Deadly Duck,* right? The nickname of our products was "Games of the Century," and it was part of the company logo. We then got on track with Fox Properties and released such memorable favorites as *Revenge of the Beef Steak Tomatoes* and M*A*S*H.

The next big show was CES (Consumer Electronics Show), so we flew the sales and show teams to Vegas on one of Fox's corporate jets to get our psyche up. We were introducing several new games, but M*A*S*H was the lead cow. Our booth was themed as the M*A*S*H bunker and tent. Obviously, we had access to all the Fox TV props. We created quite a stir by parading the M*A*S*H vehicles down the Strip: the M*A*S*H Red Cross ambulance and the M*A*S*H Jeeps. We even flew in Jamie Farr on an old Army helicopter. It was quite a show. We were able to sell to the major chains, gaining broad distribution. We were also able to produce large quantities of game cartridges to meet and satisfy the initial distribution and anticipated consumer demand. That was all good news.

The bad news was the market growth was slowing and the supply of new games was quickly overwhelming the market. In the mid-1980s the video game market was officially glutted. Everyone with any kind of IP licensed it for video games. My brainstorm was everyone else's brainstorm. A huge number of mass-market and specialty shops carried video games. Also, the technology in terms of graphics, sound, and game play was not moving fast enough to offset the sameness between many of the products. It was not good enough to take a popular licensed property and turn it into a game. It had to have great game play, and game play is an art.

The game play, graphics, and sound technology were not moving fast enough to sustain the market. Video game machine prices dropped, and penetration plateaued. As prices started to fall, inventories rose. It didn't take a tech genius to see the writing on the gaming wall.

CHAPTER 8

CROSS-COUNTRY SHIFTS

The entire video game industry continued its downward slide, so Paul and I took quick action to liquidate Fox Video Games. We lucked out and were able to sell the building we had bought to a start-up company from Mexico. We auctioned all the electronic equipment, office furniture, and anything else that would sell and said goodbye to all the staff who had stuck with us during the rise and fall. We kept our Jaguars but had to store several thousand units of video games that, at the time, were pretty much worthless. Paul went off to start another company with our former roommate, Jack McCaskill, and I took flying lessons, seeking some relief from the pressures of the previous two years.

As was predictable, an executive recruiter from New England had been told about me while working on an assignment for a start-up software company in Hartford, Connecticut, and out of curiosity I took his call. Barbara and I had always wanted to return to New England, and the opportunity sounded intriguing, so I flew to Hartford to meet with the private equity group headed by the CEO of United Technologies. Optionware was the brainchild of Ian Boyd, a South African entrepreneur who had developed a complete set of easy-to-use computer templates for small businesses, which were distributed by mass retailers instead of sold in computer stores. Ian was CEO and had recruited a group of very bright software developers, but they needed a seasoned president to manage the company and work with the investor group. So, Barbara and I packed up and moved to Hartford, temporarily staying in a small, cramped company-rented apartment downtown. During this time, in 1985, our first son, Shaun Colter O'Connell, was born in Hartford, and we were able to move into a rented home in Farmington just up the hill from the famous Miss Porter's School.

The challenge was to beef up the software development effort, gain distribution, and hope the investors would continue to support the company. Ian was a high-spirited guy who had lots of rough edges, not to mention a hot temper, and he could exhibit it in the boardroom when the investors came to meet. At one such meeting, he started chasing the lead investor around the table. An hour after the meeting ended, I got a call from the investors, telling me that I would be CEO and that Ian was out. As you can imagine, this did not go over well with Ian, but I had a company to run, and we were facing numerous challenges.

Eventually we cut back the employees and gave up our office space. I moved the remaining crew to our home in Farmington, where they would show up every morning and work through the day, continuing the development work on the software. We changed the name from Optionware to Shaun Software, something the programmers suggested, and registered the company in our newborn son's name. But as with other experiences, the handwriting was on the wall.

The investors were reluctant to continue funding, and I met with them and agreed that the company was not viable. But I still have the Shaun Software stock certificates!

While closing down Shaun Software, I heard about a position at HBO Video in New York from a friend running Fox Video (the highly successful video distribution arm of Fox Broadcasting), so I contacted the recruiter conducting the search. HBO Video sold prerecorded videocassette tapes and was a joint venture between Time Inc. and Thorn EMI (a large UK entertainment company). They wanted someone with a consumer products background, anticipating that the business would start to move from strictly rental to retail sell-through. They saw themselves as an entertainment content company that didn't know retail. Not a bad fit for my skill set, and movies are something for which I felt I had some passion.

The search objective was to find a CEO to put in over the current president, Nick Santrizos, who had been the president of other video companies (Vista, Miramax). Nick was, in many ways, the founder of HBO Video. He was a good guy who knew the business and was close to the distributors. However, the board felt he did not have the vision and skills to take the company to the next level. This was, understandably, not easy for Nick to accept.

During the interview process, they flew me to London on the Concorde for lunch with Gary Dartnall, the head of Thorn EMI's Screen Entertainment Division, which included HBO Video. I liked Gary, as he was easy to talk with and a nice balance to Michael Fuchs, then chairman of HBO, who was much more focused and driven. On my flight back on the "sharpnose," I was sitting near Steven Spielberg and his wife, the actress Kate Capshaw. It seemed like a sign that sooner or later everything "goes to video."

I joined HBO Video as president and CEO of the division of Time Warner. The board of HBO Video was made up of ten people, five from EMI and five from Time Inc., with Michael Fuchs as the chairman. When I asked him to describe the job, he said, "You are the lion tamer; your job is to keep the board members on their stools. Once they get off their stools, your job is to get them back on the stools as quickly as possible." Steve Scheffer, who eventually spent twenty-seven years at HBO, was president of film programming, my day-to-day contact, and the person negotiating the video rights. He was personable, smart, supportive, and critical to acquiring the right content on profitable terms. The board was very hands-off (or perhaps stools-on), and since it was a JV, EMI and Time/HBO stayed dynamically balanced and let me run the company. Also, we were doing very well generating a lot of cash, which helped.

Barbara and I packed up the house and took Sean, who was ten months old (we changed the spelling of his name to the traditional Irish version) and left for New York City. We found a very nice tenth-floor, three-bedroom co-op apartment at 815 Park Avenue and Seventy-Fifth Street with a doorman, just a couple of blocks from Central Park. From there, I could walk to my office at HBO Video on Sixth Avenue and Fifty-Sixth Street.

Immediately upon signing my employment contract, I met Nick Santrizos at the Union League Club, where he was a member. I liked Nick and respected what he had built. I think we both knew immediately it would be hard for me to run the company together with him as president reporting to me as CEO.

The fact that the JV was in a separate building (Sixth and Fifty-Seventh) from HBO and Time Inc. helped preserve our independence. I had a great office on a high floor, which I had furnished in a contemporary fashion with a glass table as my desk. I had always had a distaste for "executive wood," as I used to call it. I have always hated desks. Just like office sizes, corner offices, and parking spots, it reeks of class distinctions and sets up barriers to communication. These are mere tools, not symbols of power. I was a big believer in open office space, giving the best views near the windows to the administrative and support people, providing workstations for everyone, and eliminating assigned parking (the earlier you arrive, the closer you get to the door). I have always fought against the privilege culture of the C-suite.

Despite the apparent lion-taming advantages on JV's, I have come to feel that they should most often be avoided. I would advise anyone to avoid running a JV if possible. The partners' objectives, appetite for risk/growth, and agreement that each is making a fair contribution to the enterprises value are seldom in sync. There is generally not an agreed-upon and well-articulated strategic plan and exit. This makes it difficult to manage as a CEO, as you are often getting pulled in various directions by the partners. The partners generally end up suing each other or struggling to dissolve the JV. Strangely enough, this was not the case with Thorn EMI/HBO Video. Both contributed significant TV, movie, and other content, with HBO being the operating partner.

Back at HBO Video, Nick had hired everyone in the company. Initially some of the team made it clear that they weren't interested in a new CEO coming in over Nick. The head of sales was a particularly close friend of Nick's. He made it blatantly clear he didn't even want to talk to me. I insisted, as I normally do, on immediately visiting key distributors. In the first distributor meeting, the owner said to me, "Putting a CEO in over Nick was like putting an alarm clock in the middle of a wet dream," so that was my welcome to the industry.

Eventually, the distributors embraced the new team, as always happens, and from their standpoint, it was all about having good content to distribute/sell in their rental stores. I should have realized that those outlets would be the same dodo birds that computer software stores were becoming. Every bird has its day, but species-defining events will always lurk in the shadows.

It was quickly apparent to Nick that I wasn't going to tolerate his waning support and that I was going to put a new team and culture in place. I remember him coming to me one day and saying, "I have learned that once you have made a decision one direction, you move quickly to execute." Good observation, Nick; I think that's what a CEO is supposed to do. This was the turning point, as Nick was really signaling he had decided to leave. He had done an excellent job building the company up to that point, but what was the expression? Oh yeah, every bird has its day. I guess I'm not always the nicest lion tamer in town.

My intent was to turn the company from a video rental distribution and content acquisition company into more of a video entertainment and consumer product company. The difference should be obvious. Well, at least it was to me. Having been exposed to the entertainment industry through Twentieth Century Fox and Fox Video Games, hanging out a fair amount at the studio and being exposed to career entertainment executives, I used to wonder if it was really a business (or at least a well-run business).

This was the beginning of my amusing myself, questioning whether entertainment was a real business. There was so much Hollywood all around us: extreme preoccupation with looks, image-centrism, recognition craving, connections deploying, and partying. Oh, the partying. Everything Hollywood, from the press to the air-kisses, seemed disconnected from the real world. I considered myself fortunate that I never got caught up too much in the circus. I wasn't puritanical about it. I always found it amusing from a distance, but I never wanted my life to be dictated by all the fluff.

On the other hand, it made good business sense for me to know who the celebrities were. I wished it weren't so, but you can't take a crash course in celebrity-spotting. While not disrespectful, I never ogled celebrities or went out of my way to meet them. Barbara used to say that I wouldn't recognize a celebrity if I fell over one; it was the business that intrigued me, not the face on the screen, or being seen in *Variety* or having a power lunch at 21. It was a fun industry that was very entertaining. Others may have gotten more fun out of it, but they might also have been put in harm's way in situations I naturally avoided. The video business is driven by content and distri-bution with little regard for understanding the consumer audience or marketing. Not that I was bothered by it, but many of the lives in the industry are governed by extraneous things, like seeing if they are mentioned that day in the *Hollywood Reporter* or other publications.

I brought to HBO Video a consumer products approach and a young but strong consumer products team that I'd recruited. HBO Inc. also had a good team of existing people to work with. My small group of direct reports were top of their class and helped us achieve success across the board. Tracy Dolgin, Ellen Stolzman, Jerry Ruttenbur, and Eric Kessler were hardworking, fun, sophisticated, talented, and experienced, and we worked well together. We were blessed with inheriting an incredible advertising agency, Cadwell Davis. Frankie Cadwell, then in her late 60's and a Cornell graduate, was an icon as one of the first women to own a national ad agency who was a strong advocate of change in the image of women in advertising. She once sent me a live chicken named Francis for my birthday. Francis lived a happy free-range life in our neighborhood in North Carolina. Her agency designed unique advertising campaigns, which, along with other marketing moves and public relations, drove our video cassette volumes to levels not seen before in the industry. I also hired a great PR firm, HWH, a leading international public relations company that was co-founded by Lois Whitman-Hess and her husband, Eliot Hess. Lois was an expert in entertainment and consumer electronics PR with a wide range of powerful media connections, leading us to some phenomenal campaigns. Later, I hired Lois and HWH to create PR campaigns for other companies I was running, and we have remained close friends to this day. She currently has a popular blog, DigiDame. Altogether, it was a true dream team that worked well together.

At HBO Video we began to employ several consumer product techniques that the industry had not seen before. We no longer believed that a film's success in home video should be judged by how well it did in the theaters. We didn't accept the old myths such as "a film will do proportionately as well in video distribution as it did theatrically." We started using advertising to expand the market for a film in video and to influence the rental retailers to buy more cassettes to cover the initial peak demand. We concentrated on consumer promotions and advertising to drive cassette rentals deep into VCR penetration. We found that we could often broaden the audience in video in ways less malleable than in theaters. There seemed to be an insatiable demand for certain genres, such as horror films. I'm not sure we knew why, but it was relatively easy to run with it anyway. We found ways to help the retail rental stores carry heavier inventories during the new release, high-demand period. Halloween was a very big deal to us.

HBO video grew rapidly and became extremely profitable. The stories from these halcyon days are plentiful and often used as case studies. There was a fight over the video rights to *Platoon*, the Oliver Stone Oscar-winning Vietnam War film from Hemdale Films. This pitted HBO and Vestron against each other, as both claimed to have video rights for the film. Like all good firefights, there was a show-down, but not in the rice paddies. It was at the Las Vegas video retail show. Oliver Stone agreed to come to Vegas and talk to the retailers about *Platoon*, but he asked us to rent him a convertible to drive from LA instead of flying him. No problem, Hollywood was Hollywood. Then Vestron, a leading prerecorded video competitor, said they would sue any retailer buying *Platoon* videos from HBO Video. This time, I flew in a Time Warner lawyer, who looked and talked like he was straight from central casting. He announced to thousands of retailers during our presentation that we would legally indemnify anyone who bought *Platoon* from us.

This was an unprecedented and strong maneuver. The legal battle ended up holding the video off the market for eleven months. During that time, the publicity and scant availability drove up the eventual demand. We priced *Platoon* at ninety-nine dollars, an unheard-of retail price then, and the industry was shocked, but we sold out. *Platoon* was also the first film where there was a commercial section (meaning an ad) at the beginning of the film. That's when we used Lee Iacocca, chairman of Chrysler, which then owned Jeep, showing him sitting on a Jeep and saying," I hope we will never have to build another Jeep for war."

Vestron was eventually paid $15.7 million in a settlement. Like many battles in history, everyone goes home once tribute is paid.

Not all promotions are so dramatic, but funny stuff was everywhere. When the movie *Hoosiers*, the story about a winning, small-town Indiana basketball team, was released to video, we asked Dennis Hopper to come out to Vegas for the retail distributor show. Dennis was already a well-known bad boy from his roles in *Cool Hand Luke*, *Easy Rider*, and *Apocalypse Now*. We asked him what compensation he wanted. He said just to put a couple of thousand dollars in a velvet bag so he could use it to gamble. No problem, Hollywood was Hollywood.

And then there was Cannon Films, the vehicle of the legendary Israeli owners Menahem Golan and Yoram Globus, cousins known in Hollywood as "The Go-Go Boys" for their annual burst of film releases. Menahem and Yoram were initially known for producing low-budget films, many in Israel. They had been in business for over twenty years and produced as many as twelve movies a year. They produced TV shows as well, as their video film company had bought the rights to several classic libraries. They did a slew of Chuck Norris films. As a result, they had a huge library of popular potential video content. They burst onto our screen in an up-close-and-personal way when EMI decided they wanted to sell their half of our partnership. So, Cannon Films decided they needed some more "cannon fodder" and wanted to buy 50 percent of our JV from EMI. I had finagled my way into financing ventures, and I liked the business enough that I decided I wanted to buy EMI's piece. I asked and got permission from the board to bid.

To everyone's dismay, Cannon made an announcement at the Cannes Film Festival saying they had bought 50 percent of the JV from EMI and were now HBO's partner in the JV. Cannon was culturally about as far away from Time Warner as you could get. I remember Yoram calling Time Warner the "Ivy League of the entertainment industry." As soon as Time Warner saw the Cannes announcement, they went to the press, essentially saying they would never be a partner with Cannon. A press release war was brewing, and I was the monkey in the middle. I was quickly in touch with Yoram. My group analyzed their known library, finding it massive. With some sifting, we felt it contained some very valuable video content. I immediately wrote to both partners (Time Warner and EMI), taking a positive view of the JV's value based on the combined libraries. I essentially pleaded with both of them to get out of the press and let Cannon make the next move. If they returned, I wanted to get both parties in a room and review what we saw in the libraries and their intentions on making those available to us. My own bid was sidelined. No problem, Hollywood was Hollywood.

The meeting was rational and successful. There was a funny aspect when Yoram and Menahem would have sidebars speaking Yiddish to each other, not realizing that one of the HBO people in the room also spoke Yiddish. Classic. During the break, we downloaded their library. Everyone saw the value in a deal and decided to get down to business. The biggest issue was resolving which name would be on top in the logo. It ended up HBO/Cannon Video, which was the logical business choice for consumer recognition.

This was the beginning of one of the most fun, successful business ventures of my career. I enjoyed dealing with two diametrically opposed cultures. HBO's buttoned-up professional culture and Cannon's completely chaotic, high risk, relationship-driven culture were pretty diverse. Menahem and Yoram would often say, "Fraankh, you are family." I don't mean to sound cynical, but those calls would usually come when they were trying to get me to wire money, like $1 million in cash distribution to the partners out of the JV. To them, someone who gave them money was like family. Cannon and Time Warner weren't very interested in talking to each other, which was a distinct advantage to me, as the conversations would always go through me.

I would screen the Cannon films and other content at night to determine potential for the video market. I'd often come home with a bag of videos that Cannon had sent me. Yoram would always say, "Fraankh, these are *fantastic!*" Despite the hyperbole, much of what they sent me was great for video, especially those cheap horror movies. There were also plenty of films that were totally bizarre and inappropriate. A memorable example was a Cannon video of a transgender affirmation surgery. Yoram called me the next morning and predictably said, "Wasn't that *fantastic?*" I'm afraid I had to tell him, "No Yoram, that was definitely neither Hollywood nor Main Street." That belonged nowhere other than in the library of some obscure Swedish medical college.

And did I mention horror films? I became fixated on horror films. They were true business anomalies. I learned there was an insatiable market for really bad horror videos. It didn't matter how poorly they did at the box office. In fact, there might have even been an inverse correlation. My favorite was *Howling II: Your Sister Is a Werewolf*, where a guy whose teenage sister is killed by werewolves runs around looking for the monsters who killed her. Now that's entertainment!

Selling videos to consumers after the rental window, thereby making video stores into retail stores, became a big later-stage goal. Initially, new films were released for the rental market about six months after they were shown in theaters. We then began experimenting with selling videos in retail stores three months after the rental introduction. There was substantial demand for various videos, depending on the content. This became a lucrative stand-alone business. I'll bet you still have some VHS tapes you bought, lurking somewhere in your basement.

We advertised on TV and in movie theaters. We pioneered advertising prior to the release of the video. This was geared to get consumers to go into their video store and sign up on a reservation list, but mostly to get stores to buy more copies to meet the initial peak demand. The ability to take the same content and sell it first in theaters, next to video rental stores, and later to consumers in retail stores produced a tremendous revenue stream. Various other business models arose on that downward slope of the product life cycle, like skipping the rental window (and now even the theaters) and going directly to retail sales.

Eventually, the convenience of cable TV with its on-demand capabilities emerged as a threat that proved insurmountable. Videocassettes and even their successors, the smaller, crisper DVDs have shrunk to a small business. Videotapes now live with 8-track tapes in the depths of our memory.

HBO Video acquired the video distribution rights for Jim Henson Associates and his Muppets, which was obviously a valuable asset. I established a close relationship with Bob Savage, the new president of Jim Henson Associates and the former head of Compton Advertising. Building social relationships with people in your business and linking that to your spouse and family is often touted as a questionable practice ("Don't mix family and business"). I have always felt otherwise, though the trick is in picking your friends as friends and not necessarily as leverageable business assets.

It is so much easier to conduct business when there is a familiarity and relationships are founded on trust. Also, hopefully you can find a spouse/partner who enjoys your business and business associates. That may be easier when you choose wacky businesses like I seem to, but remember, I met Barbara while in the boring old food business. There is nothing more powerful (and here I mean jointly in a personal and business sense) than hosting a dinner at your home or being invited to a business associate's home. Relationships between business spouses can be equally important.

Here I will mention that we welcomed our second son, Thomas Mackenzie "Mack" O'Connell into the family in 1987. The girls were grown, graduated from college, and charting their own paths. Beth had married and Kim had met her future husband. The family enjoyed all the videos I would bring home and were continually entertained by my involvement with HBO Video. Barbara had raised the girls first and then focused on raising our second family of boys. She had moved with me multiple times and now we found ourselves living in NYC. It helped that she was somehow able to handle all of it. She will tell you that her most profound mentor was my mother, Virginia.

I always say to young people that the choice of your spouse/ partner is probably more important than your career choice. And I don't just mean in terms of life happiness, but also in terms of career success. Today, in most cases, by the time they marry, both partners' careers are well underway, and both more or less know the road they are likely to travel. In my day, most marriages took place in or shortly after college, at the beginning of careers. I believe those marriages face more challenges, as the growth of early careers may or may not cause couples to grow together. Given today's two-career households, people can go in eyes wide open and have a better chance of getting mutual support and involvement in each other's careers. Quite simply, that improves the chances of success and happiness. Maybe I should go into marriage counseling next?

Since content is king, the competition became fierce for video rights and video distribution deals for movies (including older film libraries). TV programs and other video content were also part of the equation. Eventually, the installed base of VCRs got so large it was the main driver of entertainment release. During my three years at HBO Video, I saw and was involved in many changes in the entertainment business. Because of the dramatic pace of change, it felt like I was at HBO much longer than I really was.

It's nice to be in a growing dynamic business where money is being made. That rapidly growing base of VCRs in the home definitely helped propel the business. Many businesses in the US today are not growing, which puts you in zero-sum game share fight. This is harder and not as much fun. It forces you into declaring war against your competitor to win.

I found that I perform best when I have good strategic agreement with my backers and board and then am given the room to operate with my team. If the supervision is too close, I start to overthink how my superiors are going to respond to a decision. This cuts the speed of my decision-making and often impacts the boldness of innovative moves. I suppose if there's too little guidance (hard for me to imagine), there's the risk of misalignment with owner goals. HBO Video was a near-perfect balance. The JV partners supplied the content, and we were responsible for getting it distributed. Entertainment companies are much better at content generation than they are at dealing with retail distribution. The JV structure, in this case a success, was partly responsible for creating the autonomy. Also, the management team was highly respected (if I say so myself) and of course, the business was going well and cranking out money.

I was not interested in moving up into a position at Time Warner. The politics were not my cup of tea. I liked being in a separate building at HBO, many blocks away from Time Warner, where we were independent. HBO Video grew rapidly, generating a lot of cash, and I was well-liked.

A few months before my three-year contract was up, Steve Scheffer began discussions with me regarding a new contract. We had developed a respectful, professional working relationship and he seemed pleased at my personal success at HBO Video, not to mention that of the business. He had a long history with HBO and, in my opinion, approached the entertainment business pragmatically, not getting caught up in the hoopla. He was confident in a universe filled with insecurities and was considered quietly powerful in a room full of major movie moguls. So when we met, he offered that his idea was to design an arrangement that was more entrepreneurial both from a range of responsibility and an incentive plan. But since it was a JV, there was no stock or options. I was happy at HBO Video, but perhaps getting a little bored and feeling like I was bumping up against a ceiling, and I needed to think about it.

About this time I was approached by Joe LaBonte, who had moved on to become the president of Reebok International up in Boston. Joe was formerly the president of Twentieth Century Fox Film Corporation and our direct report for Fox Video Games. We had developed a close relationship and worked well together. Maybe it was time to put on my running shoes?

CHAPTER 9

THE HUMAN SIDE
OF INNOVATION

I have always felt that this story is an industrial psychologist's field day, set on the stage of a leading cultural trend of the era, the running and exercise trend. While many have provided their versions, this is the first time I am providing mine.

Let's start with why Paul Fireman, the founder and major shareholder of Reebok, wanted to hire a president of all corporate and international *and* another president of Reebok North America, and what delineated the positions. Even with the benefit of hindsight, I feel like I am still speculating, as the mind of a successful entrepreneur is often a cipher, and I am not entirely sure Paul really wanted to make these hires at all. He certainly never wanted to really relinquish control. Earlier, he had had a heart attack and his wife, Phyllis, strongly encouraged him to pull back from the company and spend more time at their home in Florida, smelling the roses and playing golf, a game to which he seemed almost addicted.

Reebok's culture under Paul Fireman's reign is often characterized as "tribal" by those of us who lived it. Paul was the prototypical tribal chieftain, followed by a tribe of idealistic athletes, both amateur and professional. We were not slaves, but there was a certain feudal nature to the place, with Paul the only lord of the manor. This approach works less and less well as the organization gains scale.

While Paul pretty much controlled the board, they certainly pressured him to get professional outside help, as the company was starting to lose market share to Nike and the earnings were falling off. That is probably enough justification to satisfy the issue of bringing someone in. As to why to split the jobs as he did, all I can guess is that Paul needed a corporate guy to run the bigger company functions and a marketing guy to run the "ground game." In addition, like many founding entrepreneurs, Paul had never run a large business and thus, with Reebok growing toward the billion-dollar sales mark, the board felt it was time to add some larger company experience.

Reebok had grown, but Nike was growing faster, especially due to the category-blasting Air Jordan shoes. Also, Reebok was in a distribution squeeze where Foot Locker stores accounted for fully a third of Reebok's volume and Reebok accounted for fully a third of Foot Locker's volume. There's a Harvard case study in that balancing act alone, probably with both companies feeling alternately vulnerable and dominant, depending on the day of the week.

It was common for me not to see Paul for weeks at a time and then, unannounced, he would appear and start to unravel some new product design or call the design team together with some idea he had thought about while he was away. "We make athletic shoes. Golf is a fast-growing area of athletics. I know Greg Norman from Palm Beach. Greg is a high-profile golfer. We are going to make Greg Norman golf shoes." That was that.

When I reflected on taking this job, I saw Reebok as an impressive executive opportunity, but, as I came to see it, this was not another case of teaching the elephant to dance better or faster. This was more of a turnaround. Reebok was in more trouble in 1988 than the outside world understood. I think it was Gerry Roche at Heidrick & Struggles who described the challenge to me as rebuilding a rocket in flight without letting it drift to the ground. I wish I had been astute enough to realize the brand didn't have enough definition and was thus losing share. It didn't have truly differentiated new products. There was nothing significant in the product pipeline, and the long product development cycles and lack of new shoe technology made this even more challenging. I might have still taken the job, but I would have better girded my loins for what was to come. Finding novel ways to innovate would be the key.

Once again, Barbara sold the co-op apartment on Park Avenue, and we packed up with Sean and Mack and moved to the South Shore of Boston, to the bucolic seaside suburb of Cohasset. While living on the South Shore, I bought my first Harley, a 1991 Springer Softtail. A couple of years later, I bought Barbara her first motorcycle, a 1993 Harley 883 Sportster after she completed the Motorcycle Safety Training Course. (She later gave her Sportster to Gail for Christmas when she upgraded to a 1994 Harley Heritage Softtail Nostalgia.) The need for this alternative lifestyle experience was ingrained deep inside no matter where I went or what I did. It helped keep me calm and connected to a sense of freedom.

I joined Reebok as president of Reebok Brands North America. I was forty-five years old. I was responsible for development of product worldwide. I was also responsible for distribution in the US. I was not responsible for international distribution. This construct, like so many situations in business, was a case of the organization chart getting drawn for people or political reasons rather than for what made the most sense for the business. So while international distribution was not in my brief, I got very involved with the international distributors anyway. Form tends to follow function in business, and I just did what was necessary without concern for job specifications.

Technically, all functional areas and subsidiaries reported to Joe, but it was made clear to me from the start (and with Joe's full understanding and agreement), that I really reported directly to Paul. I preferred reporting to Paul because he was the decision-maker. I wanted to learn directly from him why Reebok had been successful and about the culture he had built. If I was to help change the company, I needed to understand these two foundational issues. But it didn't matter what I wanted; Paul called the shots. Culture is the element that characterizes how a company functions or why it's dysfunctional. It's the most critical element in a turnaround or in growing a stagnant company. Most executives have never taken a company through a cultural change. It is one of the business attributes least understood by most executives, probably because it is intangible. Furthermore, it is rarely taught in business schools or executive seminars. Figuring out the optimum business strategy is much easier than orchestrating the cultural shift necessary to successfully turn around or grow a company. What was an esoteric notion in the 1980s is now considered a mainstream and necessary ingredient for success.

Paul had considerable strengths, but I felt that the business acumen to run a fast-growing company of this size, up against a worthy competitor like Nike, was missing. Strategic planning, proper budgeting, and real accountability were missing. Serfs do not feel accountable. This is not to say that the company shouldn't have been entrepreneurial, fast-moving, and flexible. These are good things but hard to control in larger companies. Paul had always been an entrepreneur. He had never worked for anyone else, nor worked at a larger company, where he would have been exposed to such best practices. In some ways he made up the Reebok best practices based on what he (and usually, he alone) believed.

What a funny role reversal for me. I was the guy who forced stodgy big companies to dance to the entrepreneurial tune. I had rarely been the one to say, "Wait a minute, we need to do things more systematically." I was pushing for consistency and some modicum of predictability, but not advocating a highly disciplined management style where the organization would be left gasping for air. The tribal culture fostered more emphasis on guessing what the chieftain wanted, rather than independent thinking about what was best for the company. I wanted to see a management team aligned on a path to reduce the chaos. I felt that the needed discipline could come most easily through hiring people from other, more sophisticated (that is to say, more evolved), companies.

Reebok was also "Party Central." There was a plethora of lavish parties often associated with retailer-themed events. Managing "Party Central" had some interesting tribal sub-chieftain duties. At one sales event in Chicago, we had hired Paula Abdul as the headliner. She got a bad case of stage fright (surprising for a big star, I thought). I had to spend twenty minutes talking her "off the ledge" while the audience of shoe retailers was stomping their sneaker-clad feet. During another TV shoot with her, she ran off to sit in her Jaguar and cried because she thought the commercial, and the outfit she was supposed to wear, made her look fat. This is serious stuff to an image-oriented celebrity.

You can make this stuff up, but I didn't need to—I was living it. The company was populated by predominately young, attractive people. Athletic footwear was like that. With that came a lot of internecine relationships and affairs. In addition, since the marketing and product development teams were often traveling to Korea (the site of our production partner) for weeks or a month at a time, it provided an environment for collegiality, socializing, and the inevitable full array of hookups.

Our attitude in those days was "live and let live." If it didn't have some direct impact on the company and seemed consensual, leave it alone. If I had started firing people for occasional affairs, I probably would have lost a lot of my management team. In not too many years, things have changed with increased legal liability requiring generally reporting these types of incidents to a central HR function that acts independently.

Paul Fireman had built an enviable and successful company, so I don't mean to be overly critical. I learned a lot from him and his willingness to make fast changes and bold moves. But it's hard not to wonder what Reebok could have been like if it had tackled the issues of growth and business maturity a bit differently.

What business was Reebok really in? What did the brand stand for? These are classic questions that I think Reebok struggled with and never got exactly right. Maybe it was a performance athletic company, an athletic footwear company, a fashion company, a health and wellness company, an entertainment company, or a cross-training footwear company. Not so easy when you consider the breadth and dimension of the industry.

Only one-third of Reebok shoes ever see any form of athletic competition or conditioning workout. When we did the research, we found that the Nike brand stood for sweat and athletic performance. Reebok didn't stand for anything, which was a serious problem.

By way of historical background, the company was founded by Bill and Joe Foster in England, selling shoes through the mail to Olympic runners. It was at a sporting goods convention where Paul Fireman spotted the Reebok shoe and made a deal to start licensing and distributing the product in the US in 1979.

Out of capital in 1981, Paul sought additional financing so that he could fund production of the aerobic workout shoe, which was a total breakthrough and turning point for Reebok. In a deal that has become a company legend, he sold a majority share (55 percent) in

Reebok for $77,500 to Pentland Industries, a London-based holding company led by Stephen Rubin. When Rubin asked Fireman what kind of compensation he wanted, Paul asked for a relatively high annual salary with no further incentive, but Rubin wanted to minimize their risk as well as create a potential for unlimited incentive. They settled on a formula: a $65,000 base salary plus 10 percent of pretax earnings over $100,000. That resulted in a modest $65,695 bonus in 1982, $217,000 in 1983, and $1.2 million in 1984. By the time I arrived in 1988, Paul was being paid a bonus of $15,066,700—forty-two times larger than his annual paycheck.

By 1984 the partnership was so successful, Paul Fireman and Pentland bought the company from the Fosters for $700,000 and renamed it Reebok International. Reebok went on to purchase several other brands and companies: Avia, Ellesse athletic and leisure wear, Rockport Shoes, Greg Norman Collection, and On-Field. They also manufactured footwear under the Ralph Lauren label.

Every good brand needs a niche from which to build. Initially, Reebok didn't really have that, but it could have. The biggest missed positioning opportunity for the Reebok brand was the women's market. Reebok was struggling to find its way when it caught the aerobic craze. The tipping point was when Cybil Shepard lifted the skirt of her black strapless gown at the 1986 Emmy Awards to reveal flaming orange Reebok high-tops. The female market was big and getting bigger with women's sports, such as tennis, running, training, and the explosive growth in aerobics. Remembering that most Reeboks are worn on the street, aerobics put a lot more Reebok feet on the street (whether heading to aerobics class or to Dunkin' Donuts).

In studying the Nike versus Reebok brand strategies, there were stark differences. Nike owned the tough, aggressive, male sweat-performance image and could only go so far on the female side before it started to dilute the male image. In the case of Reebok, the brand was much softer and thus could move a long distance in both the male and female directions. Reebok, because of the aerobics craze and later the adaptation to step aerobics, developed a very strong female brand loyalty with the introduction of the Reebok Princess Freestyle aerobics shoe in 1982. Other female-oriented shoes had come and gone, but the Princess was a hit, made of garment leather, which was very thin and very soft. But the toe covering always wrinkled during the fabrication process, and the production managers tried unsuccessfully to eliminate the wrinkle. That turned out to be, however, one of the endearing features with female consumers, who bought them in white to wear as a fashion statement. At one point, Angel Martinez, who headed new business development, brought STEP Aerobics to Reebok. He had been introduced to Gin Miller, a fitness expert in Los Angeles, who had invented and developed the STEP. Known as a revolutionary and highly effective cardio workout device, it was combined with the Reebok Freestyle Aerobic Princess Shoe. STEP Reebok later designed an entire line of footwear and apparel. Angel Martinez later became the President and CEO of Deckers Brands.

Nevertheless, even at Reebok, the female side of the business always played second fiddle to the men's. That made no sense to me. The reasons are hard to pin down, but I suspect it went back to Paul's vision. He always seemed to see himself in a personal battle with Phil Knight at Nike. This blinded him in some ways and often caused him to go head-to-head with Nike, whether it made brand sense or not. What he should have been doing was working harder to dominate the female market and perhaps thereby help define what Reebok meant as a brand. While I was in charge, I split the male and female businesses and put a woman in charge of the women's market. My hope was that this would satisfy Paul's Nike demon and still allow the brand to gravitate toward its natural female side.

Being the tribal chieftain at Reebok, Paul Fireman and his personal quirks were the subject of a great deal of observation and speculation. One can suggest that these should be superfluous to running a good company, and as much as that may be so in a more evolved organization, in a tribal organization the movements, actions, and even affectations of the "big man" often determine the direction and strategies of the company. It's a game of second-guessing what the chieftain wants, and while it doesn't seem professional, it is the reality with which the management team must contend on a daily basis.

Paul was a quintessential entrepreneur in the best sense of the word. He did not have much respect for education, most likely because his success was not a function of education. He had dropped out of Boston College and finished his education "on the streets." Strangely enough, from where I stood, he was *not* a hard worker. This is unusual for a driven entrepreneur. He would say things to me like, "You work too hard," and "You don't take enough vacation." That made him very human to me. At the same time, he might declare, "All vacations are cancelled, we've got a product to launch…"

Paul loved product and would drive the organization crazy, making changes late in the product development cycle, sometimes wreaking havoc with timelines, costs, promises to the trade on delivery, etc. Reebok was often as much as six months late after giving retailers a delivery date. He also believed strongly in the quality of the product and used to instruct the sales organization to present each shoe as if it was worth a million bucks. But this was often with disregard for the implications of any of the changes he was making. Product differentiation and quality were king, and he would forsake everything else, including retailers, for the sake of those.

I would say that Paul was hyper focused on product differentiation, which was music to this marketer's ears. That is often the hardest thing on which to get buy-in from management, since it is often the riskiest part of the consumer marketing equation. New and differentiated product can be massively misguided and very costly, not to mention make everyone involved look very stupid.

Unfortunately, over time, the Reebok products lost their points of differentiation.

Strangely, Reebok was simply not a performance-oriented environment. This is an unusual feature, especially in a large corporation like Reebok. Being a successful executive is difficult enough, but the more unusual the culture, the more difficult it becomes. At some point, executive performance got overtaken by concern about culture change. Paul would not tolerate anyone trying to change his company's culture.

Paul seemed to need to battle for acceptance in the big leagues of his chosen businesses. The halls of the company were abuzz with a story in *the Boston Globe* that Paul's membership had been rejected at the Oyster Harbors Club on Cape Cod. If it was true, his rejection probably could have been the reason for his buying the Willowbend Club on Cape Cod and, eventually, placing a big bet to buy the Liberty National Golf Course in New Jersey, where he is involved in a controversial attempt to convert the adjacent land and bird sanctuary into additional holes for the golf course.

Paul's tight-knit family orientation always struck me as a contrast with his vulnerability to gurus and management fads. At one point, he put the entire company through "est" training with Werner Erhard. He seemed always to be most influenced by the person with whom he last met.

Shortly after I arrived in 1988, I learned that Paul had agreed to have the company sponsor an Amnesty International Concert Tour, called "Human Rights Now!" It was funded with an estimated $20 million from the Reebok Foundation. Barbara and I found ourselves involved with some of the concerts, like the ones we attended in Philadelphia, New York, London, and Tokyo. The entire tour went around the world. We met Bruce Springsteen, Tracy Chapman, Sting and The Police, Bono, Peter Gabriel, U2, Santana, and a whole host of other top-name entertainers at the time. Joe LaBonte became deeply involved with Reebok's global human rights program relating to that company bugaboo, apartheid. Reebok was incorrectly rumored to be a South African company, which triggered occasional consumer boycotts. It's hard to be the inner-city brand when you are associated with apartheid. Reebok ran famous rumor ads to dispel this notion and entered into a massive campaign, including sponsoring the concert tour with Amnesty International. I found myself troubled by the focus away from the business and questioned if our consumer could really relate to this cause.

Paul was very honest and outspoken. He certainly did not have much regard for retailers, whom he thought were sheep who had never built a business for anyone. He was fixated on Phil Knight and was always declaring war on Nike, wanting to challenge Phil to athletic contests like a tennis game (I'm glad he didn't do that, since I suspect Phil might have won or Paul might have died trying). Phil apparently had his own demons, as he never forgot having to lay off people at a moment when Reebok was kicking Nike's butt. But we didn't line up behind Phil, we lined up behind Paul. And Paul was often blinded to alternative competitive strategies other than going head-to-head against Phil.

The situation I found when I joined Reebok in 1988 was that they had no new or differentiated product. Given the two-to-three-year development cycle, that was decidedly not good news. There was no exciting product in the development pipeline. That was strange since Paul was quite tuned in to that issue. I thought that was why he had hired me in the first place. The athletic footwear industry is driven by technology, design, and entertainment, much more than people might suspect. Reebok was suffering from a lack of new product, and Nike was killing us. My view was that the Reebok designers had gotten insular and were no longer designers but stylists, simply making refinements or changes to tired designs. When I would make tours of shoe stores, I would find the Reebok brand just sort of lying there.

I visited stores like Foot Locker (our main channel) that carried most of the Reebok line. I'd look at the shoe wall and conclude all our shoes were looking more and more alike. We were nuancing the line to death by stylizing, but not innovating. I also felt the line was too black and white, lacking color as a differentiator and method to better penetrate the lifestyle element. Again, most athletic sneakers are worn for casual use, so they must work stylistically with clothing. The casual users do want to look like an athlete, but a stylish one.

The lack of truly differentiated design in athletic footwear between the leading companies continues to amaze me. I feel certain that if I took the logos off the shoes and arrayed them up on a display wall, most athletic footwear consumers couldn't identify the brands. The exception to this is in places where technology has driven a different form factor, such as with the Pump. Still, the external associations with the brand remain paramount based mostly on league licenses, star power, and distribution channel connectivity.

Reebok suffered from major production quality problems as well. I knew this from general user knowledge on the street. I was a jogger and worked out regularly in competitor shoes for comparison. I had consumer surveys done and was astounded that 20 percent of the customers were reporting quality problems. These could be so severe that there were regular claims of the shoes simply falling apart. Given that premium shoe pricing had consumers paying over $100 for their shoes, this was a serious problem. Obviously, this caused greater than normal brand switching.

Strangely enough for a globally-oriented company, Reebok was also geographically insular. Reebok was headquartered in Stoughton, Massachusetts, a suburb south of Boston. Most of the employees were from the East Coast or had gone to East Coast schools. New England is not known as a hotbed where many lifestyle trends start. Trends such as fashion, fitness, health and well-being, new food choices, and others have mostly started elsewhere. Thus, there are fewer style innovators in the area.

This may sound strange, but cultural traits like innovation are somewhat driven by what is locally or regionally the norm. Most of the trends relevant to athletic footwear and apparel start on the West Coast. Fashion trends often come from other fashion centers in the world. Reebok did not have a diverse group of designers from all over the US and the world. They weren't aware of trends until they had surfaced and at least partially played out. They didn't have employees who daily lived different lifestyles and could spot trends before they surfaced.

Having moved numerous times to different parts of the country, including New York City, Los Angeles, and San Francisco (twice), as well as mostly being involved in leading-edge trendy businesses, gave me a fresh perspective. In some ways, I think I was generally a better trend spotter than the overall Reebok design team. The valid question would be whether the trends I tended to identify were appropriate to pursue or profitable paths to follow for the company.

The Reebok product development process had bogged down into a layered bureaucratic system. It took three years to develop a new style, the first year to conceptualize and develop prototypes, the second year to refine design for manufacturability and costing, and the third year to produce selling samples, solidify manufacturing process, make test runs, and eventually production runs. That is a *long* lead time for a sneaker!

The Reebok brand had a big problem. It was losing its positioning. The early signs of this were in its being heavily discounted to sell. To maintain the revenue levels in the face of weak new product, the trade was loaded with classic product, which forced heavy price discounting to sell through to consumers. Reebok was also over-distributed, including to discounters and trans-shippers. It had, in essence, lost control of its brand.

I remember saying that our dominant advertising was "20 percent off on Reebok" in every store window where we were sold. As part of my walk-around marketing approach, I went to Disney World and walked around with my head down, looking at the footwear people were wearing. I was concerned by the amount of classic black-and-white Reeboks I saw on all the wrong (that is, nonathletic) body types. I felt that image being a key driver in athletic footwear, this trend stood a good chance of effectively killing the brand altogether.

The "cool" people were wearing Nikes and looked like they had just come from a workout. In other words, they were positioned to succeed, and Reebok was positioned to fail.

The Reebok apparel business was losing $10 million per year, with no real direction or plan for where apparel should fit into the overall Reebok strategy. That wasn't helpful to the brand's plight.

The biggest overarching issue was that there was no real strategic plan, formal or informal, at Reebok. If you asked key people in the company about the strategic direction of the company, no one gave the same answer. While this is not an altogether uncommon problem in many companies, good companies make it a priority to have a basic and pervasive understanding of their mission and plan that permeates throughout the company. At Reebok, the management and staff's answer to this important question was that there was no plan, or they would repeat the simple and primordial war cry of "Kill Nike!"

A culture based on the tribal chieftain ran rampant through the company. Reebok's chieftain had the credentials of having built an $800 million-dollar business, which was no mean feat. In general, the organization tried to anticipate what the boss wanted instead of what the market needed. For the most part though, this was all very dispiriting to the quality managers in the company. What was required for change was a heavy dosage of take-charge people willing to live by results rather than the good graces of the chieftain.

Reebok, as I saw it, was looking down the barrel of a gun. There were heavy retailer inventories lurking in the tall grass. There were shoes that were falling apart, so returns were out of control. There was ubiquitous discount pricing, which is the death-spiral for a consumer products brand. There were Korean factories colluding to raise production costs. There were no real differentiated new product or technology in the pipeline and a three-year development cycle to make matters even worse.

It struck me that three years is about the average term of a CEO in the corporate world. It would take a winning team to correct the course. But this chieftain-following team seem to have lost its mojo. I wasn't seeing an innovative kick, awareness of trends, or a sound marketing touch with the consumer. Even the mundane things were hurting Reebok. There was a new automated warehouse where the software that ran it went haywire. We lost control of the data regarding the content of incoming containers. We had a yard full of containers but didn't know what was in them. We couldn't load the warehouse and then couldn't ship small orders.

Job one was that I needed to hire a new professional management team. What was called for was to get West Coast-oriented people, sports-minded and design-oriented but still truly professionals. I needed to hire people from Nike. Nike represented the best practices in the industry, even though we couldn't totally emulate them if we were going to beat them. We hired Chris Walsh, to be the head of Operations. He had been at Nike and was currently working for a consulting firm. I ended up making numerous trips with Chris to the Far East, as he educated me to this unique contract manufacturing culture. I hired Kim Kelley from Pepsi to head sales. A critically important hire was Mark Goldston to head marketing. Mark had been the CEO of Fabergé Cosmetics. He was smart, a sports aficionado, and an excellent marketer with a good product sense and a plus-size ego. He later became the CEO of LA Gear, United Online, and other major public and private companies.

Making management changes under a chieftain is tricky. Some work and some don't. Mark very quickly made major contributions, including marketing of the Pump, but was so disruptive that he was starting to change the culture of the company. Chieftains don't like that shit. Eventually, Paul wanted Mark fired and made it clear that if I didn't fire him, I was going to be fired. It was one of the few times I have had to fire someone who was performing. Chieftains will be chieftains and hired guns (in this case, me) don't have many silver bullets that work on chieftains.

In the meantime, we needed to make moves to minimize the discounting problem. We refused to support retailers if they sold below MSRP. We needed to regain control of our retail distribution, even if it required pulling out of certain retailers. We had already stopped selling to discount chains or trans-shippers. It was time to draw the line on distributors who violated our pricing policy. We decided that we were not afraid of retailer legal action if it came to that.

We hired new, young design talent fresh from art school and other industries like the dwindling automotive sector. Many of these designers were in our target market and had an intuitive feel for our consumer. They were also CAD literate, where many of our old designers were still sketching on paper. We hired outside designers on a contract basis to get diversity and to retain flexibility. We redirected the internal design staff so that they spent their time holding creative sessions to review outside design ideas rather than create them.

I deemed that technological innovation was critical to our success, but there was an attitudinal shift needed at Reebok in that regard. I put out the marching orders: *don't delegate innovation*—it's everyone's responsibility. I initiated an intensified search for new technology, including letting the inventor community know we were open for business. I had learned from my experiences with the Media Lab at MIT about innovation on demand as a concept espoused by MIT.

The efforts started to bear fruit quickly. One evening, a project manager named Paul Litchfield came into my office and asked if I could go into the conference room and meet a pair of outside inventors, saying he didn't know how to proceed. The two inventors from California had a material whose molecular shape was a hexagon. The material was used on the skin of airplanes. They had found that when applied to the sole of an athletic shoe, it would collapse but quickly recover. The hexagonal shape was graphically interesting. It was very visually interesting and could be colorful. As an athletic shoe sole material, it was quite functional with an interesting and unique story.

The inventors wanted to produce and supply the material for Reebok while keeping the production technique protected in a "black box." Their agreement furthermore called for them to be the single supply source, which is always problematic. Nevertheless, we found common ground and made a deal. We incorporated this honeycomb material, which was called Hexalite, and flexible concept into our product line, and it was very successful. Even though the inventors later sued Reebok, claiming breach of the single source covenant, this was a first technological step to revamping the Reebok lineup.

While we were tinkering, we needed to solve the problem of keeping the Reebok brand in the consumer's top-of-mind awareness until we had new product to sell. Footwear advertising generally centers on introducing a specific new product, not on generic brand advertising. Chiat Day advertising agency developed an innovative and esoteric approach to this highly controversial $80 million advertising campaign "Reeboks Let U.B.U." This was also an attempt to make the brand stand for something: freedom and individuality.

We needed to keep our awareness up and at least get consumers to consider (and perhaps reject) us before buying competitor athletic shoes. We reasoned that when we eventually introduced exciting new products, the consumer would at least have us top-of-mind. This was a very controversial campaign within Reebok because it was all image branding with little to no product attached. It was corporate overhead versus product cost. Much has since been written about the campaign, including a Harvard case study. The retailers were cool on it, since it wasn't driving consumers into the store to buy a new line of shoes. The fact that we didn't have any new shoes seemed irrelevant.

The Reebok brand remained amazingly resilient through ups and downs and various periods of mismanagement. Paul never stopped being Paul. At one point, he actually declared war (internally) against Nike and Phil Knight. He thought it was a good way to focus the organization. Probably the best that came out of it was to declare that it was a two-player game, obviously leaving out other large competitors such as Adidas, New Balance, and Converse.

Meanwhile, I was working to review, diagram, and modify the product development process to shorten it, streamline group decision-making, take out legacy unnecessary steps, generate earlier consumer feedback, install a tracking system to identify critical decisions, and take out slack time. I have redesigned the product development system in every company I joined and always found it well worth the effort.

Given the Reebok "youth culture," I decided to send the design and marketing people around the world with petty cash to purchase cool, trendy products for review. I made it a sort of contest by giving them each $1,000 and sending them to the trendsetting fashion centers of the world: Florence, Paris, Milan, etc. Upon their return, each person made a presentation to the group.

I put a small, fast-moving group of "skunk works" in Venice Beach near Santa Monica, California, to monitor trends and infiltrate the entertainment community. It was run by Angel Martinez, who had been with Reebok since the very beginning, which seemed appropriate (Angel in Los Angeles). My theory was that once a trend started on the beach, it would symbolically cross the Pacific Coast Highway and go all the way to the East Coast. That's what happened with step aerobics, and it was my thinking that for athletic shoes, this was ground zero. As Angel had managed a running store in California before joining Reebok, he was back home. Angel was not really a business guy but had a great sense for style and a knack for spotting trends. He deserves a lot of credit for Reebok's success and survival.

If you think being president of Reebok was all about marketing, you would be wrong. You can't market what you can't produce and deliver. And you can't market what you can't price competitively, which is a result of the production process. And you can't market for very long what falls apart due to shoddy production. So, yes, I needed to pay attention to production.

I mentioned already that the company got into cash tightness in the mid-80s and didn't have the depth of working capital to support the needed aerobics shoe inventory, much less the broadening of the product line. The need for aerobics shoe production financing resulted in two dramatically impactful contracts. The sale to Pentland of the majority stake in Reebok brought with it a production deal. Stephen Rubin, Pentland's controlling shareholder, in combination with a partner, Patrick Tang, had an agency (ASCO) that negotiated with and placed Reebok's production in factories in the Far East for a handsome fee. The volume was nearing 65 million pairs of shoes annually. Balanced against that somewhat onerous contract was Paul's compensation contract, which proved to be so large and equally onerous on Pentland and Rubin that it all begged to be a driving force in the company's strategic future.

Paul did not like going to Korea, despite this being where our critical production partnership resided. He was not an adventurous or sophisticated eater, and Korean food was a challenge for him. He was neither worldly nor interested in being worldly. He hated travel, even in the company jet.

Reebok had serious quality issues. I directed the marketing, operations, and product-line managers to go into the warehouse in Stoughton, Massachusetts, and inspect product that had supposedly passed inspection at the plant in Korea (that would be plants positioned by Stephen Rubin). We found that the reject rate was over 20 percent (not unlike what we heard in the market). I had to notify the plants that they were now the proud owners of $11 million worth of defective product. They went berserk, saying I didn't understand doing business in Korea. Perhaps, but I said they didn't understand our consumer and were destroying our business and brand. Let the foot stomping begin!

This quality battle was also accompanied by a little pricing tango as well. I had been in the company only about four weeks when we received a fax from the Korean factories that they were going to raise prices by 10 percent, with the implication that if we didn't agree, we wouldn't see the product. These guys were simply asking for more money for shoddy product—or else.

The plan was that Paul and I and others would fly out of Hanscom Field in the corporate jet and head to Korea to renegotiate this mess. For reasons I have never understood, right after takeoff, Paul had the pilots turn around and take him back. Chieftains will be chieftains. As I recall, he mumbled something about liking cheeseburgers but not kimchi.

This left me in an interesting position of negotiating a complex multilayer arrangement that indirectly involved the primary principals, Paul and Stephen, who would be sitting on some proverbial hill watching us all do battle. I have always liked the expression that when the elephants are dancing, the monkeys should stay in the trees. In this case, this monkey was also working without much contextual knowledge, so imagine an ill-informed monkey running in between the legs of the dancing elephants.

Just to keep things interesting, I thought I would arrive at the plant unannounced to inspect the production process. The Koreans were way ahead of me. I quickly found out after landing that everyone was in cahoots: the plants, the hotel staff, the airport arrival crew, everyone. Nothing was left to chance by the very astute South Koreans.

I scheduled each plant's management to meet with me in my hotel room. Divide and conquer! Wasn't I the tricky American? The thing was, whatever move I seemed to make, they seemed to know it before I did. It was enough to make me wonder if athletic shoes were worthy of high-level industrial espionage. Maybe I had a mole in my midst. At one point I took a break and went out into the hallway. As I looked down over the railing into the atrium lobby, there they were—the various, supposedly competing plants were sitting talking…colluding. I tried to hear what they were saying, but it was all Korean to me.

The next day I called each plant back and thanked them, saying I had found a plant that would produce at the old price, pretending not to know that our controlling partner had a deal with these plants. Sometimes being the stupid little monkey is useful. They went crazy, trying to determine which one of them had broken the nefarious agreement. The following day they each came back, saying they were willing to hold their prices. Now the little monkey was up in the tree throwing coconuts down on the heads of the elephants.

We could see the handwriting on the wall that prices were eventually going to increase. Korea was a developing country (technically one of the Asian Tigers) that was beginning to produce electronics and such with a more highly trained workforce that was receiving higher and higher wage rates. When the factory workers started to steal shoes because they could sell them on the street to fellow

Koreans, that was the sign that the market had emerged. Time to look for a new country to develop (dare I say, exploit?).

When I made my first trip to Korea to visit plants and vendor suppliers, I was completely blown away by the young age of many employees. When visiting vendors, I was also struck that many employees were working under unhealthy working conditions. I clearly remember going into a basement production operation where they were working with chemicals in open vats with poor ventilation. This was before Nike and many other apparel and shoe manufacturers were attacked for these conditions in their contract plants. I recall coming back to our headquarters saying, "We are killing people." I believe this was far more prevalent in many industries like ours than was ever exposed. I'm glad to see these practices have changed and wish we had done more to improve conditions thirty years ago.

Through contract manufacturers, Reebok was employing fifty thousand people a day in Pusan, Korea. We were making 85 million pairs of shoes a year. Making athletic shoes was still a very manual process, requiring roughly 125 hand operations to make one shoe. Automation has not progressed far for a variety of reasons, the dominant one being the availability of cheap human labor. What is the right thing to do? Taking the work away certainly doesn't help the laborers. Improving conditions (and costs) cuts production and thus employment. Automating costs jobs. Moving locales just shifts the problem to another cohort of laborers and hurts the departed. It's a difficult conundrum with no easy answers, especially for an executive with a clear bottom-line mandate. Maybe that's what made Paul turn around and go home—he had seen it all before.

One of the two big reasons for the visit was quality control. Visiting the plants confirmed my team's evidence about the serious quality control problems that existed. Poor quality was killing the Reebok brand.

As the president of Reebok Brands, I was treated like a celebrity, as were other key management members. We were picked up in Mercedes sedans and arrived at the plants to a chorus line of beautiful young women holding flowers towards us in outstretched hands. This extended to the finest meals and drinks at the best traditional Korean restaurants. All this attention also meant that my movements were constantly closely monitored.

My focus was on digging into quality control. When we toured the plants, we got the carefully planned and guided tour to ensure that we saw only best practices. I did the "ugly American" thing of getting up early the next morning and arriving at the plant unannounced. It created quite a stir, as people madly ran around trying to find a high-level manager to corral and communicate with me. This was not in the Korean playbook.

I started to walk the lines and check shoes. Then I began to dig by asking about quality, which appeared to be politically incorrect. I wanted to be taken to each QC station on the line to see how they were inspecting and against what standard. Then I wanted to see the rejects and where they went. I wanted to get copies of what reject reports were being generated and find out who saw them.

As I picked up shoes on the line and inspected them myself, finding defects that had supposedly passed inspection, the supervisors did the traditional maneuver where they called over the workers and showed them the shoes, admonishing them loudly in front of me as the workers bowed their heads. I had no interest in criticizing the workers, as they were simply following management instructions. The management process, on the other hand, could use lots and lots of criticism.

Many of the quality problems emanate from running the lines too fast due to pressuring the workers to meet production goals. Sort of a classic "haste makes waste" problem. When a quality problem is found, it most often requires stopping the line until it is resolved and then restarting at a slower speed. This had a double whammy on the production output.

I asked where the inspection reports were kept, requesting to see yesterday's batch. I looked at each inspector's reports and took one report and quickly added up the number of shoes he supposedly had inspected. It came to an impossible number of over a thousand. Obviously, they were falsifying reports.

We did have our own inspectors (peer reviewers) who were paid directly by Reebok, but often they are paid off by the plants and thus rendered worthless. Even our own Reebok employees who oversaw the plants were moved frequently to minimize their developing collusive relationships with the plants.

Establishing a new quality culture was critical. As the president, I had to set the focus and standards for quality and needed to do it "hands-on." I had to be willing to be disruptive and perhaps a little culturally rude, as well as be willing to change suppliers if necessary. I also needed to get an independent read from my end users (the vaunted consumer).

Remember those poor underpaid workers who were doomed to be replaced by automation or efficient outsourcing? It made an impact. We decided that Reebok needed to embark on a major human rights campaign. Why, you ask? Reebok was still desperately trying to find something the brand could stand for—something the consumer could become passionate about and associate with the brand.

As we know, someone had decided, and Paul had approved, that our message should be about human rights. This was an issue. First, there was the consumer to consider. It was reasonable to wonder if human rights were important and relevant to athletic shoe consumers. Despite the righteousness of the stand, you needed to ask if it would translate to shoe sales. Was it a sustainable point of differentiation? Second, there were the shareholders. The annual cost of the campaign was approximately $20 million. That was a cost that came right off the bottom line. It's noteworthy that Paul had the view that he didn't care about the stock price and investor's view of how he was running the company. He often said, "If you don't like what I am doing, sell your stock." So I guess both consumers and shareholders could just vote with their feet (as it were). Third, which I don't think was considered at all, were the employees. Were they ever consulted? Which ones? Just the US or the global employees? Did they understand what it meant? Did they believe in the human rights mission? This was a touchy business.

The objective was to raise the awareness and fight against human rights violations around the world. This was why Reebok joined hands with Amnesty International, to show support in its efforts to prevent the abuse of human rights, more specifically to obtain the release of people unlawfully imprisoned. It is not something most people remember Reebok for, and it was a huge business risk on many levels, but miraculously, disaster was, for the most part, avoided. Again, it was just another example of the randomness of the Reebok strategy and culture.

The Pump. A whole book could be written about it, and several have been. It was the vehicle that brought the brand back to its original luster. What I like about this story is that it's all about design and product development, which were the vital organs of the athletic footwear business. And we nailed them both.

There is just nothing like a high-profile product success to energize a brand and its employees. My number one focus was purposely working to come up with breakthrough innovations. I knew revitalization wouldn't come from doing more of the same in the current system. None of it was an accident or just good luck.

Still, the Pump's success did not immediately give birth to a clear positioning for the brand. The consumer still could not tell you what Rebook stood for, even if they liked the Pump and the bungee jump. Further, Reebok had a history of a constant stream of new advertising campaigns. But often the campaigns weren't varying executions on a positioning strategy. They were different positionings altogether for the brand. Thus, millions spent on advertising wasn't going toward reinforcing a differentiated positioning that Reebok could own. It simply jumped all around in the consumer's head like a bungee gone wild.

Product innovation can give an energizing boost, but it won't solve for the lack of a strategy, process, and organization that can sustain growth. Random hits do not a strategy make. There needs to be a process, organization, and sustainable, differentiated strategy that is constantly turning out innovative product. If I sound pedantic, that's okay. Successful businesses are a product of replaying successful tactics if the market appetite exists and being ready to move to the next innovation when that appetite wanes.

It is often difficult for an entrepreneur to find that path and stay on it. It would be interesting to learn why and how some have done it. It is hard for many entrepreneurs to put their faith in others' ideas, as they attribute their success mainly to themselves and their ideas. Also, many have never had the experience of moving from their ideas to building an organization and installing process to capture a broader and more sustainable array of ideas.

I need to reflect favorably on my competitor, something rarely done in the heat of battle. Why did Nike achieve sustained growth where Reebok did not? Both were started by entrepreneurs. But as I see it, early on Phil Knight started to build a skilled organization and delegate authority. He was a legend but did not allow himself to become a tribal chieftain. His management team was rather stable, which provided a training ground to grow managers from within. The brand had a clear athletic, sweat-performance positioning, driven by innovative technology. He allowed himself to succumb to professional process.

Paul Fireman, on the other hand, had, in my experience, a pattern of constantly changing executives moving in and out of the company in a disruptive fashion. He also didn't believe in process, budgets, and certainly not MBAs. Paul did have an outstanding feel for product and would make bold moves which, incredibly, built a multibillion-dollar company. But over the long haul, Reebok was no Nike.

I don't know what demons inhabit Phil Knight, but I found Paul to be a complex guy carrying a lot of baggage. I found myself often thinking like a psychiatrist. I concluded that the combination of being burdened by a difficult relationship history with his father and generally too easily influenced by his advisors made Paul a challenging leader to follow.

My relationship with Paul proved to be the guiding force throughout this chapter of my life. I had been sponsored by Joe LaBonte, my long-time business colleague, and vetted by Gerry Roche at Heidrick & Struggles as a part of the search process. I never felt Paul was excited about having high-powered executives from the outside come into "his" company. Reebok had lost share, and the board and shareholders were putting pressure on him to change things up by bringing in executive marketing and management talent. I was, in some ways, simply a Band-Aid on a business problem.

I was neither hired to change Paul's ways nor expected to solve all the strategic direction issues the company faced, though some stakeholders certainly hoped I would push things in those directions. Branding and market presence were on wobbly legs. The new product funnel appeared empty of any real exciting technology. There were serious quality problems. There were underpinning contractual arrangements that were a hindrance rather than a help. Being an avid golfer, Paul wanted to spend more time at his home in Florida during the winter. And, of course, he didn't really want to give up much, if any, control of the company and its culture. This was close to becoming a managerial nightmare for the new guy.

I had learned throughout my career that there was no substitute for a strong personal relationship at every level of management. I have watched many qualified people interact with their bosses. The one who builds the relationship will weather the inevitable storm (in whatever business or interpersonal form it comes) and become the successor or get promoted. Those failing to forge the necessary relationship get cast as poor performers or cultural "bad fits" and get fired. Paul was mostly private and close to his family and a small circle of friends. There was a handful of people who he brought in at the start of Reebok's growth, and they remained close to Paul. But he didn't leave much room for others who were outside that circle, and it was a challenge to socialize or build that ever-important personal connection with him.

While Paul spent significant time away from the company because of health issues, I was busy recruiting a professional staff of executives. These were people with a passion for sports and fitness, but more importantly, professional and experienced businesspeople. There were significant operating issues that needed tending while at the same time trying to create a spectacular new product out of thin air. It was what I felt the company desperately needed.

Paul's management style created a dynamic which required that I take independent action, but action without his involvement bred distrust. Paul's randomly moving in and out of the company created havoc. This formed a dangerous gap where he may have felt he was losing his grip on the company. And chieftains have a habit of using the time-proven solution of "Off with their heads!"

One day, Joe LaBonte walked into my office and told me he was leaving. While it was positioned that he wanted to go back to California, I knew that was not the case. Things like this would often happen right after Paul came back from Florida. Joe said I would need to carry on with me being kind of anointed as the key senior executive, as Joe's position wasn't going to be filled. Joe had gained a lot of respect and loyalty in the company and, given how threatening this would seem to Paul, I wondered why Paul would want to do that all over again. I immediately thought, for many reasons, that I would be the next to go. The handwriting was on the wall.

I had developed a theory about working with Paul and the issue of trust. The way I saw it, the closer you got to Paul and the farther up the executive ladder you climbed, the closer you were to being on the path to termination. It was what could be called the Icarus Theory, except this wasn't about overarching ambition but rather about being on a stairway up to the firing squad, whether you liked it or not. I was not alone in this thinking. Executives who were promoted at Reebok would kid about how long it would be before they were terminated. It was, I thought, all about paranoia regarding losing control and seeing the culture change.

At one point, I used to advise certain managers to never host the company holiday party at their house. Joe and his wife, Donna, had hosted the company holiday party at their beautiful brownstone on Commonwealth Avenue in Boston. Shortly thereafter, he was gone. Well, I forgot that advice and after Joe left, we had the next holiday party at our house in Cohasset.

After Joe left, I was given a new contract. This was sort of perfunctory and really didn't give me much added confidence about my status. But I recognized that the severance package had suddenly become more important.

During this time, the Pump shoe was a raging success along with several other new-technology-based shoes. There were four million pairs shipped, generating more than $500 million in sales. The *New York Times* declared that if the sneaker were its own company, it would be the fourth-largest in the industry. This pushed Reebok revenues by more than 18 percent, to $2.2 billion. Nine additional categories of Pump shoes were spawned, including ones for golf, aerobics, and tennis. Analysts predicted that revenues would increase to $2.6

billion in twelve months on the strength of these innovative products and pointed to the Pump as the main force in the turnaround. The West Coast skunks group called one day regarding a new aerobics program known as Step Aerobics, a relatively new exercise actively featuring low-impact aerobics that uses a step stool, which Reebok also began to sell. We jumped on the new trend, which rejuvenated the aerobics industry. Things were going well.

Then one day Paul returned from a trip from Florida and came into my office along with Paul Duncan, the CFO. Reinforcements are always important. He said few entrepreneurs get two bites at the apple. He was referring to the condition of the company when I joined and the current turnaround. I didn't hear too much after that, because it was clear that what he meant was that he would be resuming direct control of the company and I was being terminated.

I felt that with the success of the Pump, I might have gotten beyond the period where I expected to be the next to be fired. It was not totally unexpected; however, the recent signing of a new contract did throw me off track.

Getting fired is hardly uncommon, but it rarely feels good. The reasons and rationalizations don't make up for the sense of unfair abandonment. Sensing my frustration and need to understand what had just happened, Barbara urged me to contact Paul immediately to meet with him. He was golfing in Kiawah Island, South Carolina, before heading to Reebok's big sales meeting and footwear show in Atlanta. We (Barbara wanted to join me) flew to Atlanta and headed for the hotel where Paul had agreed to meet me. We tried to slip in undercover but were discovered by a whole group of Reebok employees, who were shocked and dismayed at the news. We felt like thieves in the night, like we had done something wrong. It was a very eerie feeling.

Paul Fireman arrived around 11 p.m. with his sidekick, Paul Duncan the CFO. They went up to Paul's hotel room ahead of us and summoned us to come up after ten minutes. It was a weird situation. Paul had ordered a pizza and expected us to chow down with him. An uncomfortable tension filled the hotel room, so eating pizza seemed hardly appropriate. Barbara could not be restrained. She asked him straight out why I had been fired, given all of the success of the company, the Pump, and the turnaround. With a mouthful of cheese pizza, Paul shrugged and said, "It was just a difference in management style." He wiped some sauce off his chin with his hand. The die had been cast, and nothing was going to come out of this meeting.

When we departed the hotel early the next morning, we ran into Kim Kelley, the head of sales, who had been summoned by the chieftain. He was also being terminated. We all laughed nervously as we headed for the airport back to Boston, agreeing that we needed to rack up a hefty liquor bill on this, our last Reebok trip. Paul had eliminated the four outside professional executives who had been hired only two years before. He promoted John Duerden, managing director, International Operations, to COO. John was a very experienced executive, a good guy who didn't rock the boat. He was later named co-president with Paul, and then he was out. After John left, his duties were realigned between Paul Fireman and Paul Duncan, the CFO, the company being run again by the old guard.

I was fortunate to have had a brilliant employment attorney in Boston, Steve Carr, who worked wonders with the employment contracts I had signed at HBO, Reebok, and others to follow. It's not something that you look forward to having to rely on when the axe falls, but in this case, my contract had just been renewed favorably for me, which gave me some breathing room to consider the next turn in the road, the next adventure, the next challenge. I was forty-nine years old and had experienced more than most do in an entire lifetime

Paul sold Reebok a few years later, at the right time, to Adidas for a nice high price. It still pains me to see the mismanagement and deterioration of the brand that has taken place, first through neglect and then through corporate repositioning. There have been a stream of attempts to change the positioning of the brand. It has fallen all the way from a powerful, full-fledged athletic performance brand to the growing, but small, cross-training segment.

I was then in Kübler-Ross's five stages of grieving process about my premature Reebok departure. I couldn't help but think that if Paul could have accepted a partner who could have brought the right amount of discipline and strategic architecture, Reebok today might still be Nike's biggest challenger. It might even be larger than Adidas and the upstart Under Armour. The question unanswered is what might have happened to Reebok if this professional team had stayed together or bought the company.

Yet the dogs bark and the caravan rolls on into the night. Gypsy trails lead away from the chieftain.

CHAPTER 10

PLAYING THE RIGHT CARDS

It was a warm day at the old, run-down American Tobacco warehouse on Blackwell Street in Durham, North Carolina. As the strange-looking Shred-It trucks pulled up between the warehouse and the old Durham Bulls Athletic Field, four black Chevrolet Impalas came in behind them with dark-suited men. The accounting firm of Coopers & Lybrand had come over en masse from their offices in Raleigh. None of the accountants from the forensic operations squad had ever been on an assignment like this before.

The warehouse foreman came out to meet the entourage, along with a man wearing a shirt that said "Impel Marketing," with the name "Bob" over the pocket. Bob held a clipboard with a two-inch-thick stack of green-and-white computer paper that listed all the inventory in the warehouse. He handed the clipboard to the older gentleman from Coopers & Lybrand. This man handed it to his adjutant to his left, who opened an accordion briefcase and brought out a matching stack of computer paper. Then the loading dock doors swung open, and the first of many pallets of shrink-wrapped trading cards were loaded onto the platform.

The shred-it crews were ready and waiting. As the shredding trucks began their grinding operation, the accountants checked and verified the destruction of thousands of registered trading cards.

Bob took a long pull on his Marlboro Light and said, "I just hope they still need an inventory manager. We're shredding 90 percent of what we have in the warehouse." He then walked over to the shred-it gang and pulled out half a dozen heavy-gauge plastic bags. He handed them to the crew and asked them to fill them up with the first of the shredding. When they asked why, he explained that the brass back at the office wanted it for something. The crew shrugged and did as they were asked. As they handed over the filled bags, they reminded Bob that the rest of the shredding would be taken to the pulp mill and incinerated. Bob just nodded in the knowledge that his job was done.

After shaking off being spurned by Reebok and Paul Fireman, I got down to the business of "What's next?" As a company in the habit of dumping its executives, Reebok had retained the services of an outplacement service. And what a lovely and inspiring name they had: Challenger, Gray & Christmas Inc. The name had all the elements of motivation, mood description, and a pleasant and surprising ending. So I met with them.

Some people think it's like having to resort to a dating service and that outplacement should be done by yourself. This is very silly and narrow thinking, and I figured there was nothing to lose in seeing what it was all about. After all, I had sent fired executives to similar services and knew only what their own promotional literature had told me about them. I went to their office in Chicago for training on how to conduct a job search. That's where I encountered one of the best books on job searches, *What Color Is Your Parachute?* I recommend it to anyone doing a search.

One of my Challenger, Gray & Christmas assignments was to do a detailed writeup of every job I had taken in my career. What was the situation when I walked into the job, how did I address it and change it, and how did the people and personalities influence that? Barbara and I decided it was time for a vacation, so we made arrangements to head down to Barbados for a week to sort things out. I holed up in the hotel room for five days, taking breaks only to eat meals, in order to write this *magnum opus* (thank goodness Barbara is good at amusing herself). The document was hundreds of pages long. The experience of producing this document was a reward unto itself, but it also came in handy at a later time.

This process served several useful purposes. First and foremost, it was a great catharsis after twenty-five years in business. Second, it helped me see what I enjoyed and liked doing, and what I should avoid. Third, it brought to the surface my accomplishments and how I had handled various situations. Fourth, I was able to boil down my career into vignettes or soundbites that allowed me to interview more effectively by being able to give solid examples. I highly recommend this process but recognize that most people will find it much too tedious to do.

After a full year of sorting through various opportunities, the right situation came along. I was recruited to be the president and CEO of Impel Marketing in Raleigh-Durham, North Carolina. The offer came with a nice sign-on bonus, which helped ease the pain of change. At age forty-nine, Barbara and I and the boys sold our beautiful oceanfront home in Cohasset, packed up, and moved to a newly built house in a subdivision in Cary, North Carolina, a suburb on the outskirts of the Research Triangle.

One of the first tasks when I took over Impel Marketing was to change the name to SkyBox International, which was a much more invigorating name, and then start with the job of restoring the products' perceived scarcity. The business was trading cards, and it was losing $80 million per year. Another early decision I made was to move from the expensive leased Research Triangle Park office to a refurnished tobacco warehouse in Durham near the old Durham Bulls baseball field. It somehow seemed altogether appropriate. Not only was it cheaper rent, but the charm of the old brick building created a cohesive environment in which to work and get focused on turning around the business.

We needed to destroy tons of card inventory in a high-profile fashion so that the collector market would take notice. It was a bold, innovative, and expensive move, for which we hired Coopers & Lybrand to oversee the destruction, sort of like having an accounting firm count the Oscar ballots. We invited the retail trade to a dinner in which waiters dressed in tuxedos served shredded trading cards in bags on silver platters to our guests. It got the point across with panache.

Next, we pulled out of mass distribution, including withdrawing from Walmart and retreating to card, hobby, and comic bookstores. It may be the only time someone has walked out on Walmart, a place most wholesalers kill to get into.

Soon after, we cut the workforce from two hundred to seventy-five people (including warehouseman Bob) and began a rebuilding process. This was a lesson on how to do a gut-wrenching housecleaning in order to survive, my first experience handling a major layoff. I think it's best handled through honesty, directness, and constant communication with the entire organization. It is also about compassion for those losing their jobs and the often-forgotten stress of the survivors. I brought in my former associate at Mattel, Joe Zaccaro, who headed a professional human resource consulting group in Denver, to assist in this effort. He was extremely instrumental in advising me on a smooth transition. I have had to take this action many times since in my career and have learned valuable lessons, such as it's better to cut deep and sharp in the first round in order to minimize the need to do it again or have the slow, nagging pain of continual layoffs. This is not without risk, but it has always worked better for me.

I had gone from food, to video games, to entertainment videos, to athletic shoes, and now to trading cards. Marketing had been a big part of all my prior businesses, but I was now going into a business that was almost entirely about marketing versus intrinsic value. It was a fascinating new challenge.

Impel Marketing was a division of Liggett Tobacco Company, owned by the Brooke Group, a public company with an infamous owner and major shareholder, Bennett LeBow. Sports trading cards started years ago packaged in cigarette packs. They went through the tobacco distribution system, which was extensive. They eventually were also packaged with bubble gum for kids.

Major, well-known licenses were the keys to success for the business, and Impel had the nonexclusive rights to the NFL, NBA, NHL, and, very unusually, the exclusive rights to all the Diamond and Marvel comic book characters.

One weekend about a year after I joined SkyBox, Barbara and I were invited to Fisher Island just off the shores of Miami Beach for an evening event featuring an auction of Russian art. Eduard Shevardnadze sat on the fantail of *Stefaren*, the 177-foot yacht owned by Ben LeBow, the principal shareholder and CEO of our parent, Brooke Group, and named after his two daughters, Stephanie and Karen. He had a pocketful of sterling silver slot machine tokens with Ben LeBow's smiling face on them. Shevardnadze was then the high-profile leader of Soviet Georgia, and he was one of a dozen important Russian diplomats being entertained on the luxury yacht, moored at the even more luxurious Fisher Island home of the LeBows. The yacht had a story—Ben had commissioned it and in so doing precipitated the bankruptcy of the Brooke Boat Yard, such that he bought its remains, including the almost-finished yacht.

The house had a story—Metropolitan Life had financed the development of the island as the latest, greatest playground for the rich and infamous. It had almost gone bankrupt and been bailed out by LeBow and other well-heeled wheeler-dealers who loved nothing more than to pounce on the misfortunes of others at their most vulnerable moments. That evening, even the name of LeBow's company that was sponsoring the lavish Russian art auction was intertwined in the art of the deal: Brooke Group. Eduard Shevardnadze, as a newly minted Russian oligarch-in-the-making, was impressed on many levels.

I was just a simple farm boy from Ovid, New York, but here I was bidding on expensive, original Russian art while standing shoulder to shoulder with Shevardnadze. With my new art purchase under my arm, LeBow grabbed me and asked me to explain the trading card business to Eduard. We were already on a first-name basis even though it was all through a Russian interpreter.

"You see, we create these cards and convince people, mostly children, that they are special and unique. We hold a few back in our vault. We make money on them and then they start trading them, bidding the price up. When the price is high enough, we might sell some of those in our vault to make more money."

The interpreter struggled to explain this and then returned Shevardnadze's reply: "And what are these cards used for?"

My reply was simple. "Nothing."

Even without interpretation, he just stared at me, then burst into laughter, pointing at the painting under my arm. "So just like that painting.... I love capitalism." Once he was laughing, it was okay for all his subordinates to join in on the joke. He slapped me on the back and handed me a water tumbler of vodka.

Ben LeBow was a true financier. He was a man of great influence, a tobacco magnate, a real estate investor, and a corporate raider as good as any. Rarely a day went by when he hadn't done a deal or two. While some of his attributes can be likened to and presage our esteemed ex-President Donald Trump, I would posit that Ben LeBow had more swash and less buckle than Donald.

Ben began his career assigned to a general as a computer science specialist at the Pentagon. He had graduated from Drexel University in engineering and attended Princeton. He parlayed his Pentagon computer experience into a software company that he sold successfully. He made his first big money in a takeover and turnaround of Pantry Pride, a supermarket chain. His lavish lifestyle (boats and planes) and aggressive, on-the-edge business dealings always kept him front and center in the press.

Ben was the sort of entrepreneur who would do things no one else would ever do. Risk was not, as they say, a four-letter word to him. He was smart and very creative in his dealings. He would get into turnaround situations that were so messy that no one else would touch them. He used litigation as a powerful tool. He was continually suing and being sued. He was the sort of combatant who worries less and smiles more the nastier the battle gets.

As a negotiating method, Ben knew how to side with the enemy, which is an unusual and unique trait. This disarmed his enemies and certainly jangled the nerves of his allies. He once described to me how he felt true venture investing wasn't present any longer in the US. Ben loved doing business in Russia. Very early in the post-Glasnost era, when most people stayed away because of the unstable and constant regime changes, Ben was happy to invest there. He was comfortable dealing with an unstable political regime. His Brooke Group (whose name changed to The Vector Group Ltd. in 1999), made many real estate investments in Russia as well as buying the Ducat tobacco company. Ben formed a combined tobacco company with Liggett Tobacco called Liggett-Ducat.

One night I was with Ben in his stretch limousine. He turned on the limo's TV to a news clip of a snowy cold day in Russia showing

Ben wearing one of those fur hats, a "ushanka," and facing protesting workers who were renovating one of his buildings. "They stole every last goddamn toilet," Ben was yelling on the TV. "I'll fire all of you unless those toilets are back here by morning!" He lit another cigar and turned to light mine. We'd been to three nightclubs already, and I asked, "Where next?" He laughed loudly and off we went.

The next morning none of the toilets had been returned, but Ben seemed nonplused by it all by then. I guess Russians do not threaten that easily. He was off on another rant about a totally different subject.

When Ben bought Ducat, he apparently loaded it up with debt, as was his game. This ignited a publicity storm in Russia, led by the former general manager, who admitted himself into a hospital from which he ran the protest campaign. Apparently, in Russia you can't be sued if you are in the hospital. Ben was constantly being sued, and he admired this original tactic. He was sued by shareholders unhappy with how he was running his public company. He was sued by Carl Icahn and other equally well-muscled investors for various business deals gone sideways. And Ben was not shy about suing other people himself. He spent a small fortune on legal representation but considered it just another cost of doing business. I once told him, "If you didn't do such-and-such, you might not be sued," to which he replied, "Where's the fun in that?"

My relationship with Ben LeBow was easily the wildest of my career. That's saying a lot for a guy who seemed to attract the wild and crazy of the business world. While I was not at all like Ben, he must have felt he needed someone with my very different profile around him. I think he needed my traditional professional background, especially if there was the possibility of taking SkyBox public. It reminds me of the Tom Hagen (Robert Duvall) character playing the straight-man lawyer/*consiglieri* to Al Pacino's Godfather, though without the illegality. I had a solid CPG reputation, and he needed me to turn Impel/SkyBox around and extract its hidden value. Many people would not have taken the job, given LeBow's reputation for brash and unorthodox behavior. Add to that the nature and risk of the turnaround, and most seasoned executives would have run away from the situation as fast as they could. Lucky for Ben, I was different and treated it all like an interesting challenge.

While I liked Ben, we were so very different. He viewed me as the buttoned-up, classically trained business guy while he was the risk-taking, hip-shooting, high-profile entrepreneur who had made a lot of money (often with the ubiquitous OPM—other people's money). Often, when he came in his private jet to Raleigh or summoned me to NYC, I would arrive with a typed agenda and written analytical summary of the business. That night in the limo while cruising around town, he screamed at me not to bring "that fucking agenda and analysis." He preferred that I just talk to him about the business.

It was refreshing that he preferred verbal communication to sending each other zillions of memos back and forth or analyzing financial statements. It took me out of my trained comfort zone and into what may have been my true comfort zone. He called me often but was very impatient if I wasn't immediately available, often screaming at the receptionist to go find me. If we were in NYC, we might meet first at the office, but then he asked that we jump into his limo and go with him to the best bars and restaurants, like the Four Seasons. Ben liked to be seen at the power tables.

He was personable, fun, honest (some might disagree, but I would not), and very direct. You always knew where you stood with him. He enjoyed life more than anyone I knew. He knew how to live. You could argue with him, and he would listen and yield if you had a superior point of view. He often came up with ideas you hadn't thought of or didn't dare to think of. That attribute alone made it worthwhile to spend time with him.

With Ben, I came to understand that, despite my otherwise calm demeanor, I have an Irish temper. It was fine with Ben, but later I had to throttle it back and work on controlling it. My temper had seldom showed up at work before this, but Ben seemed to bring it out in me, and I would get mad as hell at him and just let it rip. Ben would treat the outburst with great humor. He'd say, "Frank, you're off the reservation." He would mostly just say, "Okay, okay…" until I had unloaded all my anger. He would often call me the next day and ask if I was taking my meds and if I was "back on the reservation." He seemed to never hold these arguments against me. Our interchanges certainly did not follow the rule that if you get mad in a conversation, you lose. In any other business setting I have ever experienced, if I spoke like that to my boss, I would have expected to be fired.

Ben paid very competitive salaries and had no problem sharing the profits with his management teams if they performed. He always started by asking you how much you wanted to make. Jointly, we then put a plan together between salary, bonus, and equity to hit that goal. In the case of SkyBox, he set aside a significant share of the hoped-for profits for the management team. The terms were always generous. I actually had in my employment agreement a clause that stated that I had the reasonable opportunity to make $20 million. I had established this as the game changer for me. I made more money with Ben than in any other job.

Howard Lorber, Ben's operating guy and chairman of his holding company, New Valley—which owned Liggett Group (tobacco), 50 percent of Nathan's Hot Dogs, and various other companies—was Ben's go-to guy. Howard always had lots of irons in the fire, and Ben was okay with that. Howard was in the insurance business and the real estate business (he is currently the chairman of Douglas Elliman real estate).

While Howard was not involved day-to-day in the operations of SkyBox, he was very valuable to me. He would play the calm, good-cop, rational role when we were in a crisis. He would also arbitrate disputes between me and Ben. You see, this was not an uncommon phenomenon in my relationship with Ben. He got mad and fired me at least three times. In one case he summoned me to NYC for a board meeting, where I was sure he planned to fire me for my stance on resisting spinning the company public at a time I felt was premature. Howard eventually moderated the situation, and we got back on track. While there were not a lot of people Ben trusted, it seemed clear he trusted Howard. Ben drew a sharp distinction between his family and others. Howard was "family."

Richard Ressler was an active advisor to SkyBox. In many ways, he was the person besides me who was most involved in SkyBox's turnaround strategy. He was always all over the numbers, as one might expect of a brother-in-law to Leon Black.

Richard was smart, young, and fun. He had made a lot of money and was destined to make a lot more. He was involved in a limited number of Ben's deals, but clearly, with his connections, he had access to capital and could put his own deals together whenever he wanted. Richard was always careful to stay on the right side of the line, especially given Ben's willingness to approach it sometimes. Eventually, Richard amassed a fortune in Los Angeles real estate. He drove around LA in an old station wagon and wouldn't dream of having a limo. Hanging around "deal guys," you quickly see who has a knack for the deal and who is more likely to be an operator or flunky. Richard had a knack for the deal.

Mike Rosenbaum, the vice chairman of SkyBox and the guy who was most involved in recruiting me, didn't spend a lot of time in the company, but he was involved with the NBA and NFL licensing arrangement. He also made an initial contact with Earvin "Magic" Johnson that led to a landmark agreement with SkyBox as the first company to sign Magic after he announced he was HIV positive.

The first thing I learned about the collectibles business was that it operates on perceived scarcity. Supply limitations drive demand. But to have a successful collectibles market, demand must exceed supply and there needs to be a perception of scarcity. This fundamental economics 101 precept creates the chase for rare cards and especially the urge to complete the collection of full decks.

The market is driven by secondary trading value. That means the price for which you could sell a card, or better yet a full-deck collection. Historically, there was a published guide called *Becketts* that tracked secondary transactions for a wide range of current and previously produced cards. Today, eBay is the standard value clearinghouse.

Swapping or trading cards is a big aspect of the social entertainment element of the market, with kids and adults trading cards actively. Kids who weren't particularly good at math knew the value of cards and became shrewd traders. During times there were trading card shows on weekends or swap meets, kids went to trade or buy cards. It was a sport to them.

New sets of cards (new releases) are continually being produced, but once the initial print run is complete, generally that series is never printed again. This is where the scarcity value is derived.

Manufacturers print limited card quantities. The actual production quantity may or may not be made public. The cards are randomly packaged and sold in small (seven cards)packages that are often made of foil. They will produce fewer numbers of some cards to increase the difficulty of collecting a full deck in order to create a buying frenzy that keeps consumers buying packets until they have collected a full deck. Needless to say, the subject matter of the cards must appeal to the collectors, whether sports figures, celebrities, or other entertainment personas. In the case of special releases, the manufacturer may decide to uniquely number the cards and publish the quantity of the cards actually produced.

Cards started out being sold in hobby stores or in little trading card shops that bought and sold cards. There was a lot of negotiation with the proprietor as well as knowledge transfer to the collectors.

It works in the reverse manner as the traditional CPG business. When a new release is successful, which means it sells out and therefore demand exceeds supply, you don't produce more or you will kill the value of the cards consumers bought. They also won't trust you on the next release, thinking you will overproduce. So in some ways, the more successful you are, the fewer units you produce. It takes a special thought process to optimize against it.

Still in the cost-cutting mode, we made plans to build our own printing facility under the premise that it was necessary to control the production and protect the random distribution of cards in the individual packs. In addition, the printing and insertion of very valuable and rare hologram and celebrity cards needed to be controlled. Theft of valuable cards was always a concern.

Another key factor for success is to bring in a top-notch management team. Whenever anyone asks me about the key to success in a turnaround, growth strategy, or market leadership situation, the answer is always the same: the people. I brought in Jay Ladd to head operations, Jerry Ruttenbur—who had reported to me at HBO Video—to take charge of sales, Scott McCauley for marketing, kept Tommy Smith as CFO, and hired George White's PR firm to help us establish ourselves in the market. He eventually joined us and became the entertainment and comic book licensing guru.

New products were also called for. We created the Entertainment Trading Card business new category. We introduced innovation via hologram technology. We also made a major promotional push by signing Magic Johnson to be our spokesperson and bought the rights to the 1996 US Olympic Basketball Team, the "Dream Team." We started licensing very different types of properties like Disney movies and Star Trek, which certainly already had its own cult following. We went about establishing the SkyBox brand.

The most important question to ask was, "What business was SkyBox really in?" I'd asked the same question at Reebok. Everyone told me we were in the sports trading card business, or at least in the trading card business. There were the normal standards given about the business, including the importance of sport licenses—especially the ubiquitous baseball cards, which SkyBox did not have. The company tried forever but never got that license. A producer of cards supposedly needed to own its own printing facility for reasons of quality and security control over valuable cards and collation of packs.

With some quick, simple consumer research and the insight of our brilliant advertising guy, Howard Rockett, we discovered that SkyBox was not in the trading card business at all. SkyBox was in the business of *connecting kids of all ages with their heroes*. This was not a subtle distinction, but rather a defining one. This generated a break-through since it released us from being myopic and focused on sports. It gave us access to a whole new category of growth and created a new method of communicating with our market.

We already had a successful comic book trading card busi-ness—DC and Marvel, headed by Superman, Batman, and Sandman—but we saw it as more of an extension of comic book-collecting, which had been around a long time. Once we realized these were also heroes to kids, the light bulb went off and we asked ourselves, "What are other sources of heroes for kids?" This led us to Hollywood and to the TV and movie studios, a patch I knew well.

SkyBox quickly became the premier Entertainment Trading Card Company. We picked the best evergreen TV and movie heroes and met with the studios. We were received warmly, as this was a new application of their characters/properties and thus a new revenue stream which SkyBox was going to build for them. There were many advantages to this strategy: we paid lower royalties because it was a new category with no track record and little competition, and we could expand the age range both younger and older based on the property—especially into girls, who back then were not generally considered much into sports the way boys were. Since these properties were driven more by collecting full sets and less about secondary value, we could produce and sell more cards, worrying less about the size of total production runs. We weren't selling to collectors and traders but to enthusiasts. Besides Star Trek, we got the category killer by licensing Disney characters.

One day I was sitting in the Park Avenue office of David Stern, commissioner of the NBA. He was in front of me, talking calmly on the phone with one of the team owners: "It'll be fine. He's only one player and besides, he's doing the right thing." I had no idea what the topic was. All I knew was that the NBA licensing deal was a huge and symbolic part of our card business. Our NFL license paled by comparison, and we had never been graced with the MLB license.

I knew it would be a difficult meeting as we were not meeting our minimums with the NBA, and they wanted no part of the talks. We needed not only to retain our license (the other card companies were hanging around the hoop waiting for a quick rebound), but I needed to negotiate improved terms.

Stern put the phone down and turned to me and said, "You're off to a good start. Now, I've never had to trade down an NBA agreement, so let's not let this be a first."

This was the beginning of my many negotiations with David. He was a lawyer and a tough negotiator. His reputation was well-known in this regard. After some painful negotiations, we were able to reach a compromise that improved our economics and helped us turn the company around.

David (we had gone to first names by the end of the first hour) explained very succinctly, "I'm helping you out here, Frank, because I don't envy you working with that gang over at Brooke. This should give you something to build on and look good to Ben, but you and I will be doing many annual renewal negotiations, I hope, and I'm getting this all back from you down the road, understand?"

"Fair enough." I knew when to be gracious.

David recaptured any lost ground and then some in a multimillion licensing transfer fee to Marvel when the company was eventually sold. This is a case where long-term greedy beat out short-term greedy to our mutual advantage.

Before I left David Stern's office that afternoon, he told me to be sure to watch my TV tomorrow. The next day from my hotel room, I turned on the TV to hear Magic Johnson announce he was HIV positive and would be leaving the NBA. So, that had been the topic of David's earlier phone call. It shocked the sports world and was named as ESPN's seventh-most memorable moment of the previous twenty-five years. A couple of weeks later, Mike Rosenbaum was on a flight to LA and sat next to Magic's agent, Lon Rosen. That led to a conversation about the possibility of SkyBox signing Magic to an agreement. We did some quick research on how he was viewed by kids and their parents. The results were predictably positive. In general, he was seen as a hero.

SkyBox became the first sponsor to sign Magic Johnson following his HIV positive announcement. It was a big risk in many ways. We were able to negotiate an arrangement we could afford, which would not have been possible prior to the announcement. In a way, we needed each other and served each other's purpose.

It was truly the beginning of a great relationship with Magic, during which Barbara and I got to know him and his wife, Cookie, personally by traveling together to many events. He bent over backwards to make public appearances, attend sales meetings and calls with buyers, and help us make unique cards. He was always personable, down-to-earth, and fun. While on a promotional tour that brought him to Raleigh-Durham, he even came to the office to sing happy birthday to one of our sons. If you knew him, you called him Earvin, not "Magic."

One memorable event took place at a high school across the street from the SkyBox offices. Durham High School had about the highest dropout, truancy, and pregnancy rates in the country. After some promotional meetings in the office, Magic agreed to speak at the high school assembly that afternoon. When he took the stage, he asked every kid wearing a hat to take it off. This was a sign of respect, and he deserved it. He zeroed right in on their attitudes and the fact that many were there because they had to be, not because of his message. He delivered one of the most direct and relevant talks on behavior and personal responsibility I had ever heard. He could pick out the troublemakers in the audience and zero right in on them and their attitudes. The kids gave him a standing ovation, and no one was wearing a hat.

Magic always wanted to have me teach him about business. In a conversation with Barbara during a promotional trip, he confessed that he wanted to have an office with a desk where he could put his feet up on it if he wanted. He said he already owned a Mercedes Benz, but he wanted to be a respected businessman. He soaked up every opportunity with the SkyBox management team to learn, frequently with a barrage of questions. I'm not sure we ever taught him anything, but he was exposed to many of the facets of our business, and we talked business whenever we were together. It was a great experience to have him around as much as we did.

The Magic sponsorship directly led to SkyBox getting the rights to the Dream Team Trading Cards, as the team would be playing basketball in the 1996 Barcelona Summer Olympics. Few events have ever garnered the attention and spirit of the Games for the US audience as did that one. It was also the only opportunity to see the best US players on the same team, and that was not lost on the fans. It was also the perfect SkyBox medium.

SkyBox's exclusive Olympic Dream Team rights prevented the NBA from exploiting the Olympics. I will never forget getting a call from David Stern asking if I would give up these rights for "the good of the country." Nice try, David. I promptly responded that I had learned a lot about negotiating from him and if the tables reversed, I pondered aloud whether he would give up the NBA usage rights for nothing other than purported patriotism. We eventually negotiated a deal, but it was on my terms for a change. I think he respected me more for it.

Magic had a ten-year-old son, Andre, from a prior relationship. This situation was not generally known at the time, and Earvin had kept Andre out of the press. But father and son appeared to have a very good, loving relationship. One of the greatest commercials SkyBox made was with Magic and Andre. It was all about connecting kids and their heroes. The bit was touted as the best use of an athlete/ hero in a commercial.

It was a combination of a good commercial by my Rockett Man, Howard, and sincerity by Earvin. Howard Rockett and the folks at his agency came up with the idea of doing a commercial with Magic trading SkyBox cards with his son, Andre. This was designed to demonstrate the hero connection. We were very surprised when he agreed to have Andre appear in the commercial. Brilliantly written, it featured Andre choosing to trade his father's card for another player, and the interaction between them was priceless. The NBA often used this commercial to show other licensees how to effectively use players in a commercial. And yes, Magic did go on to become a very successful businessman with the creation of Magic Johnson Enterprises. I'm sure he has a beautiful desk in his office with his size sixteen shoes proudly on it.

• • •

One day I was notified that a truck of valuable cards had been stolen. Because they had been transported across state lines, we wound up dealing with the FBI on the issue. We had printed the valuable rare cards, often with holograms, in a secure contract printing facility. Frequently we used facilities that printed bank notes and stock certificates. In this one instance, we had seven trucks leaving the printer, traveling in a caravan to the collator. The collator machines randomly place cards into the retail packs so that no one can tell from the outside which cards are in the pack. However, kids have devised all sorts of techniques for trying to detect if there are any rare cards in a pack before they buy them.

Only six out of the seven trucks arrived at the collator. Obviously, we were very concerned, as these were valuable cards that would screw up the market if they were sold through the black market. After a week went by, we got a call from the FBI that they had located the truck. Then the most bizarre negotiation with the FBI took place. Bottom line: we had to pay $50,000 to get the cards back. They wouldn't tell us who had stolen the truck or allow us to prosecute, saying they needed to protect the identity of the undercover agents. This made no sense to me and forever raised questions in my mind about who really had stolen the cards. J. Edgar would have rolled over in his grave … or maybe smiled up from it.

Swap meets were havens for traders to buy and sell cards. Also, they were frequently where stolen or counterfeit cards showed up, given all the commotion. We once got a call from a young kid who had located a dealer at a swap meet who had a large quantity of rare cards that he was selling at a substantial discount. The kid knew something was wrong. He bought a few and then contacted us. Since the rare cards are uniquely numbered, we knew they were stolen. He could have easily bought all the cards and resold them at a huge profit. In this case, we were able to confiscate the cards and arrest the dealer. We voluntarily decided to pay the young kid a reward that substantially contributed toward his college education. Kid—1, FBI—0. Go figure.

When Ben LeBow bought Liggett & Myers Tobacco Company and formed the public entity Brooke Group, he was sued by shareholders for loading it with debt. It was forever considered a troubled conglomerate. In fact, it became one long integrated name in the press ("Brooke, the troubled conglomerate"). LeBow came to an unusual and perhaps clever (some would say, outrageous) deal with shareholders. This was a guaranteed floor of sorts, that if the shares were worth less than nineteen dollars per share on November fifteenth, 1990, he would make up the difference in cash or kind. Again, Ben was nothing if not creative. He would do bold things like this that others would never dream of, at times coming right to the edge of legality.

SkyBox was a separate, almost hidden, business entity inside of the Brooke Group that few shareholders knew anything about. Progressively, as SkyBox turned from a loss to a profit, it became more valuable. The thought of spinning out SkyBox into the public market was suddenly on the screen.

As the November fifteenth date approached, Brooke's stock was still far below the threshold. Ben's solution was to value the now-profitable SkyBox and spin it public and grant sufficient share to Brooke shareholders to cover the gap.

Ben called me to New York and sat me down with Howard next to him for reinforcement. There would be no backchanneling this time. After minimal pleasantries, he got right to it. "Frank, it's time to spin your baby into its own public company." But I didn't feel we were ready and that we needed a few more quarters of success before we would be considered credible. I told Ben my perspective, but he didn't want to listen to logic and a colorful exchange ensued.

Howard Lorber jumped in at this point and suggested to me that we have Houlihan Lokey begin a valuation of the company and see what they came up with. He asked me to just consider it. Howard knew how to pull victory out of the jaws of defeat. So I agreed.

When we got into the necessary disclosures required for a public offering, the subject of my contract hit the radar screen. It contained a clause about "a reasonable opportunity to make $20 million." I was forced to eliminate the clause in a revised agreement to appease the shareholders. But Ben was still aware that this was my number.

When we spun SkyBox public, the shares traded around four dollars per share, far short of Brooke's independently backed appraisal estimated at fourteen dollars. Ben took the position that the contingent rights holders should receive only enough SkyBox Contingent Value Rights (CVR) valued at fourteen dollars to make up the gap to get to Brooke's target nineteen dollars. The CVRs were issued one month before the promised nineteen dollars a share. Making matters worse, when Brooke announced plans to spin off SkyBox, Brooke's stock dropped to $3.75. Oops. Seems the market knew it was there all along.

Normal people would find it rather stressful being sued and owing millions in loan payments, but not Ben. This was maybe the most fun time I had with him. I would have meetings with him in NYC quite regularly, and he would gather various people and run around NYC to high-end restaurants and bars and party like there was no tomorrow. But for Ben, tomorrow was just another day in high-finance, high-wire paradise.

Because of Ben's unusual on-the-edge maneuvers, his numerous lawsuits, his ownership of a piece of Big Tobacco, his dealings with the Russians, and his being a former Drexel gunslinger, he was constantly in the press. His turnaround acquisition targets were often described as ugly ducklings. Heavily leveraged and risking little of his own cash didn't help this image. He was described in the press as being "short, pudgy, but sociable." I was with him once when he was reading a scathing article about himself. He said the only part of the article that was true was he was indeed "short and pudgy." You've got to love a guy who was so self-effacing. Compare that to my friend at Reebok. He had a great sense of humor.

Ben and I had an ongoing dialogue with Ron Perelman and his crew at MacAndrews & Forbes about buying SkyBox before we took it public. Importantly, Ron controlled Marvel, and when he bought Fleer in 1994, it signaled the end of SkyBox's valuable Marvel license for trading cards. Ron's lieutenants were quite a group: Howard Gittis, Don Drapkin (who later sued Ron and won $16 million), and Bill Bevins. We met often at Ron's headquarters at 35 East Sixty-Second Street, known as the Townhouse. The building was very secure, staffed by ex-FBI agents. Ron held weekly breakfasts at his Townhouse/office, often inviting an eclectic group. They were fun and the other attendees were often icons of business. It was totally a big elephant dance with this monkey just trying to keep from getting stepped on.

It was during those sessions with Perelman that I met the guys from Toy Biz, a toy manufacturer owned by Avi Arad and Isaac (Ike) Perlmutter. I knew Ike from my days in the toy business at Mattel, where he was a well-known liquidator. Ike sometimes carried a gun, which could be mildly intimidating when you were negotiating. Toy Biz exchanged equity for exclusive, perpetual royalty licenses to make Marvel toys. A good deal for both: Toy Biz escaped costly royalty fees and Marvel got valuable equity in Toy Biz.

In the end, we stopped going to these breakfasts. Also, Ben never believed Ron would pay us enough for the company, so we found other breakfast joints.

One of my reasons for getting involved with SkyBox from the beginning was to buy SkyBox to use it as a platform to build a unique entertainment company. After we spun SkyBox public and the stock price was low, I went out to raise the money to buy it from share-holders. My first stop for financing was Dick Cashin, then at Citicorp Venture Capital. I had gotten to known Dick over time, initially through Bill Achtmeyer at Parthenon. Dick was not your typical investment banker. At six foot four, he was a Harvard man and a two-time (1976 and 1980) Olympic team rower. He is one of the most funny, honest, and straightforward bankers I have ever met. He is a guy who will always take your call and try to help you. If you met in his office and asked for help, he immediately picked up the phone to find a way to help. I had trouble finding a room in NYC one night and I stayed at his condo with him and his family. He speaks slowly with unbelievably dry humor.

With Citicorp backing, we made a bid for SkyBox. Immediately, Ron Perelman who controlled Marvel, got into the bidding process. At one point Ron called me and said I was working heavily with debt financing and that he had the cash to outbid me, which he did. Since I had stock and options plus a new contract with a good severance package, I was a bit ambivalent. Also, Ben retained a decent portion of stock when we spun off, so he stood to benefit, and I felt I owed him that much. Marvel already owned Fleer Trading Cards and Panini, an Italian collectables and publishing company, and bought SkyBox at a nice price that I helped to underpin with my failed bid. They merged the two trading card companies under their umbrella and called the company Fleer-SkyBox, relocated some employees to the Fleer operation in New Jersey, and shut down the Durham office.

Soon thereafter, Ron Perelman called and asked me to meet him at the Townhouse on the Upper East Side. When I arrived, after clearing the security checks, he was chewing on his cigar as usual. Basically, he got right to the point and commented that he realized I had experience in most of the industries in which he had acquired companies. He said, "Look, we are deal guys. We don't know anything about operating companies." Without hesitation, he asked me if I would consider joining MacAndrews & Forbes and have various companies report to me. I told him I'd like to think about it and perhaps talk to some of his CEOs.

I quickly learned that he had tried this before and that many of his new hires had lasted a short period of time. As part of my due diligence process, I contacted a couple of people and got the straight scoop.

It didn't take me long to figure out that the last thing the company CEOs wanted was to report to someone under Ron who was experienced in their business. I could easily relate. I decided that life was too short to take this assignment, and I called him to decline his offer. By this time in my career, I was getting better at spotting a bad deal before I entered into it. Incidentally, Perelman never gave his lieutenants equity, but he was very generous with salaries and annual bonuses.

At this point I had a failed bid to buy the company and was still the CEO but running SkyBox as a division of Marvel. After I turned down the job with Perelman, the guys at Marvel contacted me saying they wanted to put in a friend of the firm as the CEO of SkyBox to give him operating experience. I had suspected as much.

It was time for me to move on, and since I had a very lucrative severance arrangement, I was happy to leave the company in their hands. I was fifty-three years old when I left as president and CEO of SkyBox with a pocketful of money from a solid contract and sale of my shares. I did go through some tough negotiations with my contract but came out very well. This included up-front payments, retaining some equity but also two more years of monthly severance payments. My final meeting with Ron's lawyers in NYC was tough, but I was amazed at how well I did. Maybe it was all that screaming I had done with Ben? When I left the lawyer's office, I celebrated in what has become my tradition when I feel I have had a real victory. I went to an outdoor café in New York and ordered champagne and mashed potatoes. Don't ask me why.

On December 27, 1996, Marvel filed for bankruptcy. What took Marvel down? Books have been written on this subject (*Comic Wars*), but basically, they paid high prices for several companies, loaded the company with debt, and suffered the consequences. The baseball strikes dampened trading card enthusiasm. Comic book collecting waned, and, in fact, all sports and entertainment collectability began to slow down. It happens.

One of the burdens cited as a reason for the Marvel bankruptcy was a high fee paid to the NBA regardless of sales. I assume this was the transfer licensing fee David Stern extracted when Marvel bought SkyBox.

The baseball strike became a killer to the sports collectability business. I have a definite opinion of how baseball, the once most popular sport in America and creator of heroes, through greed, arrogance, lack of willingness to change, and disconnect with their fans, eventually lost its relevancy with young people. Far fewer kids grow up today playing baseball or looking up to baseball players. The salaries paid to players grew to unreal levels, supported by ticket prices climbing to levels that are out of reach for many families, not to mention assorted steroid scandals surrounding high-profile players. All of this has created resentment with fans. The games are often too late and too long for children who fall asleep early. MLB has also been unwilling to change rules to make the games more exciting from a spectator's point of view.

When I was at SkyBox, we had many meetings with MLB in an attempt to get a license. I tried a researched-backed approach with creative ideas on how to help close the gap between players and fans. The research showed that baseball players were seen as disconnected, arrogant, and caring only about money and not their fans. They grew up as star athletes, starting on an arrogant path in high school. The research showed this was in stark contrast to NASCAR, which was the fastest growing sport with a 40 percent female audience. The drivers grew up working with their dad in a garage, scraping and scratching to get enough money to race. When they got a sponsorship, it involved a lot of work placing them in contact with their fans in all sorts of events from store openings to local fairs. They were not high school heroes. As a result, the drivers are seen as more down-to-earth and approachable. The fans, including women, are emotionally attached to their favorite driver.

We approached MLB with a series of novel concepts, one being a trading card series to help make the players become more approachable. In the most basic way, they needed to touch the hands of their fans. The concept was a free card series that would be handed out by the players to the fans. This flew in the face of all sorts of myths that needed to be broken. There were many ways to make money on this concept, but it would force the players into contact with their fans.

MLB rejected this along with many other ideas. There were various reasons, but I found the licensing group was comprised of a group of lawyers and others whose job was to optimize the short-term value of the players and teams. It was always, "How much are we going to make on this?" Not, "We have a long-term problem we need to solve." The strike said a lot to fans who showed that they are ultimately in control. The sport has never really recovered.

Most important to Marvel's bankruptcy was the demise of comic book collecting, which was a somewhat self-inflicted wound by over-distribution through Hero's World and the proliferation of comic book versions. I learned the hard way from SkyBox that the collectibles business is very different from any other consumer product business. It is essential to preserve the sanctity of rarity and genuine scarcity and trust with the consumer that you have not flooded the market. This is totally contradictory to the CPG philosophy of producing more flavors and quantities when you have a success.

Perelman also did several financial maneuvers when Marvel was doing well that benefited him but not necessarily shareholders. I am constantly amazed at what you can do legally to take advantage of shareholders, especially by coming up with creative, complex financial vehicles, particularly through holding companies. Also, both Perelman and LeBow are big bank clients who want to borrow lots of money, and so goes the overleverage story.

Months before Marvel went into bankruptcy but was in a loss position and having serious cash-flow problems, their lawyer approached me. They asked if I would suspend my monthly severance payments and convert the obligation to a loan with interest. Without any hesitation, I said *no*. In essence, I figured Ron Perelman had a lot more money than I did, and it didn't make sense for me to take the risk of loaning him money. I probably collected another $1 million before the bankruptcy. Unfortunately, my management team that was still in place at Fleer/SkyBox did defer their salaries, which they never fully recovered. One of my rules: never defer your salary.

The Marvel bankruptcy took on a life of its own. I will not forget turning on my television on December 27, 1996, to hear that Marvel had gone into bankruptcy and I was still owed a couple of million dollars. At the time I was the lone unsecured creditor among a group of others whose stake was secured by one thing or another.

Enter Carl Icahn. When Marvel was clearly in trouble, Carl bought a large number of junk bonds. When Ron Perelman tried to restructure the company, Carl blocked him, which paved the way for bankruptcy. At one point Carl gained control of Marvel, but his control was eventually thrown out by the bankruptcy judge. In 1997 Toy Biz and Marvel Entertainment Group (MEG) merged to take the company out of bankruptcy. So Ike Perelmutter and Avi Arad of Toy Biz ended up controlling Marvel. They changed the name to Marvel Enterprises.

Meanwhile, because of the unsecured amount of money I was owed, I ended up on the creditor's committee. We joined a lawsuit with former shareholders, claiming Ron Perelman had made $553 million in "unjust enrichment" from junk bonds. This was a full-time job working with the lawyers and the committee to try and recover some of the loss.

It took two years to reach a somewhat thinly veiled settlement. We recovered some of the money that was rightfully ours and were given warrants in the newly formed company as it came out of bankruptcy. We assumed our warrants were valuable, but Barbara had to spend a huge amount of time trying to trace down the warrants. At one point she was told that they had been cancelled, and later that they had actually been destroyed. Even working with various law firms, we never felt we got accurate information on who cancelled them and why they had the authority to do so. It's a bit of a cloak-and-dagger story; suffice it to say, we prevailed somewhat in the end but left a good amount on someone else's table.

That summer after the company closed its offices, Barbara and the boys and I returned to our second home in Woodstock, Vermont, which we had purchased the year before. As the summer came to an end and we prepared to return to our home in Cary, North Carolina, the boys asked, "Why do we have to go back to North Carolina? Why don't we just live here in Woodstock?" We didn't have a ready answer for them but soon realized that we could certainly live in Woodstock, a place we had all learned to love for its beauty, peacefulness, and remoteness. Barbara enrolled the boys at the Woodstock Elementary School, returned to Cary to pack up our personal belongings, and put the house up for sale.

Simultaneous to running SkyBox and eventually its sale to Marvel and my exit from the company, I was serving on the advisory council at Cornell's Johnson Graduate School of Management. One of my advisory cohorts was a fellow named Rich Marin, who also had gotten his undergrad and graduate degrees from Cornell and went on to work in the financial industry at Bear Stearns, Bankers Trust, Deutsche Bank, and as a founder of Beehive Ventures, among other stellar executive positions and start-ups.

One day during the council meeting, we began talking and soon learned that we had a shared love of motorcycles. Having spent part of his youth in Italy, motorcycles were a way of life for Rich, and he owned several bikes that he kept in New York or at his home in Park City, Utah. He had spent many summers riding the beautiful roads in southern Utah and was planning another trip, this time with some former business associates. He asked if I would like to join them. I went home and told Barbara about the trip, she gave me her blessing, and off I flew to Salt Lake City.

Rich is a bear of a man, standing six foot five, but he is an experienced and graceful motorcycle rider. We gathered at his home in Park City: me; Rich; Andy Forrester, a former Bankers Trust associate; Arthur Einstein, Andy's neighbor in Katonah, New York, and a successful advertising executive; and Larry Klane, another bank associate. In addition, there were two strong-looking young women, Deb and Mardi, who drove the chase vehicle pulling a small trailer, into which we could put our gear. It also contained their massage tables, which I learned later that day were for us to climb onto and have them massage out the kinks and knots of the day's ride. Rich had the whole thing planned, from the maps to the motels in which we stayed, places to eat, places to gas up, and the appropriate overlooks where we could stop and take in the monuments and stark beauty of the southern Utah mountains. I called Barbara from one lookout during a pit stop and told her, "You would love this trip." She was an avid motorcyclist in her own right, and I knew she would have been speechless with the trip, the planning, and the camaraderie.

When I got back home, I shared the photos of our trip and vowed then that if there was another trip the next year, I would try to get an invitation for both of us. Meanwhile, Rich had begun to plan for such a trip, but this time he wanted to explore the Green Mountains of Vermont and, with the help of a good friend in town— David Beilman, who also was an avid rider—they planned a group ride for the next year. This time we agreed to meet at our home in Woodstock, and I invited my friend Walt Lynd, Bob Kirby, and Stan Robinson, who had been working for us since we bought our home in Vermont. Stan was a local with a Harley in his barn.

The group of ten gathered at our home for an initial meeting, as we were all strangers and had to figure out just how this was going to work. Suffice to say, the group got along famously, dinner and bottles of wine were consumed, stories began to unfold, and by the end of the first night, we hadn't even had wheels up yet but we ceremoniously crowned Walt as chairman of American Flyers Motorcycle Club with our motto, "High Mileage, Low Expectation."

This isn't a story about the AFMC, but it is a story that is worth mentioning, as it became the backbone of mine and Barbara's deep and important friendships over the years with like-minded riders, all of whom came from various walks of life and backgrounds. By this time Barbara had become an excellent rider with her own stable of motorcycles. What held us all together was a deep trust in our riding ability, the knowledge that someone always had our back, and the love of travel that took the Club on exciting rides all over the world on all sorts and sizes of bikes. Like a fraternity of brothers—although this one included a few women riders—we shared an unspoken love for one another, the thrill of the ride, the enjoyment of each other's company, the consumption of too many bottles of wine, and the stories of rides gone by—stories that were repeated over and over because they confirmed that we were connected and knew we were a unique group of riders. When I make mention of someone who was a member of the AFMC, it's because that person impacted my life in a way that no business experience ever could.

CHAPTER 11

(1996–2000) ENRICHING THE GREETING INDUSTRY

After the SkyBox episode, which was a gift that kept on giving through my creditor committee work, I spent some time reflecting. As before, I kept in touch with my friends at Heidrick & Struggles. It was they who brought me an opportunity to become president and CEO of Gibson Greetings in Cincinnati. Gibson was an interesting company in an interesting business at an interesting time in the evolution of an interesting country. *Interesting* means challenging, and challenging requires something special—perhaps something innovative.

I flew out to meet with the board of trustees, who were conducting the search, as they had made the decision to terminate the current president. Once I received the formal offer, we had a family meeting at our breakfast table in Vermont and decided to take a trip to Cincinnati to check it out. The Information Age was in full force by 1996, and we were already at the beginning of the compact laptop era. Both boys were big video game players (I wonder where they got that from?). As soon as they learned that a possible school they could attend, Cincinnati Country Day, was very progressive and that each child had a laptop, it was game over. They said, "Okay, Dad, plug us in. Let's do it!" Contract negotiations began, and I accepted the position as chairman, president and CEO of Gibson Greetings. I was fifty-three years old.

In an all-too-familiar pattern, Barbara and I and the boys buttoned up our Woodstock home, packed our personal belongings, and moved to Cincinnati into a lovely home in the Indian Hill section of the Cincinnati suburbs.

Gibson Greetings has a rich but somewhat troubled history. It was the third-largest greeting card company in the industry. It had a significantly smaller market share than the leader, Hallmark, and the second largest, American Greetings. Business wisdom, as paraphrased from Jack Welch of General Electric fame, is that if you are not one of the top two market share leaders in any business, you are always behind and playing catch-up. You were really an underdog. When I became CEO, Gibson produced greeting cards, box cards, gift wrap, calendars, and also had over one hundred retail stores.

I recognized (eyes wide open) that Gibson was really a turn-around and that it was a company rapidly losing ground. Gibson was the monkey in the middle between two giants (Hallmark and American Greetings) who had a lot of money to keep the monkey as the monkey. The one, Hallmark, was a private company and the other, American Greetings, was a public company controlled by

Morry Weiss and his family. Hallmark was the larger of the two and combined they had about an 85 percent market share, with Gibson coming up in the rear with about 9 percent. To make matters more complicated, there were several smaller and alternative card companies, reflective of the changes underway in the industry.

Gibson's costs were out of line. They owned their own printing facility (SkyBox all over again) and it was non-union, but their labor rates were higher than union shops, since they would raise their wage rates every time there was a unionization threat. Their printing presses were generally older in the print industry, where technology was moving rapidly with higher speed, better quality, and faster change. The company had been "milked," with little or no money reinvested in its plant. In addition to a progressively obsolete printing operation, the information technology infrastructure of the company was near the crisis level of breaking down and losing control of the company. There was a lack of integrated systems, and many of the interfaces were manual. This extended to the old pull-card approach (no scanners) for reordering and controlling in-store inventory. The warehouse order-inventory-control systems were inadequate. Overall, major obsolescence problems had not been faced.

The Gibson card line was tired, and so were the designers. The cards were looking more and more alike. The biggest gap was in the humor-themed market, a critically important element in the card business. Gibson card humor needed to be radically different and more edgy. The line was still dominated by a lot of long, syrupy verse with flowers on pink paper. Most all of the cards (both verse and graphics) were created inside by employees in a big cubicle-filled atrium. This group included people that painted flowers. One big happy family sinking together in the changing marketplace.

Gibson had pioneered selling greeting cards in supermarkets. Initially, this was a successful strategy, with Gibson often having the exclusive rights in all stores in the chain. However, Gibson was at a serious disadvantage buying shelf space from retailers, as they had no way to outbid Hallmark or American Greetings with their much larger wallets. The card industry method of distribution and retailer economics is unique. In essence, a retail chain accepts bids for a three- or five-year contract to provide their stores with greeting cards. The contract will specify the number of stores and the linear feet of shelf space. The second element is exclusivity for any individual store and/or the entire chain. The contract generally calls for a substantial up-front payment (into the millions), for a 100-plus store chain. Then there is added money for the retailer on each card sold, at some percentage of the retail selling price to the consumer. The card vendor has all the responsibility for inventory, selection of the mix of cards for each store, and shelf merchandising. In Gibson's case we paid for around ten thousand retail field merchandisers. If you want to know why the retail price of cards has increased so much, it is not the cost of creative, printing, or paper, but the distribution costs and up-front payments to retailers.

The strategic flaw that Gibson had to work around was their own very unique competitive position. It's what made this such a difficult turnaround. No matter how superior the consumer appeal of the card itself, if Hallmark or American Greetings set its sights on one of Gibson's distribution partners, their strong cash position gave them the necessary muscle to push out Gibson. Consumer preference was simply a secondary factor in business success. Hallmark or American Greetings could also take an account at zero profit or a loss if they felt they could increase prices later and recoup. In market parlance, this is called having a predatory advantage. Gibson's lower share, higher costs, and creative issues simply made matters even worse. Having the financial horsepower to fight the two industry leaders was critical, but that was a hard thing to achieve, given Gibson's precarious cash position.

This became a financial deal game with decreasing emphasis on serving the consumer. The up-front cash overpowered the product. Hallmark had developed a brand, and American Greetings was known for copying Hallmark and having strong retail relations based on economic deals. Progressively, the consumer was more interested in the appropriateness of the message on the card and the price. This disconnect was both troubling and an opportunity.

The retailers worked the card oligopoly to their favor to maximize their economics. In some cases, they moved from an exclusive card company for the chain to an exclusive by store, splitting to increase their negotiating effort. We started to feel like the retailers were trying to keep Gibson marginally in the game to put more pressure on Hallmark and American Greetings. What is that they say in poker? If you can't spot the sucker at the table, that sucker is probably you.

Hallmark and American Greetings got so far away from serving and understanding the younger consumer that the alternative card companies sold through smaller retailers such as gift shops, and independent card stores grew and started to take share from the big guys. These companies were also very profitable, as they weren't buying retail shelf space. In most cases they did not have people physically visiting the store or merchandisers stocking the shelves. They phoned the stores, took orders, and shipped UPS to the stores. Eventually, the consumer demand for alternative cards became so strong and unfulfilled by the big greeting card companies that mass retailers needed to carry those cards.

If you're thinking what I'm thinking—you just might want to perform extensive due diligence before you tackle a turnaround— you would be half-right. Clearly, some diligence is a must. But I am not entirely certain how much worthwhile diligence can be done until you are on the inside working the problem. These insights may seem obvious, but they never are at first glance. Also, so long as you understand going in that it's a turnaround, part of the deal is that you are there to find and identify the problems and then fix them, whether they seem unfixable or not. I, for one, seek the challenge rather than shy away from it. I regret nothing, and I guess I was meant to run into the proverbial burning building.

Gibson was my third turnaround, after Reebok and SkyBox. I was confident coming out of those situations that I could turn around about any consumer product company through innovative product and bringing in a strong management team.

We started by improving the management team. We made bold operational moves, such as closing our fifty-year-old printing operation and outsourcing production, which significantly reduced our costs and improved quality. We outsourced a long-established group of illustrators and writers and went directly to the Internet, where there was a wide range of freelance people and other creative resources who we dealt with electronically. At great cost and management time, we installed an integrated accounting and cost-management system. We made a few mistakes, too, such as transitioning to an automated warehouse, which proved to be much more difficult than expected. In general, though, we began to put the company on a more competitive footing.

Here's a good lesson that seems obvious now: don't let internal production people head up an outsourcing analysis. When I suggested the possibility of outsourcing our printing, the internal group gave me several older studies that showed it was more expensive. When I looked at the analysis, I realized it had not included several costs that could be avoided by going to the outside. I finally hired a woman who was an expert on printing to get quotes from the outside and she correctly redid the analysis. The new study showed a substantial cost advantage to outsourcing and, of course, it avoided a large capital expenditure to update our printing facility. The newer outsourced presses offered higher quality as well. I am generally a big fan of outsourcing production, particularly when you need to increase and speed up innovation.

Alien from Fox Video Games

Platoon, the movie by Oliver Stone, released by HBO Video, 1986

The HBO Video Team: Jerry Ruttenbur, Ellen Stolzman, Tracy Dolgin, and Frank O'Connell

Jamie Farr of *M*A*S*H* joins Frank O'Connell at CES in Las Vegas to promote the *M*A*S*H* video game from Fox Video Games

The original Pump Basketball Sneaker

Sugar Ray Leonard with Frank O'Connell at the White House celebrity tennis tournament, sponsored by Reebok, 1988

Barbara and Frank on the lawn of the White House at a celebrity tennis tournament hosted by the First Lady, Nancy Reagan, 1988

Frank O'Connell at the White House celebrity tennis tournament.
Reebok sponsored Nancy Reagan's "Just Say No to Drugs" campaign.
He presented a special Reebok sneaker to President Reagan.

Donna LaBonte, Chuck Norris, Frank O'Connell, and others
aboard the Reebok jet returning from Las Hadas resort in Mexico
after attending a celebrity tennis tournament, 1989

Cornell Enterprise
Magazine, featuring
Frank O'Connell,
"Reebok's Man in the Shoe"

Frank O'Connell and rock star
Joan Jett at a Reebok event

Frank O'Connell and "Magic" Johnson at Skybox International

Frank O'Connell delivers a presentation of SkyBox
at a card collectors convention in Hawaii

"Magic" Johnson, Frank O'Connell, and David Robinson with Skybox Trading Cards

Frank O'Connell and Jim Kelly of the Buffalo Bills with SkyBox International

Frank O'Connell and "Magic" Johnson with SkyBox International

Walt Lynd, Barbara and Frank O'Connell, and Sandy Lynd ride to
the Harley Davidson 90th Reunion in Milwaukee, Wisconsin

Frank and Barbara posing with their children (left to right), Sean, Kim, Mack, and Beth, at the Outstanding Alumni Awards Ceremony at Cornell University

Mack, Barbara, Frank, and Sean, 2004

Frank with his two sons, Mack and Sean

Virginia and George
Govern at their 40th
anniversary celebration

Frank celebrates "Mother's" 85th birthday with the
help of the folks from Gibson Greetings

Frank O'Connell
on the cover of
IndustryWeek.com
about the return of
Indian Motorcycle

EDITED BY TOM POST

UNEASY RIDER

Indian Motorcycle has attracted yet another bike buff who wants to make a buck off the old brand. Have there been too many promised comebacks?

BY KELLY BARRON

Indian's new chief: Frank O'Connell is revved up to ride the classic bike back to glory. But is he too late?

Frank O'Connell featured on a 2001 Indian Chief

Frank and Barbara ride
their Indians in the hills
of Gilroy, California

Mack, Barbara, and Frank complete the Indian 100th Anniversary
Ride, pictured here with Barbara's 2001 Indian Scout

Frank, Mack, Barbara, and Sean O'Connell join Branscombe Richmond
at the Crazy Horse Monument in the Black Hills of South Dakota

Jeff Gordon, winner of the 2001 "Driver of the Year" award, receives
a customized Indian Motorcycle from Frank O'Connell, CEO
of Indian Motorcycles, and Branscombe Richmond

Branscombe Richmond and Kenny Olson, lead guitarist for Kid Rock,
perform at the Indian Motorcycle concert in Gilroy, California, 2001

Branscombe Richmond, Tim White of Audax, Peter Fonda, Frank O'Connell, and Rey Sotello celebrate the end of the Indian 100th Anniversary Ride in Gilroy, California, standing by the 2001 Indian Scout that Barbara rode 5,000 miles across the country

Arnold Schwarzenegger on his Indian Chief Motorcycle

Frank and Barbara O'connell at an Indian Motorcycle Event

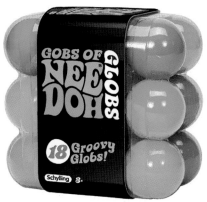

One of the top selling items at Schylling Toys, Nee Doh, sells millions of units each year

Richard A. Marin, co-author of Jump First, Think Fast

Frank O'Connell and Bill Achtmeyer, CEO of Parthenon, enjoy watching the New England Patriots football team from the Parthenon suite at Gillette Stadium

"BREAKFAST WITH THE CHAIRMAN"
(and a few outrageous friends)

Frank O'Connell and his "Silly Slammers" friends, Gibson Greetings

Frank O'Connell and Oscar Robinson, "The Big O", at SkyBox Trading Cards

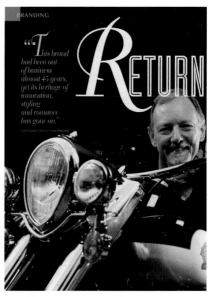

Frank O'Connell featured in an article about the return of Indian Motorcycle

In this time of accelerating change, nimbleness seems to over-rule long-term, fixed-asset, cost-based thinking. It frees you from running the business backwards from the plant's capability versus the market's need. It requires better planning and forecasting, as typically a company-owned plant is whipsawed and receives the blunt force of last-minute changes resulting from constantly updating forecasts. Also, it frees you from being trapped in your plant's current technology. It also frees management's time, which is quite valuable in a turnaround situation. One further lesson is that an internal production team rarely knows how to run an outsourcing operation.

In the end, we could not overcome the retailer's short-term desire to sell their shelf space for big cash payments, and Hallmark's and American Greeting's willingness to pay it. I quickly learned we were in the banking business, financing retailers, rather than being a CPG company being granted shelf space based on the consumer demand for its product.

Should I have discovered the fatal strategic barrier to success that I couldn't overcome during my due diligence process? Maybe. There were signals I should have taken more seriously and investigated more in-depth. Gibson was losing distribution, and there was little I could do about that. But I was in this up to my neck now, and I needed to find some ways out for the company and the shareholders.

I learned lessons about the board, even during the interview process. One member asked me in the interview how I planned to stop the bleeding. He probably knew more about the company's condition than I did (one would hope so). The first lesson is to make changes in the board immediately, if you can. When I went to Gibson, I was the president, CEO, and chairman of the board. I was asked if I wanted to make changes in the board beyond filling one open spot. I should have taken the time to evaluate the board and brought on people with a fresh perspective who could really help. Opportunity missed.

It wasn't that it was a terrible board, but they had been through a lot and were burned out. One of the board members took over as interim CEO when the prior CEO was terminated. This had set up a weird set of dynamics. Many things happened on this board's watch for which the shareholders at some point should have held the board responsible.

To fill the one open spot, I brought in Bob Kirby, my former boss at Arnold-Oroweat, who knew me well and was a big help, especially with his knowledge of the supermarket business, since those were our largest accounts.

It's imperative that you have a well-balanced board with the expertise needed to guide the CEO and the business. Boards are hugely important, as it is always lonely at the top. In public corporations today, boards have taken on substantial responsibility, often matched by liability. This should not be a game of mutual manipulation. CEOs often fear that a board member wants their job and thus are competitive versus supportive. The board should also not be made up of a group of old cronies and "yes" people. It's important to get it right.

It isn't always easy to find people with the right expertise who know how to be good board members, especially if they have been in an operating role. Coaching, versus grabbing the wheel, is an art. Not all board members know how to do that.

Also, a good board is diverse. I often find consumer products companies that have products sold principally to women often do not have enough, or any, women on the board. Greeting cards fall into that sales category, yet there were no women on the board at Gibson. I feel the same about the lack of representation of African Americans, Hispanic Americans, and other cultural groups.

• • •

I had a few moves up my sleeve for the Gibson problems, so let's take a ride through that process. The trick was to get several "moves" to cascade into a trend towards success.

Move Number One: Start by knowing the consumer. Conduct a major consumer segmentation study. To my knowledge, no one in the greeting card industry had ever done an extensive segmentation study.

We learned a lot from the study there were other areas that led to confusion. We clearly saw that we were in the relationship business. People wanted cards that reflected their personality and were highly relevant to their relationship with the recipient. We saw the major bifurcation as being between older and younger consumers. With the explosive use of the Internet, there was also the early but rapid growth of electronic greeting cards. That was a potential game changer of massive proportions. We came up with a very different way to break down and view the market. Blue Mountain Arts developed one of the fastest-growing brands in America by giving away electronic greeting cards on the Internet. This all had to be factored into our thinking and segmentation.

Move Number Two: Develop a new strategic plan. I had learned this lesson progressively over my career: it was wise to spend the time and money at the start to put together a strategic growth plan. The plan should be heavily fact-based, analyzing the internal business, the product lines, the channels of distribution, the customers, and the external market drivers, including, of course, the competition.

Move Number Three: Increase scale and fill in some gaps in our product array. We specifically started trying to buy a series of alternative card companies, like digital greetings companies. The consumer did not want to send their mother's greeting card to their friends. The Big Three in the card business just did not get it.

Gibson could see the alternative card companies taking share, but they were always focused at ground level on taking accounts from Hallmark. We tried unsuccessfully but could not acquire the best alternative card companies, like Recycled Paper Greetings and Blue Mountain Arts. We quickly learned that they were very profitable, which was a tad surprising to us. They suffered no up-front payments to retailers, no cost for in-store merchandisers, card development and printing was outsourced, and their limited sales force typically phoned the stores and took orders.

Move Number Four: Develop our own alternative lines under new brand names. Simultaneously, we began a move toward using freelance card designers. This effort was headed by George White, a very talented guy who worked for me at SkyBox handling PR and helped us to acquire many of our licensing arrangements.

We developed edgy new brands such as Buzz Cuts, Ripple Effects, Bulls Eye, and Life As We Know It. We borrowed several pages out of the alternative card companies' book. This was the beginning of outsourcing development on the Internet.

Hallmark was not totally asleep at the switch and did introduce the Shoebox brand of humorous and more irreverent cards. This new line had done well but still did not fill the alternative card gap, which was widening.

With further understanding of the consumer, Gibson also became the mass-market leader in multicultural cards: Hispanic, Jewish, African American, and other card lines.

Move Number Five: Use licensed properties. Gibson owned some interesting properties such as Far Side, Dilbert, and Chicken Soup for the Soul, but we needed to make a real point of difference, bordering on turning the greeting card section into an entertainment aisle in the store. Some of the TV, movie, and sports properties we licensed were *The Lion King, Jurassic Park, The Simpsons, Home Improvement,* World Cup Soccer, *Mad Magazine, Sesame Street,* Mickey Mouse, and *Aladdin.* By 1994 we had more than fifty individual licenses.

Move Number Six: Convert the card aisle into an entertainment center. Drive traffic down the greeting card aisle, particularly in supermarkets where the volume buyers were every day. We knew that cards are often an impulse sale and consumers will buy multiple quantities for future use, so it could be a big sale.

We built a store-within-a-store. This included gift and collectible product. We experimented with putting TV monitors in the aisles playing TV or movie trailers of properties associated with Gibson cards.

Move Number Seven: Distribute other alternative card companies' product. This was heretical on so many levels. It broke convention in the traditional and alternative arenas simultaneously. When we couldn't buy an alternative card company, we offered to distribute their product in the mass distribution market.

Move Number Eight: Develop an umbrella concept called "relativity." It meant to suggest those things that were most relevant to the consumer. Under this umbrella we distributed numerous brands in a spinner rack. In many cases the alternative card companies did not want their specialty store brand (their main identity) on the product sold via mass distribution, so they used another brand name. This is hardly a new marketing concept, but it was relatively new in the greeting card game.

Move Number Nine: Dismantle and sell The Paper Factory, our 150-store chain of card, gift wrap, party goods, and collectibles stores. Running a retail chain of stores takes very different talent than running a manufacturer and distributor. It also requires capital to build and maintain stores at the quality level we needed. It was like running two different companies, and we could not afford to do that.

Move Number Ten: Digitize the entire library of cards to monetize whatever value there was in that intellectual property. This required us to convert the Gibson archives of thousands of cards, both graphics and verse, from film to digital. While somewhat costly, this eliminated the need to move printing plates around in preparation for using contract printers.

Coming from the trading card business where we were continually innovating and printing millions of cards, I had met many printing experts. One was a woman who was herself very capable of running the existing presses but was also up to speed on the ever-changing printing technology. I hired her to consult at Gibson, especially to cut through some myths. I recall one incident when I was in the press room and one of the older pressmen said something couldn't be done. Even with her small frame, she climbed up on the huge press and began adjusting. Before long she could make the press achieve the "impossible." She became a vital link in moving to contract printing.

Move Number Eleven: Outsource printing, which would eliminate four hundred jobs. We needed to cut our costs, reduce our capital expenditures, improve quality, and enhance new product development. This was a difficult decision, as there were three and four generations of family members working in the printing plant, which had operated in Cincinnati for over fifty years. However, the analysis strongly indicated the move was essential, so we went forward.

I made the very difficult but very necessary decision to slash the workforce, primarily in the printing and production areas. The layoffs and early retirements sent shock waves not only throughout the company and the industry but into the community as well.

This was the beginning of a period of qualifying vendors and then putting each needed production run up for bid through an online network. This allowed printers with excess capacity to aggressively bid and thus helped us keep our costs down. It also allowed us to be more creative in our product design, as we didn't have to worry about the limitations of our internal production capabilities. We could go to printers with the latest technology and bid the jobs with the level of technology needed to get the job done.

Move Number Twelve: Install a new ERP system, an Enterprise Resource Planning system that would integrate the management of core business processes across the whole business. It's a critical tool in modern businesses. Nevertheless, the inevitable disaster did strike. We had carefully planned to do the implementation during the slowest business period, which was the beginning of the year. We hit a series of snags that kept causing delays. Those delays pushed us into the prime business season, with the warehouse automation implementation being the last phase. Problems arose regarding processing orders at the peak of the season, creating out-of-stocks on the retail shelves. We eventually resolved the problem, but it did impact sales and earnings. It was the price of progress—except we couldn't afford to pay for such lessons just then.

Move Number Thirteen: Gibson bought a stake in E-Greetings Network. We could see the trend among young people toward electronic greeting cards. The velocity on the Internet grew rapidly, with other companies joining in either for free or by offering subscriptions. Eventually, Internet card volume grew to a million cards a day.

We did all the neat stuff like researching greeting card occasions to identify what other purchases were triggered. We then went to those companies to establish links and a referral revenue arrangement.

Many other companies entered the electronic greeting card business with various approaches to generating revenue, from advertising to subscription agreements. No one ever really cracked the code as to how to monetize this business. American Greetings eventually bought up and consolidated many of these companies. While not profitable, electronic greeting cards have broadened in appeal and taken a slice out of the printed card market.

Move Number Fourteen: Diversify our product line, and I thought we should diversify into toys. One bright idea was Silly Slammers, a different kind of social expression, which was called "a beanbag with an attitude." This was a hand-sized stuffed beanbag plush character with a sound chip that said something funny when slammed down. An example would be a Silly Slammer that looked like a lawyer saying "trust me" when you slammed it down. There were many other characters in the line. There was also an element of collectability that we hoped would catch on. We looked for ways like this to use our extensive distribution system, sales, and ten-thousand-person, in-store merchandising force to sell other products.

Silly Slammers quickly became popular. We expanded the line through licensed properties, creating a new category of toys. Many of the characters were featured on popular TV shows like *Regis and Kathie Lee, The Rosie O'Donnell Show,* and *Talk Soup.* They were chosen as one of the best children's toys by the Institute for Childhood Resources in San Francisco. The volume in year two hit an amazing $60 million and was very profitable.

Most toys have a two-and-a-half- to three-year life cycle unless there is a connection to an evergreen property, those that last a long time as opposed to those that just come and go. The first year is introductory as it gains distribution and popularity. The second year is characterized by rapid growth, typically accompanied by production shortages.

In that critical third year, we overproduced, generating excess inventory we eventually were forced to sell at a discount. This is a lesson I have learned several times, and I stay very close to the sales forecasting process, especially towards the tail end of the life cycle.

Despite all these moves, the handwriting was still on the wall. Hallmark and American Greetings were still eating our lunch. They seemed unstoppable and would just keep eating up our shelf space, buying it from retailers. We were doing everything imaginable to innovate and differentiate our card line from Hallmark and American Greetings by providing alternative card brands to the mass market and expanding the industry by providing appropriate product to young people. This was not outweighing the onslaught of being outbid by competitive up-front payments, which were being funded by continually rising prices. The cost of the paper and printing the card was actually small in relation to the distribution costs.

Move Number Fifteen: Expand internationally through acquisition of a United Kingdom card manufacturer, with distribution in Australia and New Zealand. These were English-speaking countries where the per capita consumption of greeting cards was four to five times what it was in the US. Gibson bought 60 percent of INK Cards in the UK, which was well run with an excellent management team. They were good at product development and had excellent retailer relations and great distribution, including in all post offices.

Move Number Sixteen: Initiate a radical cultural shift. We shut down the old, established operating plant and administrative office in the quiet Cincinnati suburb of Amberley Village and moved into new headquarters across the Ohio River in Covington, Kentucky, with beautiful views across the river to downtown Cincinnati. Because of our change to outsourcing printing and various design functions, we no longer needed the huge and expensive 100,000-plus-square-foot space. We also wanted to establish a new, creative, contemporary culture centered on the consumer and our retailer customers. This would also help us attract the best and the brightest employees.

As the card industry started to decline, parts of our strategy simply were not working, and Gibson failed to land some large accounts thanks to its inherent cash shortage. The constant rising prices of cards and the availability of free electronic cards on the Internet took their toll as well on the softening market. Gibson was making aggressive restructuring moves, but we couldn't stop the bleeding from the loss of accounts.

My old pal Ben LeBow, through his New Valley Corporation, bought 5.01 percent of Gibson at prices between $6.19 and $9.25 per share. The stock had dropped from $27 a year earlier. The vultures were circling. LeBow took the position that the stock was undervalued and that moves should be made to sell the company or find new paths for growth.

One day shortly before the close of the quarter, my CFO walked into my office with a bunch of pencil-scratched numbers indicating a surprisingly bad month and thus a bad quarter. I was blown away by the surprise and immediately knew the impact would be disastrous on the stock price. It was not only that Gibson was having a bad quarter, it was not knowing about it in advance and being able to alert the market. This would force us to unveil to the market our very worst problems. I was angry as hell that we hadn't seen this coming in our forecasts or had some sort of warning. But we all know where the buck stops on these sorts of things. There was no time to recover before quarter end. If you know early on that it will be a bad quarter, you have time to adjust expenses or do promotions to boost volume.

I kicked myself for not being closer to the financials to know what was happening. You can't blame your CFO for the performance, but the CFO shouldn't deliver short-term surprises to your doorstep when it's too late to act. All these innovative moves we had made, which individually were successful, could not overpower the loss of accounts to Hallmark and American Greetings, who had been outbidding us to buy shelf-space contracts. We continued to lose share, sliding from 9 percent to around 6 percent. It's always a hard call to declare defeat, but it was time to consider selling the company to retain what was left of shareholder value.

About this time, I was again approached by the president of American Greetings, Morry Weiss. He still wanted to buy Gibson. When American Greetings made their last attempt to buy Gibson, shortly before I arrived, the board had gotten an opinion from Skadden Arps law firm stating that the FTC and Department of Justice, based on antitrust guidelines, would not allow number two American Greetings to buy number three Gibson, as this would result in over 80 percent of the industry in the hands of two companies.

Gibson's potential suitors were limited, as any buyer could see that Hallmark and American Greetings would continue to take Gibson's shelf space. American Greetings was really the only potential buyer. Gibson's share would get them close to equaling Hallmark's share. They could consolidate Gibson's revenue on American Greetings' cost structure with very little incremental cost, making the acquisition very accretive.

I met with Morry and began a good, professional relationship that got us through a rocky road with our board, which was naturally skeptical that a transaction could ever take place. I found Morry straightforward and very communicative. If we had not established a relationship where we could productively negotiate with mutual respect, I doubt this transaction would have ever happened.

Would the FTC and the Justice Department allow American Greetings to accumulate a combined market share of 36 percent versus Hallmark's 46 percent share? I thought so.

With the help of our lawyers, I was able to convince our board that we could demonstrate two things to the government agencies that would be material. First, we could show that the greeting card industry had changed, requiring a redefinition as printed, plus the advent of digital greeting cards, which were in direct competition and in fact a reason for the decline in printed cards. If you included over a million electronic cards being sent each day, the share of Hallmark and American Greetings was much smaller. This meant that American Greetings plus Gibson's share didn't meet the concentration guideline trigger. Second, if American Greetings did not acquire Gibson, the company would probably continue to decline and disappear (a tricky path that could further impair value in the eyes of the acquirer).

We eventually agreed on $10.25 a share or $163 million as the selling price.

The big issue was clearing the Justice Department. I made a trip to Washington, DC, on Valentine's Day and, during the meeting, had everyone go online to send an electronic Valentine's Day card. Because the holiday volume was so high, we couldn't even get on any of the greeting card sites. That day, millions of electronic cards were sent. It was a very convincing and demonstrable argument that the greeting card market had been greatly expanded by electronic greeting cards. There were also almost no barriers to entering the electronic greeting card business. The Justice Department approved the sale of Gibson Greetings to American Greetings.

How did I feel about the Gibson experience? Bittersweet. While we had made very dramatic moves, doing everything imaginable from a consumer and operations standpoint, we ended up selling the company at a considerable discount from what the stock price had been when I took over. As the captain of the ship, it's hard to be happy with a scuttled hull. We may not have hit an iceberg, but the ship was being decommissioned, and that's never a proud moment.

My job as a CEO had been to generate shareholder value. There were a lot of ifs and buts; however, they don't and shouldn't count. I'd taken the job, I'd thought I could make the turnaround but couldn't. You never escape the feeling that there were thousands of shareholders who believed in you.

As it relates to lessons learned, a more careful inspection of a proposed turnaround should lead you to determine if the key variables are within your control. I can't tell if that's 20/20 hindsight or just wishful thinking. The next issue is whether you have the most critical skills around which turn is going to pivot. Generally, I should have learned that the combination of declining markets and several big players controlling the market, where the retail distribution is going to be hard or costly to obtain, are difficult barriers to overcome. Nevertheless, as I have noted before, regrets are for wimps. The man in the arena stumbles and gets up to fight another day.

What I love about business is that it is incredibly fair. If you generate value, you get rewarded. If you don't, you get punished. There is a constant report card: market value and share price if you are public, and profits if you are private. I love having a scorecard. It is not some elusive, intangible measure left to interpretation. In all the businesses I have been in and am currently involved with, there is nothing more exciting than working the P&L to get to the bottom line. It is the ultimate score card.

The consumer will ultimately determine your fate. No matter how many other barriers and layers are in the way, the ultimate purchaser will determine success or failure. I try to block out all extraneous noise surrounding a product to determine how it is perceived by the consumer versus how it is perceived by the competition. I am often in conversations where people are giving elaborate descriptions of the industry dynamics and go-to-market strategy. I stop them and say, "Let's start with the consumer and work backwards to the manufacturers." When a consumer product company is presented to me looking for me to invest in it, I do two things. I listen to the presentation and measure how long it is before they mention the word *consumer*. With the Internet and very inexpensive ways to reach even narrow target audiences, there is no excuse for not getting consumer feedback. This should be accompanied by basic details such as how the problem is being solved, how your product is positioned and perceived, and what is the unique differentiating feature versus the competition. These are basic and critical.

In a turnaround, speed is essential. There are always things closing in on you. In the case of Gibson, being between the two giants, Hallmark and American Greetings, was like being in a vice that was tightening. Since greeting card sales were declining, it was a zero-sum game of taking share to grow. We either needed to figure out some way to expand the industry with alternative cards or introduce some new form of product, such as electronic greeting cards. Or perhaps we could have transformed the company by using the asset base to get into another category, such as toys, gifts, or collectibles. In the case of SkyBox, we were able to build a whole new category of entertainment cards based on TV and movies.

There are more unknown factors in acquisitions than there are in mounting an aggressive new product development program. Making acquisitions profitable is among the hardest business challenges that exist. As we experienced at Gibson, internal or organic growth in a declining industry, even making bold moves, is hard to come by and takes time. A much faster way out of the box is acquisitions. We probably should have pushed harder to find the right partner that could have benefited by our direct-to-store delivery and merchandising force. Woulda, coulda, shoulda.

CHAPTER 12

(2000-04)
REVIVING THE
ENGINE

It was a scorching hot day, even for Las Vegas. The motorcycle convoy crew had spent the prior afternoon at the pool at the fabled Hard Rock Hotel, with its strippers from the surrounding clubs ("encouraged" to attend by the hotel entertainment staff). The boys from Gilroy, California, fit right in. They had more body ink per square inch of muscle and sinew than the best the Vegas Strip could muster. The crew was now all suited up to ride across the Mojave Desert. Over in the corner of the breakfast room sat a slender man in black leather pants, sipping a black coffee. He was speaking quietly with another man who was always by his side. When he stood up and shucked on his fringed leather jacket, he became suddenly familiar. If he had put on a Stars and Stripes helmet, the outfit would have been complete.

Peter Fonda isn't every Baby Boomer's icon, but he is every Baby Boomer biker's icon. With Steppenwolf's *Born to be Wild* cranking on the radio and Peter Fonda riding an Indian Chief next to me, I was only missing Dennis Hopper and Jack Nicholson in his gold football helmet to transport me back to 1969 and the days when we were all Easy Riders.

Between Primm, Nevada, and Baker, California, there are very few rest stops. Barbara was leading a pack of Indians on her Indian Scout, next to Peter Fonda, the desert scenes were reminiscent of that ride across America that Fonda made to Mardi Gras. This was as close to Nirvana as I have ever gotten. Unfortunately, Fonda was somewhere beyond Nirvana, since we were all supposed to exit for gas and he just kept on truckin' down Route 15 with the sounds of the '60s probably ringing in his ears and the mellow mood only broken by our chase sweeper catching up to him when he ran out of gas alongside the Interstate.

I was the chairman, president, and CEO, the chieftain of Indian Motorcycles, and I was working hard to revive the brand by sponsoring a cross-country Centennial Anniversary Ride (copying the Harley tradition) in 2001. Barbara led the ride over 21 days and 5,000 miles across the country with upwards of 400 or more bikes following close behind. We had an 18-wheeler transport with spare bikes and parts and a couple of "wrenches" from the factory riding the tail in case of breakdowns. The ride was sponsored by the "Make A Wish" foundation, with scheduled stops at Indian dealerships across the country, fulfilling the wishes of numerous kids with a dream of being on a motorcycle. Vitamin Water also sponsored the event and provided a truckload of product. The ride started at the birthplace of Indian in Springfield, Massachusetts, and were headed indirectly to our new home base in Gilroy, California. For publicity, we invited

Peter Fonda to ride the leg from Las Vegas to Los Angeles, where we were hosting the last in a three-week series of big promotional parties. Fonda tried to do the right thing, but just like in *Easy Rider*, we eventually had to leave him by the proverbial side of the road on account of, well ... I guess shit just happens, man. Luckily, his friend, who was *compos mentis*, stayed with him.

Indian Motocycle (the original correct spelling) may well be the most respected and recognizable brand of motorcycles in the world. What was it about the Indian experience that made it more significant than any other job I had ever had? This was especially vexing to me because it would be hard to claim that it was a successful venture, maybe helping the brand survive for a greater day. It must be something about the Indian brand that makes it so special to everyone. Of all the people in the world, I should understand that, since it was this very brand that had lured me into the rocky shoals of the motorcycle industry.

Indian Motocycle is a famous American brand whose awareness, strangely enough, ranks up there with Coca-Cola and Harley-Davidson, even though at the time, Indian had been out of business for forty-five years (1953–98). Avid fans would love to have a nanosecond of involvement in the history of the Indian brand, and while I regret nothing about it, the job did take its toll. My five-year experience was longer than a nanosecond but has taken on an oversized share of mind and heart in my career story. Can you enjoy your failures as well as your successes?

What is it about motorcycling that makes it become a lifelong passion? It's a thrill, a risk, a danger, something kind of sexy. It's always a little hard to define, as riding a motorcycle isn't rational. That may be part of the charm, breaking the constant pressure of needing to lead a rational life. It triggers the full set of senses, affords beautiful views, passionate sounds, earthy smells, and a feel of the road that screams "freedom." There is constant movement and change as you ride, with things and situations coming at you all the time. It makes you feel alive. You can see a new and different world.

I have read many of the books about individual experiences on motorcycle trips all over the world. Typically, they are about some event or short period of time or life-changing experience. There is Neal Pert, the *Ghost Rider*, riding to sort out his personal losses. There is *Zen and the Art of Motorcycle Maintenance* with its '60s message of spiritualism. And there is even the portentous *Rebuilding the Indian*, with its message of focus on the important things in life. In my case, I have been riding consistently since 1965, or more than fifty years, covering thousands of miles a year. Motorcycling has been a big part of mine and Barbara's lives. It's not an event or an experience. It's not a metaphor or even a life statement. Motorcycling is life and passion. I guess that means that it qualifies as a lifestyle.

Indian Motorcycle was my greatest disappointment and yet my most exciting business experience. Regardless of everything else in my long career, people remember I was involved with Indian Motorcycle. The obvious question is why. Why did I get involved? And why did it prove to be such a disappointment?

Indian, as a company and brand, is slightly older than Harley-Davidson. It had a larger market share than Harley-Davidson as recently as the early 1940s. An array of different owners tried to operate the company from its Springfield factory, but it succumbed to bankruptcy in 1953.

The Indian Motocycle Company began in 1901 when bicycle racer George Hendee teamed up with engineer Oscar Hedstrom to build the first motor-driven bicycle. They called their "motocycle" company Indian, to denote its American roots. In 1902 the company had produced 143 motocycles. They operated out of a facility in Springfield that they called, appropriately, if not politically correctly, the Wigwam.

The unusual thing is that the brand was as fashionable with men and women as it was respected for its racing prowess. Riders were not part of a cult like Harley, but more independent. It was a Ferrari of its day. In fact, not unlike Ferrari Red, since 1904, the Indian Motocycle Company had an identifiable deep red paint that has become Indian's trademark. Its advertising in those years was sporty and reflected the American desire for adventure. The best-known ad suggested, "Wouldn't You Like to Be With Them?"

For the decade leading up to World War I, it was the darling of the racing circuit. International speed and distance records were shattered left and right. When an Indian rider passed a Harley rider on the track, they would lift their butt cheek where they had a patch of a bucked-tooth Indian laughing. Burt Munro on his 1923 Scout, featured in the popular motion picture *The World's Fastest Indian*, was hardly the first to set speed records on the machines. As World War I began, Indian's owners decided on the "guns versus butter" route and sold most of its production to the United States government war machine. It thereby started a tradition of starving its dealer network for supply. This gave its big competitor, Harley-Davidson of Milwaukee, Wisconsin, the edge in the postwar period by allowing them to easily poach dealers and become the market leader.

When America entered World War II, it did so on the back of forty thousand Indian Motocycles. By then, it was back to selling as many motorcycles as Harley-Davidson. The company's track record with the US military was strong, and even its design elements suited the military. With all the controls on the left-hand side, soldiers could fire at will with their free right hand. The recruits being trained on Indians during a four-week course would come back from war as dedicated Indian riders. The 1948 Indian Chief, with its distinctive Indian fenders and overall look, had a huge seventy-four-cubic-inch engine, a hand shift, and a foot clutch. The Chief was handsome and comfortable. Unlike its Harley rivals, it was well-sprung and even had new telescoping front forks. It had a staggering top end of 85 miles per hour in standard factory-delivered form and over 100 miles per hour when properly tuned. It was slow off the line due to its weight, but it was a fearsome machine and, of course, sported the Indian War Bonnet light on the front fender.

The demise of Indian began in 1945 when Ralph Rogers bought controlling interest from DuPont and started making lightweight motorcycles, a strategic direction that fit neither the times nor the image of Indian.

Like all ramping economies after the war, demand shifted to more family-friendly cars, and the Indian Motocycle Company ceased production in 1953. It had been felled by geopolitics and bad long-term strategic outlook, but its brand remained strangely strong despite this.

Between 1953 and 1999 there were a series of owners and people who claimed to have the rights to the Indian trademark. While I was at SkyBox, I became interested in two things regarding Indian Motorcycles. I wanted to obtain a trading card license for Indian to complement our Harley-Davidson license and, secondly, on a personal level, I wanted to see if I could buy the rights to the Indian trademark.

The brand figuratively spent forty years wandering in the wilderness, encountering countless charlatans and hucksters that would have made the proudest Indian weep. The Indian brand was so ubiquitous that many claimed to have the rights to it. It took over forty-five years of legal wrangling before the rights were consolidated by a Federal receivership and auctioned off the brand and its logos to Summerfield Johnston Jr. of the Coca-Cola Bottling Company. So, in 1998, Indian Motorcycles emerged from the catacombs of bankruptcy, positioning itself to reclaim the lost glory of America's first and once-mighty iconic motorcycle, just as the Baby Boomers were looking for new and exciting recreational vehicles. A condition to acquiring the brand was that the winner had to demonstrate its ability to successfully bring the motorcycle product back to the marketplace. Many wanted the brand (for T-shirts and other paraphernalia), but few wanted to fight the mighty Harley-Davidson, which by 1998 was in its solitary dominance of the American heavy metal market.

Talk to anyone who knows the Indian brand, and it brings a smile to their face and a story about a ride and someone in the family who owned one or rebuilt one. The logo and distinct style still remains one of most recognizable brands, even though the company had not been in existence for the past forty-five years.

Summerfield Johnston's investment group teamed up with the California Motorcycle Company (CMC). They created a prototype and drove it into the courtroom to prove that they were up to the task. They incorporated as The Indian Motorcycle Company of America and started production in an old Safeway Stores headquarters and warehouse building in Gilroy, California, the "garlic capital" of the world. They were an agglomeration of nine companies, the most dominant of which was Rey Sotelo's CMC. Indian was set to pick up where it had left off more than forty-five years prior. For each of the first three years after reclaiming the name rights, 1998 to 2000, a new model was introduced: the Chief, the Scout, and the Spirit. During that time, the bikes were composed of standard parts that were being made for other cycles and the motorcycle aftermarket. This was a familiar approach to Sotelo, since he had used it at CMC. There was no time to design a proprietary motor chassis, since that would be a three-year development process.

• • •

After completing the sale of Gibson Greetings to American Greetings, Barbara sold yet another of our homes and she, the boys, and I returned to our beloved home in Woodstock, Vermont, to get a break from the turmoil of and end to that experience in Cincinnati. The boys were now each headed to boarding schools in New Hampshire, close by so we could see them. It was a decision we grieved over, seeing our sons leave home at such a young age, but we determined they had been moved enough and these two schools would provide stability and a great education while protecting them from being possibly uprooted again, given my history at finding new and challenging things to do in my career.

Another fortuitous phone call came one day from a friend named George Conrades, who was the chairman and CEO of Akamai Technologies. He introduced me to Robert Calhoun, a cofounder of Monitor Clipper Partners in Boston, who, upon hearing of my interests in motorcycling and the industry as a whole, introduced me to Summerfield Johnston Jr., the then-CEO of Coca-Cola Enterprises, Coke's bottler organization. Johnston had invested $100 million in Indian's attempt at resurgence with CMC, and although he understood brands, he did *not* understand the motorcycle industry. I then met a most interesting cast of characters.

George Conrades was not just a friend and influential business leader but was also on the board of Harley-Davidson and an avid motorcyclist like myself. Bob Calhoun was the senior advisor and cofounder of Monitor Clipper Partners, which was considering making an investment or buying controlling interest in Indian Motorcycle from Summerfield Johnston. During a due diligence background check, however, Bob's company had unearthed the background of Rey Sotelo, the current Indian CEO, and discovered that he had a criminal conviction in his past and, thus, they indicated that they could not invest or eventually take the company public unless it was behind an experienced CEO without blemishes could also play well on Wall Street.

Summerfield Johnston was the son of James Johnson, the founder of Coca-Cola Bottling Company, the first Coca-Cola franchiser located in Chattanooga, Tennessee. He sold the bottling operation in 1991 and became the CEO of Coca-Cola Enterprises, which consolidated bottlers. The family was deeply into polo and owned a polo farm and stable of horses in Florida. Summerfield was a soft-spoken man, a gentleman with a Southern demeanor. Obviously, he was also a very successful businessman, but he had gotten into an area, motorcycling, that he didn't know much about. He kept writing checks thinking the reborn company was nearing breakeven, but then realized after $100 million that it was going to take a lot more than he wanted to invest.

Monitor Clipper, while interested in the investment with Summerfield, backed off upon learning of the CEO's background. They had placed a fellow from Harley-Davidson, John Fitzpatrick, in the CEO seat but quickly found out from their tour of Wall Street that he didn't have the stature to raise capital.

George Conrades suggested to Bob Calhoun that they contact me to introduce me to Summerfield's financial advisor. Barbara and I had just returned to Vermont from a motorcycle trip in Provence, France, with our American Flyers Motorcycle Club and so, of course, I had motorcycles on the brain. I was also primed for a new challenge after the sale of Gibson. We were back living in Vermont, and I was spending all my time motorcycling and looking at a lot of interesting opportunities.

After a lengthy conference call, Summerfield sent the Coke Enterprises jet to pick me up in Lebanon, New Hampshire, and fly me to their headquarters in Atlanta. I remember the pilots wearing red vests with the Coke logo and pulling into the Coke hanger, where there was a full fleet of sleek jets. There was also a smaller tail-dragger plane belonging to Summerfield, which could get into small airports and dirt runways, including his ranch. He had also flown the Indian management team to Atlanta so that I could meet with them to discuss the status of Indian and determine if I wanted to get involved. Meetings at Coke's headquarters were impressive. I liked Summerfield. I liked Rey and his management team. I could easily relate to the team, being an avid motorcyclist myself and lover of the Indian brand. I was impressed enough that I agreed to visit Indian's headquarters in Gilroy. As an avid Harley owner and rider, I was most interested in riding one of the new Indians and forming my own opinion as to the brand's quality.

One of the things I learned in my due diligence phase was how Summerfield Johnston ended up buying Indian Motorcycle in the first place. Since he was not an enthusiast, this was intriguing to me. It seems he had won the bid at auction.

Unfortunately for Summerfield, the investment in California Motorcycle Company did not offer professional management, design, engineering, or OEM knowledge and skills. In some ways, it was amazing how far along the road they had gotten the company and its production of motorcycles with their limited skills and raw ingenuity. CMC and Rey Sotelo were good at customizing bikes using S&S engines, off-the-shelf engines, and bending lots of metal to make things fit. But they were not engineers and did not have the skill or understanding of how to design for quality, manufacturability, mass production, and manageable cost. This strategic error would lead to producing beautiful bikes, but very expensive bikes with major quality issues. To rebuild the bikes in the field, under warranty conditions, at far-ranging dealership shops, required millions of dollars.

My first ride on a new Indian took place after arriving in Gilroy early in the evening. I went right to the factory and first thing asked them to give me a bike to ride and a helmet to wear before having any discussion about the business. I couldn't have been more excited. My intent was to suspend any analysis and just enjoy the ride. The Chief I was given to ride was big and shiny and sleek, and had many romantic design elements reminiscent of the original Indians produced before 1953. The engine was an ordinary off-the-shelf S&S Engine, a Harley replacement which was good enough to provide a smooth ride.

I rode through the hills outside of Gilroy, which are lovely and always a good test track for me. The hills rise above the valley floor in a series of twists and turns through farms, horse ranches, and along a creek bed. In essence, this created a perfect testing road. I was totally in my element. I did notice an unusual smell, almost like burnt oil, so I stopped to check, kneeling on the ground to get my nose close to the engine. I didn't learn until I got back to the plant that it was the smell coming from the garlic food processing plant in the valley and had nothing to do with the bike.

I rode out of the hills onto the open highway on Interstate 101 to run at higher speeds. The bike had plenty of acceleration and ran smoothly at about 65 miles per hour. When I passed an eighteen-wheeler and accelerated to just under 80 miles per hour, I felt the rear wheel start to shimmy. This was not like a high-speed wobble. I backed off the throttle and let the truck pass. This problem obviously needed to be resolved, and to me it made the bike feel less than perfectly safe.

I had no background in vehicle design, engineering, sourcing, and production. I had spent a lot of time in other industries on these issues, overseeing plants and these functions. I enjoyed and was very comfortable on the factory floors. I did, however, understand establishing the right metrics to monitor and direct a manufacturing operation.

After I returned home to Vermont and continued discussions with Summerfield, my initial agreement was to go in as a consultant. I would be paid from his foundation, and I would analyze the products and company structure with recommendations based on what I could determine would be a strategy for success. Ten days later, I flew back out to San Jose, rented a car, drove to Gilroy, got settled in the Gilroy Hilton, and the next morning set myself up in a small office at the factory. Rey Sotelo's office was a huge space, the proverbial paneled corner office, loaded with his motorcycle memorabilia. John Fitzpatrick, the president, was in the office next to Rey. My priority was to find, within the organization or outside, good people who understood motorcycle manufacturing. This also meant I would need to then listen to them, agree on the measurements for success, and let them go to work.

During my initial weeks in the Gilroy plant, I met with the management team and most everyone in the company. I was looking for many things, but most keenly for motorcycle OEM (original equipment manufacturing) experience. I was disappointed with the size and quality of the engineering department. I read all the reports I could find, including financials and, importantly, warranty reports to see what was breaking out in the field, and any form of consumer feedback. The initial purchasers of the new Indian bikes so loved the brand and styling that they were willing to put up with an incredible number of problems.

One of my main concerns was looking for safety issues. I spent a lot of time on the production floor observing the manufacturing process. Again, I was astounded by their ability to keep the line moving. This was good and bad, as there were times the line needed to be shut down to solve a problem and ensure quality. I was also focused on how robust the final inspection check and test ride were before the bikes were shipped. I could observe from consumer and dealer reports that bikes with problems were getting shipped and sold, knowing it would impact customer image and satisfaction plus result in a costly fix in the field. I met with local dealers and talked with owners in dealerships. The ultimate test was taking various random bikes coming off the production line and riding every afternoon. The results were less than stellar.

My initial top ten key observations were:

1. There was a big gap between running Indian as an OEM quality assurance assembly operation and the current large, customized manufacturing shop.
2. The bikes needed to be redesigned and engineered for quality, cost, and manufacturability. There were too many vendors to control and a lack of primary vendors supplying complete modules, which are essential to quality and running a strictly efficient assembly operation.
3. The company needed to close the back door by preventing any bike with a quality issue from being released. One hundred percent rigorous testing of finished product was a must. Reworking bikes on the line was not as expensive as in the field, plus the company needed to avoid creating a bad consumer experience.
4. The company also needed to comply with warranty fix requirements, which were running into the millions and sapping the time and energy required to reengineer and produce new, quality bikes. This was like trying to run two companies simultaneously with the same people.
5. There was every indication that the Indian brand was very healthy. Buyers were putting up with a lot of problems but still loved the bikes.
6. This came as no surprise, but many potential Indian Motorcycle buyers saw them as a Harley clone and would continue to do so until Indian made its own proprietary engine and stopped using S&S engines.
7. Indian needed more of the right, more broadly experienced motorcycle engineering and manufacturing talent. There was also a bias among the well-tattooed crew against engineers and designers from sport bike companies, which limited recruiting. Gilroy, California, is a tough place to recruit talent to with little vendor support close by.

8. Indian should not have been making its own apparel and accessories but rather licensing it to other manufacturers. There were too many SKUs and loads of inventory that couldn't be sold through to Indian dealerships. There was no one in the company with the proper apparel and accessory experience.
9. The culture needed to change from doing anything possible to get bikes out the door to practicing extreme quality consciousness.
10. Indian needed to bring money! I was not experienced in vehicle manufacturing, but I could see that it was going to take a big investment in talent, design, and manufacturing to deliver a bike that could live up to the Indian brand.

The conclusions drawn from my several weeks in Gilroy were summed up in a report that I sent to Summerfield and his advisors with my ten observations. I wrapped it up by saying it would take a lot more money and a huge cultural shift to turn the company around and properly engineer the bikes to become a true OEM. The company needed to transition from a manufacturer to an assembler, which meant less passion and more business. This raised a critical strategic question about the best path for the company. Serious consideration needed to be given to the alternative of having some other company such as a motorcycle, sport utility, or another type of vehicle company produce the bikes for Indian.

Indian could be the designer, marketer, and distribution / sales / dealer-relationship manager. The good news was that there was every indication that the Indian brand remained strong and that the demand was there for a true quality Indian Motorcycle.

I was certainly not an expert on motorcycle or vehicle design and the production of hard goods. However, I did know from years of being involved with the design and development of many consumer products, where I had spent substantial time on production floors, that the Gilroy operation was a long way from an efficient, high-quality operation. Their resourcefulness in many ways was amazing but also the root cause of the quality issues.

My mind was churning through all my experiences, looking for a solution. A few years back I had been on the board of Moto Guzzi, the Italian motorcycle company with a Ferrari-like history, which had been purchased by a private equity firm in NYC. It was a bit of a wild ride, as the Italians never wanted the Americans to own this famous Italian brand. We were the Germans, temporarily occupying Paris while the French Resistance marshaled its forces. The Moto Guzzi production was in an old historic plant on the shores of Lake Como. This was where the Italian fashionistas played, but not where hardworking wrenches lived. A little bit of Gilroy garlic would have helped the place. Moto Guzzi needed to update the manufacturing plant or move to a modern facility, but the government wouldn't let them do either. Without modern manufacturing capability, I saw no similarities to Indian other than a shiny gas tank and two wheel's worth of brand strength. We eventually sold Moto Guzzi to Aprilia, another Italian motorcycle company.

How about the radical "back-it-into-the-garage" strategy, which would be to develop and reinvigorate the Indian brand with wonderful, retro legacy apparel and accessories? It could be made into a lifestyle brand using many of the Indian DNA elements, logos, colors, signage, material (brown leather), and the motorcycle could be reintroduced later. The old bikes could serve as classy props. There are fifty thousand old Indians still registered today, so they would be easy to source. Then, after the Indian brand regained broader aware-ness, particularly among young people who ride, it could be reintro-duced to the motorcycle market on a reengineered basis, from a true OEM facility. This was worth a thought.

222 | *Jump First, Think Fast*

Some people, cold and rational as they were, believed entering the motorcycle business was simply too difficult and capital-intensive. The apparel strategy could be tweaked to allow us to strategically sell a few bikes but make money on other Indian-branded lifestyle products and accessories. Clearly, the winning strategy was to exploit the well-known Indian brand's trademark and logos with apparel and clothing accessories. Indian had a wonderful legacy of well-dressed men and women riding Indians, all with very romantic stories. If you asked anyone about Indian, they would say, "Oh, my grandfather dated my grandmother on an Indian," or, "I had a boyfriend who had an Indian." The mention of the name brought smiles to the faces of millions of people. Also, Indian's history of consistently outperforming Harley on board and dirt tracks created many stories and racing legends. The question remained how to translate this history into a winning business strategy.

Maybe it could be a bit like the Ralph Lauren retro approach? The Indian War Bonnet logo and scripted logo were much like Ralph Lauren's polo pony, but more distinctive. I had walked through the apparel warehouse across the street from the factory, looking at the stacks of apparel and clothing accessories. I was blown away by the number of SKUs and the amount of inventory, much of which I could tell from the box dates hadn't moved in weeks. This was a totally separate and complex business with no one running it, at least no one who had the necessary experience. It immediately hit me that this was a separate business, one that Indian should license out and not produce itself.

Basically, at this point, the company was financially broke. Understandably, Summerfield Johnston wanted to stop writing checks and take on a financial partner. He was in a tough spot. The brand was worth more than what he had paid for it and there was a decent dealer network, but the money he had put into manufacturing and apparel was mostly gone. The bikes produced thus far, because of quality problems, were more of an ongoing warranty liability than an asset. While the designs were aesthetically pleasing and captured a fair amount of the Indian DNA, the line was a dead end. A new proprietary Indian motor was essential yet very expensive to develop. It would be necessary to redesign down to the frame for quality and economic manufacturability. This was critical. The only thing that had been proven with Summerfield's $100 million investment was that the Indian brand and DNA could be beaten with a stick and still survive strong as ever.

At the same time, Excelsior-Henderson, an old bicycle brand that had been owned by the Schwinn Company, had attempted to design and manufacture Excelsior-Henderson American made motorcycles under the umbrella of Hanlon Manufacturing Company, founded by Dan Hanlon in Belle Plaine, Minnesota. Over a seven-year period, they built a huge factory with projected production of 20,000 "Super X" Motorcycles. They set up dealerships around the country and took pre-production orders, which created a two-year waiting list. After burning through $100 million, they were only able to produce 1,950 units. I had paid a $500 deposit on one of the 1999 Super X Models and took delivery of it later that year with VIN number 499. I still have that motorcycle in my barn in Vermont. Unfortunately, E-H was unable to raise additional capital and filed for reorganization under Chapter 11. This was a bad omen for Indian. It was an indication of how much capital it takes to start a motorcycle company. It's not $100 million, it's closer to $1 billion.

So now what? Strategically, I thought about many things, including a path that would get the company to a reasonable exit strategy. Summerfield Johnston wanted to get his money back and have a remote possibility of achieving some level of return on investment. There were at least two basic strategies for making this happen. Number one: We could grind down costs, minimize design changes, and buy as many preassembled components as possible, like the auto industry "black box" concept. With this they would consolidate vendors, allowing for a simplification of Indian's assembly line and an attempt to break even at low production volumes. Number two: Redesign the bikes for quality, thereby designing and building a proprietary Indian engine. This would require investing further in plant automation such as robotic welders, hiring the right people, and building a larger dealer network. This much higher break-even strategy required a major capital infusion from a partner and probably loss of control for the current investors.

What was the right exit strategy? It might have been possible to attract enough private capital to become a small- to medium-sized manufacturing company, obtaining cash for growth and an exit for investors. It was also likely that an existing motorcycle company would see the value in the brand and want to go after a piece of Harley's 80 percent-plus share of the large bike business. However, my guess early on was that interest would be in the brand. The potential buyer would need to start almost from zero to design the bikes to meet their quality, safety, and efficiency manufacturing standards. This, we later learned, would take well over $100 million. All of the current pain, suffering, and investment would not have much residual value. Investors would also be concerned over the warranty liability of the bikes previously sold, which numbered in the thousands, as well as the potential collateral damage they represented to the Indian Brand.

Rey Sotelo lived in Gilroy and enjoyed being in the Garlic Capital of the World. CMC and Indian leased a large building, a warehouse, and started manufacturing motorcycles from scratch, but starting from scratch was naive and an impossible task from the beginning. What worked for a customizing shop like CMC would not work for the OEM operation needed and envisioned by Indian. Gilroy, due south of San Francisco and San Jose, was an unlikely location for a motorcycle manufacturing facility, as there was no vendor infrastructure or trained workforce such as you might find in cities like Milwaukee or Detroit.

Many of the people in the operation were Rey's friends, and the average number of tattoos was high. They had hired some people from Harley including John Fitzpatrick as president and John Hagan as the head of manufacturing. But since Harley was organized by functional area, it was hard to find anyone Indian could hire for the top job who had a broad enough range of experience.

Indian had hundreds of suppliers, which were hard to qualify and control. Though Indian represented a small-quantity buyer, the suppliers knew Indian might be large someday. Nevertheless, the quality and delivery schedules afforded Indian were less than sufficient. There were also far too many individual suppliers to manage and control. Most vehicle manufacturers have primary suppliers for various systems such as a front end. That supplier deals with all the subcomponent manufacturers and delivers an entire on-spec, quality-checked front end.

As an example, Indian was stringing its own wire wheels instead of buying a fully assembled wheel with a tire or perhaps a whole front end. There are a lot of obvious problems with this approach, one being finding the responsible party when there is a problem. The finger is pointed in many directions, but ultimately Indian is left holding the bag, trying to troubleshoot. This is a costly approach because it's both hard to know your costs and even harder to reduce costs, as you must turn to hundreds of suppliers. Indian had hired some good people from the automotive industry who understood this cost-control concept, and luckily, some people trained in the automotive industry also loved motorcycles and were attracted to Indian.

Indian had highly resourceful people running the assembly lines. They were driven to keep the lines running and turn out finished product. When they ran out of a component to keep the line moving, they would try to come up with a substitute—it was common to go to the local hardware store and buy small springs, for example. On some occasions they would buy Harley parts since the early Indians had several similar components. It was a manufacturing professional's worst nightmare.

In many ways it was amazing they could turn out good-looking bikes with Indian DNA designs that actually ran. The workforce was very dedicated and hardworking. Given the huge number of components, poor or erratic quality of parts, and unpredictable delivery schedules, it was magical that they could get the pieces to work at all. Even more amazing yet was that the brand was alive and well, even though the bikes were very expensive and the quality issues were all too well-known. The bikes were in demand.

Not all of the problems were with the power plant. One of the most expensive fixes was the big S-curve fenders on the Chief, which kept cracking. This was not only an expensive proposition but impacted the brand's entire image. Dealing with the warranty issues and then redesigning the bikes to eliminate the quality problems was like running two companies at the same time.

It was clearly understood by all that we had to develop our own engine. A large portion of the market said that if we were using S&S's aftermarket engine, we were nothing more than a Harley clone with a fancy and iconic name. This was a lot to digest in due diligence.

After reading my report and having a few lengthy conference calls, Summerfield Johnston and the investors approached me to become the president and CEO of Indian Motorcycle, with the job of raising the capital and rebuilding the management team.

What are the lessons we all learned in green-lighting this decision? The hurdles were high and obvious. They had run through $100 million after having gotten started on the wrong foot. Much of that money was wasted in building the wrong foundation. They did do a good job of capturing the Indian DNA in the external design of the bike. However, it would have been easier to start from scratch and redesign the internal guts of the bikes for cost and quality manufacturability, as well as outsource the manufacturing of entire systems to enhance the ease of assembly. Changing course was going to be costly and would require a huge cultural shift to becoming a more professional organization.

Rey Sotelo had established the culture at Gilroy with himself as the tribal chieftain (yes, that old problem). He had an interesting cast of characters as friends whom he had hired. Some were qualified people from the motorcycle business and others had come in from the automotive industry. There were also good people further down in the organization and on the production floor.

The culture defied precise definition. It was a combination between bad boy Rey as the tribal chieftain (I guess that made me the corporate chieftain), a motorcycle gang with professionals tossed in for good business measure, a huge customized motorcycle manufacturing operation, and the organizational silly putty that brought and held everyone together—the passion for the Indian brand. The Indian brand cast an aura that was more powerful than money or any individual. It truly felt like you were working toward the second coming of some mythological god.

Rey, in building customized bikes at CMC for athletes and entertainers, had built a following for Indian, including members of the cast from the TV show *The West Wing*, where the bikes were featured in some episodes. The list also included the TV shows *Gilmore Girls*, *The Ellen Show*, and *According to Jim*, and personalities such as Drew Carey; Dusty Baker from the San Francisco Giants; Rich Gannon from the Oakland Raiders; Kenny Olson, lead guitarist for Kid Rock; Jeff Garcia of the San Francisco 49ers; George Clooney; Laurence Fishburne; Peter Fonda; and even Arnold Schwarzenegger.

I discussed this next opportunity with Barbara, who supported the idea, knowing how we both felt about motorcycles and that it was kind of a dream to be so intimately associated with Indian. We quickly agreed on a contract with salary and equity ownership. Summerfield and his financial advisor were honest, straightforward, and thus easy to deal with. I immediately understood that I was their only hope at getting any of their money back. I signed the contract and became president and CEO of Indian Motorcycles. I was fifty-seven years old and had never felt younger or more enthusiastic. It was simply a dream to have this opportunity. While Barbara stayed in Vermont to be geographically close to the boys who were off in school, I flew back to San Jose, checked into the Hilton, and took a deep breath while gazing out the window at the beautiful brown hills of Gilroy.

As I had done in previous companies, I needed to pull together the strategy. The company needed a fact-based strategy to focus resources against priorities. It was also an essential first step to raising capital. One of my first moves was to bring in an outside consulting group to help me. I picked up the phone and called my good friend Bill Achtmeyer, chairman of The Parthenon Group in Boston. I particularly liked strategic planning and felt it was essential to successfully point a company in the right direction. I had enjoyed the planning process, working with the management team and the insanely bright people at Parthenon who had been with me in the other turnaround battles.

I found the internal data analysis and gathering of external market and competitive information to be a fascinating discovery process. From my early days as a trainee in the market research department at Carnation, designing and analyzing consumer research reports, I was always excited by discovering insights. We ended up pioneering the design and utilization of Internet panels for decision-making as a new way to get at learning more about consumer sentiment.

Raising capital needed to be a priority. Indian Motorcycle Company was essentially bankrupt, with Summerfield and his advisor writing checks weekly to keep the company alive. The management team had just made a trip through Wall Street and hadn't been able to raise the money. In fact, several months prior, one of my Vermont neighbors had invited me to listen in on a Merrill Lynch call where they were attempting to attract investors for Indian. I think initially they were trying to raise just $10 million. I laid out a strategy for the most likely sources of capital. Tucker Anthony was also brought in as an investment banker to put together the deal memorandum and pitch book.

Since the management team had been to most of the likely suspects on Wall Street without success, the turndowns became known in the network as, "Did you look at the Indian deal?" The sheep mentality takes on a life of its own and the deal gets shopworn, regardless of its potential. The general conclusion was that the Indian management team did not have the credentials (i.e., leadership and operating experience) to give any investor confidence in the deal.

I had experience raising capital, including for my start-up at Fox Video Games. I am pretty good at raising capital when I am running the show and passionate about the venture. I'm less effective when I am trying to raise it for someone else's venture. The combination of a solid, fact-based strategic plan, my knowledge of the industry, and firsthand mileage on the seat of many bikes, enhanced by a passion for the Indian brand, produced a compelling story. I thoroughly enjoyed making the presentations and fielding the questions. While confidence with an investor audience is important, passion is a winning element.

The list of potential investors was a combination of Tucker Anthony customers, Summerfield and his financial advisor's contacts, my network, and prospective Parthenon private equity clients.

We started on a typical road show. On the second day we went to Boston where Bill Achtmeyer, the chairman and founder of Parthenon, had arranged a meeting with the Audax Private Equity Group, run by two former Bain friends, Geoff Rehnert and Marc Wolpow. Several Parthenon people had gone to work for Audax as well, making the connection even more solid. Audax had just raised a fresh fund of $500 million and was eager to make investments. Never ignore the importance of good timing.

When I started the presentation to Audax, there was only a small group in the room. I can always tell the signals when they get interested, and can equally tell when you haven't grabbed them. In this case, more people started coming in, which is always a good sign. Then the questions jumped from due diligence, to whom we had shown the presentation, to where were we in the fundraising process. If an investor is interested, these are the things they start to ask. They want to avoid a bidding war at all costs. Before I finished the presentation, one of the Audax people, Steve Kaplan, left the room. He came back with some other people and said that Audax was interested in an exclusive arrangement and asked us to give them time to do some further due diligence. This is the moment you hope for in a pitch.

The discussion turned to our willingness to give them an exclusive arrangement and a discussion of the terms. The negotiation then revolved around how long they needed and whether there would be any remuneration for the exclusive. Obviously, there is value here regarding the risk of taking the deal off the market, not completing the deal, and/or forgoing a bidding war. If there was no deal, we would need to restart the process and face a possible stigma of someone having turned down the deal. A worse nightmare would be getting the reputation that the deal has been overshopped. Private equity firms are bit like sheep in that they are reluctant to move forward after a competitor has turned a deal down.

The negotiations and due diligence moved quickly. Summerfield Johnston and the current investors knew they didn't have much leverage since the company was bleeding cash. They weren't going to invest more, and the company was still some distance away from breaking even. In a word, it was a buyer's market.

A deal was struck. Audax was willing to take over the company, putting in a substantial amount of cash. The current investors would not be paid any cash, but rather given a small retained interest in the new company, with the prospect that someday their small slice would be worth something.

Audax bought Indian. I remained as the chairman, president, and CEO, but life would be different with a private equity investor. I negotiated a new and better contract. It was a three-year contract, including equity. We needed to be lean, so I started by trimming senior staff who weren't needed.

After negotiating with Audax, Summerfield's financial advisor said to me, "Frank, your life is going to be very different now." He was warning me that Audax was going to get into every aspect of the company. I knew just what he meant. I had had free rein in my prior months running the company and making changes, but I could see that Audax's involvement was going to be substantial. This is typical of many private equity firms. Regardless of which side you are on, it is a delicate balance.

I have been on both sides several times. If I am the new private equity owner, depending on the strength of the management team, I always look for more involvement. I particularly want to oversee getting a world-class management team in place and establishing a solid strategic plan. The management team has to own it and be passionate about executing it. If I am on the management team, I'm looking for agreement regarding strategy, an annual budget, financial reporting, and support from the board, but I want to run the company day to day without diversion or supervision. I know that this balance lasts only while the company is on plan. Once off the plan for more than a short period, most private equity owners step in. Private equity firms are typically not good at running companies. They are transaction people who don't have much operating experience. There are exceptions with some larger private equity firms that have staffs and/or advisors with operating experience.

Audax's lead person, Steve Kaplan, installed a new CFO at Indian with whom he had worked before. This is always tricky in terms of a person's loyalty. Team dynamics are hard enough in a young company without a key position like CFO acting like a backdrop investor spy. It is common for a watchdog CFO to create a double-agent scenario. It can also be very productive if the CFO knows what the investor wants in terms of reporting and knows the personalities. If I am the CEO, loyalty to me and the team is an important element. Some CEOs go overboard with this and place loyalty above talent and all else.

The Audax Group in general were good people, very honest and straightforward. They sent a young, smart guy to basically live with us at Indian. Tim White was one of their managing directors, he had an impressive law degree, and he provided financial oversight for Audax.

The Parthenon Group, who introduced us to Audax, did a major study of the industry, with a focus on identifying potential Indian purchasers and making a deep comparison to Harley-Davidson. We used this in all of our subsequent investor presentations.

After raising the money, it was time to access and build the management team. Audax wanted to make clear to the organization and to Rey Sotelo that I was in charge. While Rey and I came from very different walks of life, we got along great, and I felt we genuinely liked and respected each other. He was honest about what he did and did not do well. I found him very straightforward as opposed to Machiavellian. He could get mad, get in your face, but he also listened to your point of view and would change his mind if your points were compelling enough. He was articulate and could tell stories and be very convincing. He had good relationships with the dealers and the riders, and he was a respected member of the motorcycle community. Many CMC dealers became Indian dealers, while others were under-capitalized and fell by the wayside.

Indian needed a deeper, more professional management skill base. Key areas included design, engineering, product development, marketing, sales/dealer relations, licensing, sourcing, and operations. While still a high-risk, early-stage company, Indian was an attractive place for anyone to work, especially if they were passionate about the revival of the brand.

One of the most significant hires we made was a young, very bright guy, Darrin Caddes, as the head of design. He had worked for prestigious automotive and motorcycle brands such as BMW and Fiat. At first, I was concerned that his BMW background would be at odds with the needs of Indian. Also, while BMW makes a cruiser, their line is much more sport-bike oriented versus Indian and Harley, which are cruisers. Designing for Indian required as much understanding about Harley as you can get. The two companies have been archrivals for over one hundred years. I have a library of required reading regarding the Harley/Indian wars. As marketing folks would say, Darrin grasped the essence of the Indian brand. He did a landmark analysis and presentation, identifying the key elements of Indians DNA. His presentation was one of my favorites, as it captured the key iconic elements of this famous brand. It also pointed out the unique differences of Indian compared to Harley. I have done a number of presentations on the historic differences between Harley and Indian owners, but none were better than that one.

A pro from the automotive industry, Chick Ramsay, who had been at Autobytel, Toyota, and Lexus, headed sales and the building of the dealer network. The new Indian motorcycles were initially distributed through some old legacy Indian dealerships as well as some of Rey Sotelo's CMC (California Motorcycle Corp.) vestigial dealerships. In general, these dealerships were small, undercapitalized, in the wrong geographic areas, and on low-traffic roads. Also, they were not professional new-bike brand manufacturer sales and service operations.

The new dealer network concentrated on car dealers. They were well-capitalized, which meant they could get the floor financing to

234 | *Jump First, Think Fast*

support bike inventory. They were in high-traffic locations, often with a vacated dealer showroom from a closed franchise such as Oldsmobile. They understood the importance of training, new vehicle sales, customer service, and how to make money on a service. They were often motorcycle enthusiasts and hired experienced motorcycle people to staff and manage their Indian operation. In many cases they wanted to be part of building the brand.

Next, we brought in Fran O'Hagan as vice president of marketing, who had previously been VP at Jaguar Land Rover of North America and head of sales at BMW of North America. As an avid motorcyclist, Fran understood iconic brand marketing.

Hiring good engineers who had experience designing and building an entire motorcycle was the most difficult task. Most motorcycle engineers, especially from Harley, specialize in one component, such as the frame, the suspension, or the power train, but not the entire bike. We found some of the best engineers in the countryside of England, where motorcycle and automotive manufacturing and racing is prevalent. I made a trip to England to source engineering talent. There are excellent engineers spawned both from motorcycle and automotive manufacturing and the hotbed of performance engineering shops that exist there. They are there supporting a world-class racing circuit. In particular, we hired several engineers from the British car company Lotus.

I also started searching for designers who understood retro design. I felt hot rod builders who worked with other made-in-America iconic cars such as Ford would be a good match. Fortunately, I ran into Chip Foose, the iconic automobile designer, hot rod builder, and motorcycle restorer. He was the youngest member to be inducted into the Hot Rod Hall of Fame at age 31. His father's garage was next to an Indian dealership, and he clearly understood the Indian DNA. We hired him to do some retro Indian motorcycle designs, which were very cool. He was in such demand from and so busy with car manufacturers that we never were able to fully refine his designs. He did, however, stimulate our creative thinking.

John Hagan became our VP of manufacturing and director of operations. John was all-Harley, where he had headed up the Porsche/Harley V Rod JV project. He had experience in setting up "greenfield" factory start-ups. The challenge at Indian was transitioning a job shop operation into a continuous-flow, quality culture that covered welding, manufacturing engineering, final assembly, paint, and powder coating. This was a huge challenge, including sourcing quality suppliers, since our quantities were still small. John led an approximately 450-person direct labor force and 50 professionals. As I explained, the mentality was to do everything possible to get the bikes off the line and out the door, even if it took buying Harley parts when we were short on supply. We eventually reached production of five thousand bikes a year. We could break even at around seven thousand.

One day at Indian, the front desk called my office and said Arnold Schwarzenegger was on the phone. I had met the big man while at Reebok. I answered the phone and he said, "Fraunk, this is Ah-nold." He explained that he had always used Harleys in his movies but really loved Indians, and that he would like to use Indians in his next movie, *Terminator 3*. I explained that we were a fledgling company and had no money for movie placements. Arnold said, "Fraunk, I have money." He said that if we supplied the bikes, including several that would get destroyed, he would use Indians. This ended up being a great deal for us, plus we ended up having a fun and productive relationship with Arnold.

Arnold was an avid motorcyclist and quite knowledgeable regarding Indian. We gave him a new Chief for his personal use. At one point he dumped the bike and fractured some ribs. He quickly responded that it was not the bike's fault. He would frequently meet with a group on the Pacific Coast Highway in LA for a ride on Sunday mornings with his beautiful Indian Chief.

We repaired his bike and delivered it to him at a dinner at his restaurant in Santa Monica. When we were unloading the bike, I crunched the back fender. At dinner I told him of the problem, at which point he laughed, saying it was nice to have someone tell him the truth. We had a fun dinner with his ubiquitous cigars. Then we took his bike back and fixed the fender.

Terminator 3 was a good publicity promotion. We also mixed some limited-edition Terminator paint. As a surprise, Arnold came as a secret guest to one of our dealer sales meeting in Las Vegas. We filled the room with smoke as he rode between the tables onto the stage to huge applause. On with the show.

• • •

So, what happened at Indian back in 2003 that forced us to shut it down? Progress had been made, but the warranty costs of rebuilding in the field were enormous. The originally produced bikes with quality problems were a larger problem than expected. Also, the cost, time, and talent required to build a new path to becoming a high-quality efficient designer and assembler of motorcycles required many more hundreds of millions than we had forecasted or had on hand.

We invested considerable time and resources in designing and building our own motor called the Power Plus 100, an old Indian name for a motor, using conventional V-Twin technology. The motor was beautiful and had all the design cues of the vintage Indian round bottle cap head-designed engine. Amazingly, it was completed for only a few million and ended up being both powerful and well-designed, with minimal quality issues. I still own one of the original Indian's with a Power Plus 100 engine that I rode across the country and I keep it in my barn in Vermont with my other motorcycles, and it has operated flawlessly for thousands of miles. People always comment about it, assuming it is an old Indian engine. The move from S&S

Engines to our proprietary Indian engine did help quiet down the critics and gain legitimacy. We were no longer a Harley clone, but it was all a bit too late.

Our dealer network was building momentum. Quality was improving day by day. Design improved significantly. And sales were steadily increasing. However, our cash burn was high, and we still had some distance from being cash flow positive, given our cost structure.

Warranty claims remained high and kept the company diverting cash and allocating manpower to repairing the bikes manufactured several years earlier. The "S" curve fender still kept cracking. Despite all the Indian bikes on the road with problems, the brand remained strong nonetheless.

Our investors at Audax were writing checks almost weekly and, while still believers in the potential, they were becoming fatigued in the same way Summerfield Johnston had become before them. They did what private equity firms do when things are off track, making the decision to bring in a new CEO and moving me to chairman so I could focus 100 percent of my time looking for a buyer or another investor. One afternoon Steve Kaplan from Audax flew out to Gilroy to inform me that they had hired Louis Terhar to replace me as president and CEO. Lou was from Cincinnati, a graduate of the Naval Academy, and his career had been largely in scrap metal. I think they were impressed with his having graduated from Annapolis and thought him a natural leader. He had not been in any business related to motorcycling, however. He was a perfectly nice guy but did not have the motorcycle or automotive skills and intuition to take Indian to the next level. His early hires of friends out of his former company also did not bring the required experience needed to continue the momentum while I looked for cash.

Let's be clear and call a spade a spade. This move by Audax was not a vote of confidence in me. This was obviously a difficult transition for me, moving from leading the company and running the day-to-day operations to being chairman. The term "getting kicked upstairs" is not intended to have positive connotations.

I was forced to admit during this period that it was not realistic to assume Indian could become a standalone mass-market producer of high-quality motorcycles. It was a dream too far out of reach. The amount of capital required was many multiples of what had been invested thus far. There was also a need for a much larger pool of talent, along with a cultural earthquake to adjust to a true OEM environment.

With Audax's support, I began to explore a wide range of solutions to our problems. The possibilities included contract manufacturing, various forms of partnering, and the obvious search for a buyer for the company. I was headed to the largest international motorcycle show in Milan, Italy, and had arranged in advance to meet with key people from Honda, Kawasaki, Suzuki, BMW, Ducati, and Aprilia. On the one hand, it seemed like complete heresy to consider a partnership with a foreign company. But other than Harley and Polaris, with its Victory brand, there were no US motorcycle companies that would make strong partners. It was a compromise many of us would be willing to take to allow Indian to survive.

All the motorcycle companies were receptive and arranged for senior executives to meet with me. In many cases, I had thought about what the strategy might be to either partner or buy Indian. In some cases they were sport bike companies with little participation in the large cruiser market that Harley controlled. This would also give them an American brand known around the world. There were possible dealer synergies in being able to offer both a sport bike line and a cruiser line, thus addressing two large markets. The design, engineering, and manufacturing synergies were obvious. In general, the concept was to maintain a high-profile assembly operation for Indian in the US, but with components coming from around the world. The meetings were interesting and generally filled with strategic discussions.

The perfect deal from my perspective was for Indian to control the cosmetic design, marketing, and dealer distribution with a contract manufacturer doing the engineering, sourcing, and manufacturing.

Earlier in my career, I had established a relationship with Harley's chairman, Jeff Bleustein. He, too, was a fellow Cornell grad from '60, and he had been kind enough to take my call when I was considering taking the Indian assignment. He invited me to dinner in Milwaukee, which I accepted. At this point, given their interest in selling, Audax had asked me to arrange a meeting with Jeff, which I did.

Both founding Audax partners attended the meeting. It did not go well. The Audax partners wanted a large number for the fledgling Indian Motorcycle Company, which was still well below breakeven. While we were never presumptuous enough to imply that Indian was a threat to Harley, we did hope that Jeff Bleustein might reason that if we were trying to sell the brand, a competitive powerhouse might buy Indian and start taking share. But the meeting ended abruptly.

I approached Mark Blackwell, head of the Motorcycle Division at Polaris. I discussed potential strategies involving Indian and Victory. My experience and history taught me the hard way that it was difficult to build a motorcycle brand from scratch. Mark arranged a meeting with Tom Tiller, the president of Polaris, and their entire Victory Motorcycle management team. From Indian's perspective, Polaris would have been a perfect partner. They had start-up motorcycle experience, excellent OEM engineering talent, a dealer network, American-based manufacturing, and the necessary financial assets. There were many reasons why a relationship or even buying Indian would make a lot of sense to Polaris. In the end, they wanted to just continue to build their own Victory brand.

By 2003 we were in an urgent cash flow situation with Audax, which was tiring of writing hefty weekly checks. We needed to move fast. We were going to get one shot at making a deal with most of the potential buyers/partners. There was not a lot of runway at that point for trying to troll for a high price, despite the unrealistic hopes of the Audax partners. The lesson here is to be a bit more honest in your self-evaluation, including considering the urgency of the situation. True buyers can sense blood in the water and can wait to buy the company out of bankruptcy. Once there is a shutdown, and the employees scatter looking for jobs, the dealer network collapses, and you are just buying the brand off the scrap heap.

It was necessary to think through the strategy for the potential partner and not leave it solely to them. We were more motivated to be creative than they were.

All this time, Barbara stayed in Vermont but made numerous trips to Gilroy to stay with me for a few weeks at a time. We never bought a house there, but instead rented cute little cottages down in Carmel by the Sea, about thirty minutes away, moving about every thirty days to a new dwelling. It was the relief I needed to get away from the pressures in Gilroy and to try and keep myself positive and focused on the task ahead.

I knew we were getting close to the end. The 2003 models had been released, and the 2004 models were on the assembly line. I started to make more urgent calls to the potential purchasers I had already contacted. We then received a "secret" call from a European company. They had several requests: a visit to the factory in Gilroy on a weekend, test rides on Indian bikes for several days in Northern California, and a stay in a hotel where their company affiliation was not to be identified.

The secret caller turned out to be BMW, the motorcycle company that was rolling over the US sport-touring and all-terrain markets. They sent over a small group headed by their key acquisition executive who had negotiated buying Mini Cooper. BMW obviously had great engineering and understood cruisers quite well for a sport bike maker. I did, however, feel like Indian and BMW were at opposite ends of the emotional riding spectrum. Indian was a romantic

"Rough Rider" American icon, and BMW was the rational, perfectly engineered, unemotional piece of equipment that would run all day long. After their "secret" visit, the group returned to Germany and met with their BMW team. The key executive eventually called me with his observations. He felt that his German engineers would never understand the Indian history and DNA. He said they would kill the brand with engineering.

One always remembers the big moments, good and bad. I was at Cornell giving a speech on various topics, including Indian. I remember being in the lecture auditorium when I received the call from Audax. I had to take the call in the control booth. They informed me that they were going to stop funding Indian. I immediately returned to Gilroy.

Lou Terhar was the CEO and handled the announcement to the organization. This meant the loss of jobs to hundreds of employees in Gilroy. Also, dealers had invested a good deal of money building their dealerships with inventory of bikes and accessories, showrooms, and maintenance shops. Both groups were angry and blamed Audax for stopping funding. I guess you couldn't expect the employees to see that Audax had invested and lost $100 million and underwritten their jobs for four years. I felt bad for those dealers who had invested heavily in their dealerships. It was not how I had hoped things would go.

This was a very emotional time for everyone associated with the Indian company, the Indian brand, and the motorcycling community in general. People called and cried, begging me to do something to save the company. Barbara and I had established a good reputation in the Indian family of riders, from the One Hundredth Anniversary Ride, our setup at the annual Sturgis Rally showcasing Indians, various sales and marketing events, and just riding with Indian owners and sharing the unspoken love of the brand. We felt the need to help people come to terms with the end of Indian, so Barbara and I organized a solidarity ride of Indian owners in LA, which ended with a press conference at the Petersen Automotive Museum with the theme, "Ride On!"

At our own expense, Barbara and I had banners made, along with T-shirts, hats, and other marketing materials. We contacted every dealer and rider's group in the country to create the momentum for this event. The objective was to generate a grassroots movement among Indian riders and thereby generate publicity in hopes of interesting a new investor. I hoped we could trigger one of the prior purchase candidates to step in and buy the company before it totally closed. It was a long shot. All over the country, groups formed for the final Indian ride, some riding to the steps of their state's capitol. In Los Angeles we had no less than five hundred riders who rode with us, all wearing their Indian "Ride On!" logos, waving American flags, and creating quite a buzz.

At the Petersen Museum we hired catering services to provide lunch for all who came, and the press interviewed me and other riders, getting our comments. The event appeared on the local news channels. It was an emotional, fun, bittersweet moment. But in the end, we simply couldn't find the financial support after the tales were told of the two big investors in a row failing so convincingly.

After five years of my life and psyche devoted to reviving Indian, I was looking down the barrel of a liquidation. The company went into receivership. We ceased operations; there were no bankruptcy filings. I lived in hope until the bitter end that a solid partner would step in and not let the company go down. It didn't happen. It was a tremendous loss for me personally, not financially but emotionally. I felt I was given every chance to achieve the turnaround and had still failed. The private equity firm had stayed with it through an unheard-of spend of $100 million. I felt badly for them and their investors. Audax was only two years old when they invested in Indian. Hundreds of employees who had worked hard with passion for the brand were losing their jobs. I hugged and consoled so many employees in those last days, it was worse than a funeral. Dealers who had put their life's savings into the business were left with nothing and were bitter. But beyond all the real-life consequences was the heartbreaking, broken dream of not being a part of bringing the great old American icon brand back to life. There is this unexplainable, strange feeling that you really work for the brand, and you have failed the brand.

I stayed on as chairman through the liquidation process to sign the necessary documents and be a point of contact. The company went through a California Receivership Liquidation Process. The process required an executive of the company to sign various documents and to maintain the filings around the world to protect the trademarks. Several bidders showed up during the receivership process. Surprisingly, neither Harley nor Polaris showed up to buy the brand for peanuts, either offensively or defensively.

In a proper bid process, I bought from the receiver a couple of the Indian bikes, a red 2003 and a blue-and-gray 2004 model Indian Chief with the new Power Plus 100 engine that I had ridden many times on trips and test rides. I have since ridden that bike flawlessly all over the country. I have my own twenty-two-foot motorcycle-equipped trailer with a big Indian logo on the side that still gets a lot of attention.

I spent the next year working with CMA Business Credit Services, to whom Audax had assigned the company's assets. Their job was to aggressively market the company to determine the best means for maintaining the integrity of the company and maximizing its value. Eventually, the rights were sold to Stephen Julius of Stellican Capital, a private equity firm in the UK, which also owned Chris-Craft Boats and Outboard Motor Corporation. They specialized in reviving ailing recreational product companies with strong brand names, and they vowed to resume production of the existing models of Indian. In 2006, with an investment of about $23 million, Stellican set up Indian Motorcycle Corporation in Kings Mountain, North Carolina.

By 2011 Stellican had made what was the latest attempt to resuscitate the Indian brand, but in that time frame came to realize that deeper pockets and strengths in engineering, manufacturing, and distribution to complete the mission must be undertaken. With Polaris's successful launch of Victory Motorcycles, they agreed to acquire the rights to Indian Motorcycles.

While I can't count this chapter of my career as a success, it was one of the most exciting and passionate times. Combining your passion with your job has pluses and minuses. I never felt like I was working, which must be a good thing. I loved what I did and the people I worked with. Nothing still excites me more than throwing my leg over an Indian. Nothing makes me prouder than the looks I get riding an Indian. But being too invested in a dream is also dangerous. Indian may have consumed me too much.

CHAPTER 13

(2004-20)
LIFE IN THE
PARTHENON

This is a difficult chapter for me to write because it feels like a time following a long and desperate battle where one is forced to reflect and lick one's wounds, especially because it was a heartfelt and passionate battle that was ultimately lost. Look at pictures of the Indian Chief in captivity. Other battles end in less than victory, but this one ended with no one to blame except circumstance and judgment. It was my passion. It was a tough time. There are competing needs in a time like this. One needs to get back on the horse, pick oneself up, make adjustments, and find a new path. The problem is that you need to get on the right horse, not just any horse.

The consulting firm of record, which I joined in 2004, was The Parthenon Group. With a name like Parthenon, there is a lot to live up to. The Parthenon was the peak of the power of Athens, the zenith of the Doric order, the height of western civilization. It stands as a symbol of the Hellenic victory over the Persian hordes and a more enlightened world. And yet it stood as the treasury of Athens and an armory for the Ottomans and the pillaging post of Lord Elgin and his quest for marble. The Parthenon Group meant all that and more in my seven-year career hiatus there.

I traveled home to Vermont, returning from Gilroy and all that I had experienced and left behind there. While at Indian, my beloved Mother, who had lived to be 97 years old, left us with a lasting legacy for our family. The nation had survived 9/11 while I was away, which helped me regain perspective. I was grounded in Gilroy while the FAA regained its footing. During that time, it was easy to reflect on Vermont and what a safe haven it was from the world at large. Now it would be my own personal safe haven after my battles on all fronts on behalf of the Indian brand.

I was happy to recover from the five-year Indian turnaround attempt by retreating to Vermont, settling back into the comforts I so loved about the place, being closer to my family again, riding motorcycles, and contemplating the next venture. Taking off my war bonnet, so to speak.

After a few days shaking off the whole Indian experience, a local recruiter representing a little baking company called King Arthur Flour in nearby Norwich, Vermont, was looking for a new board member. He had learned about me, so he picked up the phone and called me cold. They wanted someone with a consumer products background in the food industry, plus I had spent seven years in the baking business, so I seemed a perfect fit.

The company was an ESOP (employee stock ownership plan), the board reported to the employees, and I was intrigued with this new form of governance. I met with the then-president and the board and was offered a seat alongside others from various backgrounds, each offering their own set of expertise and skills. It was a fun little company that supplied flour, baking mixes, fresh baked goods, and kitchen equipment. It wouldn't take much of my time, four meetings a year, and it was twenty-five minutes from home.

They needed contemporary marketing to expand national distribution and brand awareness beyond the Northeast. Eventually I became chairman of the board and was able to drive them into developing a new strategic plan—which helped in expanding the brand, changing the name to King Arthur Baking Company and eliminating the knight image on the package logo while replacing it with a crown. This was easy, fun, and fulfilling, and they gave us delicious bread.

For seventeen years I had been one of Parthenon's clients, and I was their very first client at SkyBox. Later I hired Parthenon at Gibson Greetings and Indian, and I knew I was certainly one of their best clients. I had developed a strong personal relationship with Bill Achtmeyer, the cofounder and chairman, and our families were equally friendly, often skiing and spending occasional vacations together.

I was also good friends with the other cofounder, John Rutherford, who was the lead person at Bain when I was at Reebok. I knew most of the partners, many of whom had worked on my businesses. I was particularly close to Kosmo Kalliarekos, who was one of the original partners and had also worked on all of my businesses. Kosmo was a great guy, an unconventional thinker, with an IQ bigger than the room. He and Bill had always been there for me when I needed them. They always gave me credit for being a key person responsible for the initial success of Parthenon. It was common for Bill Achtmeyer to invite me to annual company meetings, and for Barbara and I to join him at the annual company Christmas party. We traveled with the partners and their wives to off-site meetings, and Bill introduced me as an advisor to Parthenon.

I was invited to speak at Parthenon's annual meeting at the Equinox hotel in Manchester, Vermont, having spoken several years before at the annual meeting in Bermuda. I generally gave a Parthenon client's point of view. In this case, I presented ten observations about Parthenon and did it with humor. I suggested that dealing with Parthenon's presentations was "Death by PowerPoint."

Following the meeting, Kosmo suggested to Bill that I should join Parthenon in some capacity, perhaps part-time to help build the consumer business. He saw value in my thought process and in my contacts. I would be the only person at Parthenon with industry operating experience. That type of partnership had been attempted in the past, but unsuccessfully. At this point I was willing to be part of Parthenon's culture, but I didn't know how to do anything part-time, and the two or three days a week turned into five or six days a week, and I joined full-time as a senior partner. I was sixty-one years old and had a lot of experiences under my belt by this time. To join Bill and the other partners at a company for which I had tremendous respect was not only a great opportunity but a humbling experience. To be brought in at a senior level, to work with so many phenomenal people who had done outstanding work for me in the past—it was an honor to be asked. Barbara and I initially leased a cool furnished apartment at the Ritz in Boston for 6 months then moved over to the top floor of the Commercial Wharf building, looking out over Boston Harbor. We were able to bring our boat and tie it up at the Boston Yacht Haven just below. I could walk to the office. The shift from operating a company to the consulting world was coming together.

I had always enjoyed working with the bright young people at Parthenon. The pillars of Parthenon's culture are smart, nice, and driven. The culture is unique and coveted by the flood of graduates from the best schools who want to go into consulting but don't want to join the big firms: Bain, BCG, McKinsey. The firm has a very flat organizational structure, is informal, offers easy exposure to the partners, and has a very collegial, team-oriented, and supportive environment.

While very performance- and customer service-oriented, Parthenon also strived for employees and partners to achieve a work/life balance. This isn't easy in a highly charged customer service business, which can require long hours and considerable travel, not always to garden spots. The culture is very much a reflection of its founder and chairman, Bill Achtmeyer, who spun off from Bain to form what was Talisman but later changed to Parthenon. Bill thought of the name as representing a Greek goddess who won battles through strategy versus brute force.

Consulting is a unique business. While I had hired consulting companies, working as a consultant was quite different. Being on the inside of the business was enlightening. I am often asked about consulting by MBAs or undergraduate students trying to get internships. I pride myself on trying to give them the straight scoop (from my view), which is often different from what others are saying. At first I found business school graduates were at times like sheep, following one another into the current trendy career path with the highest starting salary. That trendy path has led to commercial banking, investment banking, private equity, hedge funds, and consulting. It has rarely been brand management, general management, or, God forbid, manufacturing. It may be a matter of chasing money or just plain old peer-group herding.

The consulting business model works and is quite rational. Your success as a consultant is ultimately judged by your ability to sell consulting assignments and thereby get on a track to become a partner. It is also imperative that you become a known expert in some area. This does not restrict your ability to work on other areas. It is an up or out environment, like a law partnership, since everyone above you needs to keep moving up so that there are openings for talented people. The first major requirement is to be great at analytical insights (consultants are hired to make objective, fact-based decisions). Next, one must be able to manage a workflow team and, ultimately, make client presentations and build top management relationships in the process of becoming a trusted advisor.

Again, I'm not an expert on consulting, but I have observed some significant changes in the field. First, the amount of free information available on the Internet no longer requires a consulting firm to dig up information and put it into organized form. Companies can do this for themselves, especially with newly minted college grads who have high-powered toolboxes. Thus, the valuable data provided by consulting firms is the harder-to-find sort that often requires customized primary research or the construction of unique databases. I'm not minimizing the ability of consulting firms to take existing market and internal data and turn their analytical crank to come up with unique insights. But "unique" is the operative and harder-to-achieve standard. Second, the cost pressures and accountability have minimized relationship selling. Now, almost all projects go out on an RFP (request for proposals) for competitive bids, involving elaborately prepared management presentations. Third, you pretty much have to walk into a bid presentation with a compelling answer in hand to get the assignment. This means a substantial, up-front investment and risk on the part of the consulting company. My conclusion is that, like most businesses, the business of consulting has gotten much tougher. The disappearance of well-known consulting companies like Monitor Clipper attests to this trend. Parthenon had established offices in San Francisco, as well as other parts of the world. One afternoon, I was on a conference call with Bill, Kosmo, and others who were informed that the managing director of the San Francisco office was leaving to pursue an outside opportunity. During the call, Kosmo emailed Bill and I and suggested that I might go out to the San Francisco office to run it in the interim while they determined next steps. So Barbara and I packed our suitcases and headed West. We found a very cool 2-bedroom condo on Lombard Street. It had big windows with a stellar view of Coit Tower and the Bay Bridge. We had to stop traffic to back into our two-car garage. The office was located on the 36th floor of the Bank of

America building, and the views of the Golden Gate Bridge and harbor were breathtaking. For the year that I was there running the office, in addition to serving our clients, we sponsored a program for low-income women to start various businesses. Mark Loudy, a bright young Associate with whom I worked closely, was later named as managing director. We packed up our belongings and returned to Boston. We bought a beautiful condo on Chestnut Street in the Beacon Hill section of Boston, walking distance to the office and to the Boston Commons. We felt anchored to the city and the company and welcomed the familial connections we had established there. I was blessed to have a great assistant, Lisa Abbott, who kept me on track, organized, and managed my busy calendar.

When I speak of my seven years at Parthenon, I can't help but think of the Austrian mountaineer Heinrich Harrer, who chronicled his life interrupted in the book *Seven Years in Tibet*. Now, Parthenon is no Buddhist temple, and Bill Achtemeyer is no Dalai Lama, but the notion of an adventurer being rescued after a failed Himalayan ascent and achieving peace and a modicum of enlightenment in a calm and cerebral respite from the real world—that experience is hard to ignore.

I do need to separate the Parthenon consulting projects I worked on from my own outside projects, some of which I brought into Parthenon for consulting work to be done. In those latter cases, Parthenon got an equity stake, or we worked out a commission based on sales. The point is that the entrepreneurial flame continued to burn bright within me all during my seven years at Parthenon. AIRDAT is the name of a weather-forecasting technology project I brought to Parthenon. It was the primary project founded by my friend Jay Ladd. I had developed a close friendship with Jay, who headed operations for SkyBox. Barbara and I both became good friends with he and his wife, Laura.

Jay is a motorcyclist and pilot, and would-be boat captain. We obviously shared a lot of mutual interests. He joined our American Flyers Motorcycle Club and developed close relationships with the

252 | *Jump First, Think Fast*

entire gang, which continues today. Since SkyBox, Jay and I have shared many ideas for entrepreneurial ventures.

Jay contacted me at Parthenon and asked if I was interested in either independently, or with Parthenon, doing the analysis to determine the largest markets for a superior proprietary weather forecasting service. He also felt that between Parthenon and me, AIRDAT could gain access to the companies in this industry. Eventually, we made a unique deal between AIRDAT, Parthenon, and me to sell, on a commission basis, AIRDAT's service in specified industries and to preapproved clients.

This ended up being a seven-year effort, almost my entire time with Parthenon as a Senior Partner (it's a long time, but it beats wandering in the wilderness for forty years). We frequently felt like we were on the verge of selling very lucrative contracts into a number of industries. In the end, energy trading was the most interested industry. Short-term weather forecasting has the biggest impact on energy trading, and AIRDAT eventually made a very lucrative exclusive agreement with a large hedge fund that traded energy.

Throughout, my orientation was not the typical consulting approach where a client comes to you with a problem and your job is to solve it. I preferred to think of industry revolutionary ideas and then try to sell them to the company most capable of taking advantage of the opportunity. It doesn't lend itself to a systematic business model, but it was where my mind always took me.

Innovative ideas that were game changers for an entire industry were more intriguing to me than one-off company projects. I think this says a lot about how I think differently. I tend to scan the big picture. In some cases, my ideas seem half-baked, which is not altogether unfair. However, I tend to build from half-baked ideas and shift the form and thereby try to find a much larger application. There is a random thinking element to this, and I understand that random thinking is bedeviling to systematic and sequential thinkers. But it has value too. It is far easier to jump through clutter to unique solutions by being somewhat nonsequential. But articulation of the vision is then critical.

Luckily, I am typically pretty good at articulating the vision. People often say at board meetings and in other situations that they wish they could express complex things the way I do. I believe it is my random thought process that allows for this. I seem to have an unusually commanding presence when I present. People stop talking and they listen. Perhaps they have to listen carefully because of all the logic leaps I take. Nevertheless, it seems to be effective. I can tell when I have an audience in my hand. It feels like I am able to communicate deeper thoughts with greater confidence and conviction than most. I have also learned from others that I have a "radio voice," which I assume is pleasant to listen to. I know I'm good at calming babies, so maybe there's a connection.

I wait until there has been enough conversation to let me know what others' ideas and opinions are. My mind scans for insights and the right moment to present my point of view. Once again, timing is important. Calmness and courtesy are equally important. I don't criticize the thinking of others but try to go beyond the current thinking to where my ideas generally reside. Horses and board members can only be led to water; it's up to them to drink if it seems right.

The world is changing faster and faster. This is particularly so due to tectonic shifts in US and global demographics. This means that for market-based ideas, there is a need to define a vision of the future. Without that, it is hard to sell a radical idea. In order to stay in the "attention zone" with executives and board members, I try to be brief. I find it helpful to sometimes stop abruptly without ad-libbing and request a simple, "What do you think?" It is important to engage the audience, and it's hard for people to ignore direct and simple questions. I also almost always use a smattering of self-deprecating humor, which disarms people. Laughter lightens what is often a serious edginess in the conversation.

I also stress, especially with young people, the importance of "Living in the World." This means that there is a need to be aware daily of life around you. I have found one of my assets is being able to relate to common everyday life. This has been especially important during my career in consumer products. The job of a marketer is to segment audiences, but also to be able to anticipate how people are going to react to stimuli (products).

You know by now that I love and am a big user of consumer research. I have never seen it as mechanical. It is helpful if you know where to look and what to ask. Often, as with psychological research, the results require interpretation to get at their true meaning. While I am what people would consider well-educated, I have never lost my intuitive feel and awareness of the trials and tribulations (perhaps even jubilations) of the bulk of the population. I can tell almost immediately if a marketer has a personal feel for the market. It's even easier to spot one who doesn't. Growing up on a farm and having a mother who embraced and tried to help everyone has kept me grounded. I have always been comfortable and enjoyed people from all walks of life. I grew up with the utmost respect for people who worked with their hands.

Marketing is part science and part art. It's important to be able to stay on top of a fast-moving world. I always liked the definition of a great marketer—one who can spot trends before they surface. You can also argue that this means identifying and discriminating between fads and trends. I don't want to claim brilliance here since the universe always proves us wrong when we do. The universe never disappoints me—once I think I have figured it out, it throws me an unexpected curveball that makes me humble again. Like most of my generation, I grew up reading newspapers. As long as I can remember, I would daily read *the Wall Street Journal* for business, *USA TODAY* to see what my consumers were reading, and then the local paper in the area where I was living to stay abreast of my community.

And always on Sunday, the *New York Times*—a relaxing way to spend the day. I am often struck that young people, including college graduates, don't read a newspaper on a daily basis. Given the wide availability of news that is instantly updated on the Internet, I am often surprised by their lack of awareness of current events. I daily monitor a variety of sources to track trends in industries in which I am interested. If I am in a global mood, I also occasionally enjoy the *Financial Times* to get the world view. I make it a point to concentrate on India and China, as I am fascinated by these countries and their increasingly important impact on all of my businesses.

For example, rapidly increasing urbanization in the US is creating gridlock and many other transportation problems. The infrastructure of our cities is not prepared to handle this increase in traffic. This trend and problem is accelerating as young millennials want to live in cities, not in their parents' suburbs. Increasingly, their parents want to retire in the city. Contributing to the solution of this major problem has intrigued me for some time.

Working on these interesting projects intrigues me. Based on my branding experience, I tend to get involved in the normal consumer product projects, generally related to growth strategies, new products, supply chain, M&A, and various operational issues. The range of consumer products has always been wide, including the areas of toys, food, athletic footwear, apparel, greeting cards, collectibles, and more. My favorite continues to be anything with a gasoline engine or wheels including, of course, motorcycles, scooters, ATVs, snowmobiles, cars, and trucks.

In 2005 I accepted an invitation to join the board of TreeHouse Foods in Chicago. Sam Reed, who worked for me at Oroweat in Seattle years ago, had gone on to enjoy a stellar career in the baking business, running Mother's Cookies, then Keebler—which he sold to

Kellogg's—and finally starting TreeHouse Foods, which serves the private label packaged goods market. I stayed on the board for sixteen years and saw the growth of the company to more than $7 billion during that time. We went through numerous changes in both the board and executive management, but I feel I made a big contribution during that time and encountered some of the smartest people in the industry. My major contribution was to chair every committee on the board, improve diversity and quality of the board, and force the development of a strategic plan.

When Sam Reed asked me to join the TreeHouse board, I asked him who else was going to be on the board. He mentioned the name Michelle Obama, a respected hospital administrator from Chicago, and the wife of a popular U.S. Senator from Illinois. I spent the next three years, two days per quarter with Michelle at board meetings. When people asked me to describe her, I said, " What you see is what you get." She was very warm, down to earth, easy to talk to, and obviously smart with an undergrad degree from Princeton and a law degree from Harvard. She was very family-oriented and worked hard at making sure their girls had a normal life. This was challenging with Barack spending his time in Washington. On one occasion, she left early from the board meeting, rushing home to be with the girls for Halloween. One evening, while riding with her in a van on our way to dinner, Barack called her from Washington. I could tell it was a warm and humorous conversation. I was asked to coach her on my committees, as it was her first time being associated with the board of a public company. She required very little coaching, always asking the powerful and insightful questions. Barack Obama's name, for many Americans, was not quite on the tip of their tongues. But his name exploded after his famous 2004 speech at the DNC. I had many interesting conversations with her leading up to Barack's announcing his candidacy for president in February 2007. She eventually resigned when the press started to appear at the company's annual meetings.

In hindsight, I never dreamed I would spend time in casual conversations with the woman who became First Lady.

Parthenon was eventually bought by Ernst & Young (now Parthenon-EY) in 2012 and, along with a couple of other senior partners, I retired from Parthenon at age sixty-nine and transitioned out of the consulting world. Bill asked me to take an outside role as general partner to liquidate Parthenon's equity positions in various companies and private equity funds. Retirement was still a word that was foreign to me, and I had no intention of lying on the beach.

During that time, a former Parthenon partner introduced me to Phil Ivy, whose company, Crofton Capital, is a nonfunded sponsor. This is typically a small group or individuals who find good companies to buy, perform some due diligence, and negotiate a price or range. They then source a private equity fund who will put in the bulk of the investment and own the company. The nonfunded sponsor receives, for sourcing the deal, a carried interest percentage on the same basis as the private equity firm and may also co-invest a small amount of money alongside the private equity firm. The nonfunded sponsor also typically has board representation and a monthly consulting arrangement to be involved in overseeing the company, often working with management to build a strategic plan, helping get the right management team, and putting a capital structure in place.

In this case, Phil was looking at a toy company and was somewhat familiar with the toy industry but needed someone with toy-operating experience to help provide guidance and, more importantly, to attract the capital to buy the company. I had worked for Mattel, done the Silly Slammer caper at Gibson, and been on the board of Radica, a toy company we sold to Mattel. I enjoyed the toy industry, and this was a chance to sink my teeth directly back into it.

We completed a deal and bought Schylling Toys located in the northern suburbs of Boston. I was sixty-nine years old, still highly motivated and clearly not looking at retirement. I agreed to become president and CEO on an interim basis until we solidified the management team. Simultaneously, I resigned from the King Arthur Flour board, as I felt that I needed to focus on this new business while not diluting my participation at King Arthur. You can only serve one master at a time, and this was that time.

Barbara and I sold our beautiful condo on Chestnut Street in Beacon Hill, put our furnishings in storage, and moved into a cool, furnished house on stilts on Water Street, overlooking the Merrimack River in Newburyport, Massachusetts, next to the Audubon Society. The office was in Rowley, a short drive away and an easy commute to my next adventure.

After Phil and I talked to various private equity firms about Schylling, we decided to go with Gladstone Capital in Washington, DC. This has turned out to be an excellent relationship. They have been patient and have supplied excellent guidance and support, including financing our first acquisition, Lava Lamp, which is doing well. The company has enjoyed tremendous growth. During the Covid-19 pandemic, the company invented a unique compression material and created a product called "Nee-Doh Stress Balls," that is filled with this non-toxic, jelly-like compound, that comes in multiple colors and sizes. Millions of units have been sold to date and have expanded into a brand, with the help of influencers and social media. The company recently acquired the iconic Big Wheel brand, and it is being reinvented.

Schylling is a unique toy company and totally counter to my prior leading-edge technology bent. They make retro toys, specializing in wood and tin—no batteries and no electronics. They are all the familiar toys and play patterns that Baby Boomers and their parents grew up with. They are aimed at infant and preschool age. Schylling is the world-leading manufacturer of tin Jack-in-the-Box toys and kaleidoscopes, producing millions annually. We have a variety of licenses such as Curious George, Disney Pixar, and droids under a Star Wars license. We also strictly sell and distribute toys for other companies like Fisher-Price. These are known as "platform" companies versus Schylling-designed and produced propriety products, under the Schylling brand. The challenge is producing over a thousand products in twenty-three categories produced in 123 plants in China, distributed to our sweet spot, thousands of toy and gift stores, as well as the major retailers.

Early on, we had decided to promote the head of product development to the presidency, as well as bring in a new CFO. The new president, while young, had been with Schylling for six years and previously had spent several years with Hasbro and other toy companies. We knew he was outstanding at product development, but we took a risk on his ability to grow into the presidency. We kept the CEO position open as a fallback.

Both have been good moves. It drove the need to quickly get a strategic plan in place to both get us all on the same growth page and to align our human and capital resources. In my experience, it is very hard to direct the strategic planning process from internal resources, as there is seldom anyone with the experience, time, and analytic skills to achieve a fact-based plan. Fortunately, there was a Parthenon senior associate who was heading to grad school but wanted real company experience in the form of an internship. He was perfect, having all the planning process knowledge, analytical tools, and the interpersonal skills to work with the management team and board. I worked very closely with him during the process. A major thrust of the plan was to reduce dependence on distributing other platform brands and building the Schylling proprietary brand, which would drive up the value of the company.

The board has been very supportive of the new president's efforts to get the right management team in place. The biggest challenge was finding toy designers who understood retro, worked across a number of product categories, and were willing to work in Rowley, Massachusetts, forty-five minutes north of Boston on the coast. We went through a few misfires, including hiring designers from California (Mattel, Jakks Pacific, and Hasbro). This made it hard for the president, as he was working both his old and new jobs. Only recently have we bolstered the team significantly and have found a strong head of product development and head of sales. The company also moved its headquarters to North Andover, closer to Boston. Meanwhile, Barbara and I moved out of our rented waterfront home on stilts and returned to our haven in Woodstock.

Phil Ivy and I have been good partners in this venture. He has the financial skills but also good management instincts, and I have more of the operating experience, especially with production in the Far East and new product development. Subsequently, I have also invested behind Phil as lead investor in another toy company, The Loyal Subjects, located in Los Angeles. It is a market leader in art-driven collectibles with licenses for Transformers, Teenage Mutant Ninja Turtles, Mighty Morphin Power Rangers, and more. I decided, in that instance, not to play a larger role but to remain a passive investor.

There are still a number of other personal projects I work on, as numerous business plans cross my desk in any given week. I continue to pursue and track just about any kind of new opportunity that falls within, and sometimes outside of, my areas of expertise, experience, and knowledge. I have always had crazy ideas and concepts running around in my head. My boyhood best friend, Walt Lynd, and I were going to design a senior living facility for people just like us on the edge of retirement. Can you imagine? People still come to me daily with unbelievable stuff because they know I will think about it and feed them back with my out-of-the-box ideas.

CHAPTER 14

ALWAYS
A NEW DAY

After Indian Motorcycles was liquidated, at times I questioned why I was spending a large part of my time on other people's projects rather than initiating my own. This seemed to me to be particularly true, as I had demonstrated with Fox Video Games and Indian that I could passionately raise millions of dollars.

During my time at Parthenon, I was actively bidding to buy other companies, frequently with Parthenon's and Bill Achtmeyer's support. After SkyBox, for example, I was very interested in buying a collectibles company. The industry was declining and changing in form. I felt this was an opportunity to buy at a low price and take a different approach to the industry. I think we bid three times to buy the Franklin Mint from the Resnick Family (Stuart and Linda) as well as Enesco. Each time, the bid dropped significantly as these companies headed for bankruptcy. Each time, the owners or board said they were on the edge of turning them around, which never happened.

I was interested in turning around old sporting goods brands. One year, just before Christmas, I flew with Bill Achtmeyer and Dick Cashin, the head of CitiCorp Venture Capital, to Helsinki, Finland, to bid on Wilson Sporting Goods. We flew overnight to attend a formal, due diligence presentation. We arrived at their office just before the presentation, ducking into the bathroom to change into our suits. One problem, however, was that my bag had not arrived. Bill had a spare suit, which he loaned me, but it was more than a little too big, so I just pretended that it was baggy-chic and the latest style. Knowing the Finns and their proclivity to emulate, I probably started a new Helsinki trend.

I seemed to be continually approached by various private equity companies interested in buying athletic footwear and apparel brands. Also, the area of leisure athletic brands was growing. This category used athletic technology to generate comfort and press the fashion button. In most cases, these were turnaround brands that had lost their positioning. Often, larger companies acquired these brands, but then suffocated them or allocated their weakest teams, creating the risk of never returning to the mother brand if the turnaround didn't happen. These were small and large brands such as Puma, Avia (which I tried to buy when I left Reebok), and Ryka.

I believed in the value of taking older brands with good awareness that had gone in the ditch and pulling them out. I had learned that you could quickly bring them back to life by three elements: promotion, technology, and fashion. Yes, athletic endorsers and league licenses do drive sales. I was also realistic regarding the challenges of distribution. Regarding design and technology, I felt the industry was not highly innovative. I was involved at Reebok when we introduced, from scratch, the Pump and Hexalite. Regarding design, the industry is a flock of sheep, following one another around and making marginal changes. I still swear that if you removed the logos from shoes by category, you couldn't tell the difference. The shoes themselves have been manufactured in the same way for years with very little innovation. I studied many of these carefully and bid on a couple of brands or groups owning multiple brands, but never connected on price.

Despite all the swinging and missing, I have never given up on finding that just-right acquisition in one of the spaces for which I have passion. In the meantime, I spend my time productively on a number of boards and advisory groups, trying to add value, constantly learning, improving my market knowledge and contacts, and having fun. When I returned to Vermont after Schylling Toys, I was again contacted by King Arthur Flour to see if I would consider coming back on the board. They had had some key executive changes and felt that I might add value to the new company structure. I agreed to return and eventually became chairman of the board. After another six years, I resigned and turned over my chair to a solid board.

• • •

I was recently asked to join a family-owned private equity fund as an operating partner, where we are actively bidding on food companies. I continue to be interested in and involve myself with ventures where I can add strategic value, organizational structure, and build management teams. People often ask me how I stay interested and active. It's because I love playing the consumer products game. I am driven to use my extensive experience and to keep in touch with my network. It allows me to continue to mentor young people, which is a passion. I am constantly learning. I can't imagine spending my day any other way. So it's not a burden, it's not stressful, it's fun, stimulating, and exciting to see what the day is going to bring. It's still taking risks, and the thrill of jumping first into something and then, as I'm known to do, thinking fast.

I have found that my thinking is far more fluid than most people I know. It is also not sequential, as ideas come in from all angles randomly. I am always amazed with high-level executives in large companies who have never had an original idea. If you ever hear them talk at all, they speak in the obvious.

I embrace change and am terrified of boredom. I have a consistently positive attitude, no matter what. I need to keep moving. I can't sit down and watch TV. I am not interested in watching sports and am bored by them, even though I have been in the business. The same is true for entertainment. While a lot of people in the business are caught up with star power, I always enjoyed the challenge of the business the most. Nothing compares to the thrill of innovating.

• • •

Humor is critical to who I am, as well as being a powerful business tool. Have fun. Be fun. I have talked about this in various spots. If you are fun and a good storyteller and do unusual things with your life, people want to be around you. I use my close boyhood friend, Walter Lynd, as an example. He turned the most mundane things in life into the funniest stories. He always spread joy and liked spending time with older people. We used to go to Willard State Hospital together as kids, where he would play the guitar and get everyone dancing. Later he became a physical therapist and worked at Willard for years, working later as an occupational therapist in nursing homes. He would show up at 6 a.m. in the nursing home, and everybody would be waiting for him to brighten their day. When I was the chieftain at large companies like Reebok and Gibson, with thousands of employees always getting up early, I would think about how Walt was bringing joy one person at a time to the nursing home.

I have often heard wise Wall Street bankers say that the day they add as much value as a fifth-grade teacher is the day they will know that they have peaked. I liked that. To me, the day I bring as much joy to the people around me as Walt did every day is the day when I will know that I have peaked.

On the farm, life starts before the sun rises. I exercise every morning, and sometimes I run for a change, so I have seen a lot of sunrises. My farm-boy work ethic has kept me running. It keeps me working well past sundown. I feel as vital as the day I first drove my tractor into that field in Ovid. I've learned a thing or two, but I feel that there is so much more to learn. I enjoyed getting up with Dan to do the farm chores, and he used to ask me why I was grinning. I told him it was hard not to grin into the sun.

I find that I think of Walt and what he would say about my day. He would say, "Did you have fun?" I think of all the new ideas I will discover tomorrow, all the innovations waiting to be discovered, all the deals I will chase, all the motorcycles I will ride, and all the fun I will have with my colleagues, my friends, and my family. The chieftain chooses to Jump First and Think Fast.

ACKNOWLEDGEMENTS

I am sincerely grateful to everyone who helped and supported me while I wrote a 200-page outline over a 4-year period and then saw it turned into a manuscript for this book.

Thanks to ...

Barbara, my wife of 46 years, whose love and devotion has kept me centered and focused. She happily endured more than 20 moves while raising my two daughters, Beth and Kim, and later our two sons, Sean and Mack. We remained close to my ex-wife, Gail Young, and her family. There is pretty much a direct correlation between my career taking off and my marriage to Barbara. I believe there were times when I got promoted because they liked *her*. I know most spouses, especially today, would never tolerate moving every two years, but we always saw it as an adventure and took advantage of living in diverse parts of this wonderful country. From our very first date, we have shared the joy of motorcycling. An excellent rider, she has toured thousands of miles with me in the US and around the world.

My mother, Virginia Govern, from whom I learned the virtue of working hard and its direct connection to success. When my father died, I was only 2 ½ and my brother Dan was 18 months older, so as a city girl from Buffalo, for our stability, she made the decision to stay and learn to run the family farm in upstate New York. Mother would say, "The harder I work, the luckier I get." She encouraged us in every

268 | *Jump First, Think Fast*

way to be entrepreneurs, so we raised 600 laying hens, 3,000 broilers, and a herd of pigs, and we grew crops of wheat, oats, corn, barley, and beans. She believed in education and did all she could to make sure her boys went to college. She endured hardships but never lost her quick smile and easy laughter. She and Barbara became soul mates.

My children, Beth, Kimberly, Sean, and Mack, for whom I have tried to be a role model. Over the many moves we made, I was not a seven-day-a-week Dad, working constantly and seeking adventure, which I believe taught them adaptability. At times, I am sure they agreed with Mom, as she has said, "Can't we just do something boring?" Each one of them has found their own success, and I'm grateful that, when necessary, they sought my advice but did their own thing. I love my kids deeply and am grateful that we are close and can share life's adventures together. As a grandfather of six and a great-grandfather to three, their growing families are a joy to me.

My best friend from birth in Ovid, New York, Walt Lynd, who left this world far too soon, but with whom I shared my joyful childhood and adult experiences, pranks, risks, fun, and brotherly love. We rode motorcycles together, shared stories and travels, blended our families, and talked at least once a week. Our dream was to grow old together. I miss him, think of him every day, and thank him for making life so much damn fun.

My mentor, Bob Kirby, who, as a seasoned and successful businessman, took many risks with me in my early career. He gave me opportunities many would not have considered, led by example, and let me try things on my own. A keen sense of business acumen, a lifelong friend, motorcycle buddy, and true class act, Bob is probably the closest I have experienced to a father figure. He is fun, athletic, sincere, and a person whom I deeply respect.

Kandes and Cor Bregman, who have been my friends for more than 40 years. Kandes has been a huge support in writing this book, reminding me of stories that should be included and offering her advice on how to market the book. Cor, our Wild Dutchman, has always found just the right cruise to enjoy so that I could find a private corner on the ship from which to continue writing my book outline. The fun, love, and laughter we have all shared is without compare, and I am blessed to have you both in my life.

Rich Marin, who wrote this book from the notes in my outline, has showed so much support and professionalism through many versions, rewrites, and edits, and without whom this book would not have gotten finished. A master storyteller and successful author, he brought my experiences to life, gave them my voice, and added just the right amount of humor, which captures my character. An avid motorcycle rider, we formed American Flyers Motorcycle Club more than 25 years ago and have shared many experiences on the road and around the world and have learned that life is an adventure if you're lucky enough to surround yourself with interesting people. One of the most interesting people I know, Rich has shown so much patience in the writing of this book. He has a keen sense of getting the details right and still laughs at all of my stories.

Bill Achtmeyer, an expert in corporate strategy who founded Parthenon and built it into a world-class consulting company. When I joined SkyBox, I was his first client. Since then, he has worked for me at every company, and years later, he brought me in as Senior Partner. It isn't just the outstanding quality of his people, but also his insightful, no-BS, cutting-through-the-crap personality that was most valuable, often accompanied by brandy. His friendship is a treasure.

Kosmo Kalliarekos, who enjoys a successful career with a PE firm in Hong Kong. He was a young Senior Partner at Parthenon who headed many of my consulting projects. He has an IQ bigger than the room. In consulting terms, he is a case-cracker." He always had a smile, even when I first landed at SkyBox, where he came to my office to tell me that the company lost $40 million in the prior year. He never stopped thanking me for being the first client at Parthenon.

Sam Reed, who built TreeHouse Foods into the largest private label food company in the world, where I served on the board for 16 years. Sam worked for me in finance right out of college at Oroweat Baking Company in Seattle. We became lifelong friends, and he is the of godfather of my son Sean. Smart from the start, he went on to buy and build Keebler Cookies and sell it for a handsome price to Kellogg's.

Jay Ladd, who headed operations for SkyBox—a fellow motorcycle enthusiast and member of American Flyers Motorcycle Club, he became a long-term friend, along with his wife, Laura. He developed an incredible breakthrough in weather forecasting, which I tried to help him commercialize.